Trondheim
Norway

London
England

Dusseldorf
Germany

Paris
France

Chicago
Illinois

Monterrey
Mexico

Caseros
Argentina

Bloemfontein
South Africa

Santiago
Chile

Porto Alegre
Brazil

THE LATTER-DAY SAINTS:
The Mormons Yesterday and Today

THE
LATTER-DAY SAINTS:
The Mormons Yesterday and Today

ROBERT MULLEN

Doubleday & Company, Inc., Garden City, New York
1966

AUTHOR'S FOREWORD

The Church of Jesus Christ of Latter-day Saints has been given much attention by the world's press lately. A pulsing expansion in missionary activity and effectiveness, plus in some instances a somewhat overblown idea of the Church's business activities, and of course the always absorbing story of the martyrdom, the trek, and the settlement, combined to stir interest.

While the resultant articles were most friendly, they were necessarily limited in scope, usually fastening on one phase or another of the religious, social, and economic aspects of Mormondom. Thus the present publishers felt that a rounded-out account would be useful.

My original interest was in trying to help outline the contents. As the discussions advanced, I suggested that it might be wise to follow Winston Churchill's advice when approaching history and to tell it as if it had never been told before; but at the same time I urged that emphasis be given to the modern Church.

I also suggested that the book might very properly be divided into three parts; the first to cover generally the Joseph Smith era; the second to be about Brigham Young's time; and the third dealing with the period since, which would be, roughly, the twentieth century.

I expressed the hope that the book might be factual and correct but not linger over old disharmonies; that it should be neither saccharine nor sour. Most of all, I said it should be so presented that a non-Mormon would not feel he was being proselytized.

Heads were nodding in agreement and we then talked about who should write it. Suddenly I found all eyes were turned on me.

"But," I protested, "I am not a Mormon."

"No, but you know their story. We would trust you to tell it."

So, that is how it came to be.

ACKNOWLEDGMENTS

For the early portions of the Mormon story the author is, of course, completely indebted to the historians who covered the ground before him. Appreciation of these sources is made in the Bibliography and Notes as appropriate.

Much of the material relating to recent or current events was obtained from firsthand reporting, which is to say travels, observation, and interviews. Sources thus treated are gratefully identified in the text in order. In this connection it would be well to point out that these glimpses of Mormon activity must be something like stop-action photos. Mission presidents and missionaries usually serve only two or three years and so interviews at any given moment may be with a personality who has just recently come on the scene or who may be about to depart. While the players may change, however, the stage remains the same.

ABOUT APPELLATIONS

It may help the reader to follow subsequent pages if he understands that the formal, legal, and, they consider, deity-bestowed name is The Church of Jesus Christ of Latter-day Saints. This is abbreviated so that it may appear, for example, in a newspaper headline as LDS Church. Sometimes the members are referred to as LDS, as, the question might be asked in Salt Lake City, "Is he LDS?" Often they are referred to as Saints, in the early Christian meaning of followers of Christ. Thus if the statement were made "They are Saints," it would not be meant to indicate canonization, but simply to identify a group as members of the Church. Most popularly, however, it is known as the Mormon Church and its members as Mormons. This appellation was at first used as a sort of convenience, or nickname, and derived, of course, from the Book of Mormon, the name and origination of which are described in pages following.

Contents

Part Two
THE TIMES OF BRIGHAM YOUNG

Part Three
THE TWENTIETH CENTURY

Part One

THE JOSEPH SMITH
PERIOD

Chapter One

A SUCCESS STORY

Among the Mormons, all is well.

As The Church of Jesus Christ of Latter-day Saints enters the last third of the twentieth century, its membership stands at an all-time high. Its growth is the fastest in its history. Theological dissents are virtually nonexistent. Not for the Mormons the pessimistic limitations of Kierkegaard or the Deity-absence of Existentialism, for to the age-old questions "whence?" "whither?" and "why?" they feel they have eternal answers.

The early demise of the Church was forecast with the martyrdom of its Prophet, Joseph Smith, in 1844. At that time the Church had 40,000 members. Again, an early end was predicted with the passing of Brigham Young in 1877. At that time the Church had grown to 150,000 members. Such forecasts are not so common today, when it is reaching toward 3,000,000 members.

It required 117 years—1830–1947—for the Church to reach a million members. It took only 13 more years—1960—to rise to a membership of 2,000,000. At the present rate of growth it should number 3,000,000 before 1970.

In the last decade the Mormon missionary system has found ways of increasing effectiveness. In fact, individual missionaries are today about three times as effective as they were only ten years ago.[1] As the acceleration gains, it is no wonder that other denominations study the Mormons with deep interest.

This book, written by one not himself a Mormon, is about a religious movement that has had its full share of criticism and even scorn and persecution, yet has grown and prospered until today it is recognized as one of the most successful such movements in the world.

While many think of it as a Utah church or even a Salt Lake City church, the fact is that the greatest growth today is away from that center.

It has expanded in California mightily, but South America, the British Isles, all of Northwest Europe, the islands of the South Seas and even the Orient are alive and bustling with Mormon activity. The Saints are very much alive. Few realize the extent of their worldwide thrust.

International Expansion

As this is written, 12,000 Mormon missionaries are proselytizing in sixty-five countries. A world-wide building program, budgeted at $60,000,000 a year and with 868 new chapels and other buildings under construction at this time, has been underway since World War II. Some seventy-five new chapels are being built in England alone.

In Marseilles, France, a Mormon group has zoomed from eight members to 450, and this is cited as only one example among many. In West Germany, where more than 1000 missionaries work, Mormon groups involve more than 26,000 persons! One of the most active areas of the world just now for the Mormons is, as it surprises most to learn, Central and South America, where an all-time high membership of 40,000 is recorded. And this is growing by the minute. Even in the far-flung islands of the Pacific—the Fijis, Samoa, as well as Hawaii, New Zealand, and Australia—membership is now above 60,000.

Today, Mormons have basketball leagues in all parts of the Free World, including Finland. They sponsor one of the world's most successful Boy Scout organizations and a large soft-ball league. And these, of course, are merely ancillary to their Church activities on which it can be truly said the sun never sets. Missionaries are going up one street and down another in far distant towns, calling at houses, as the message is carried. Fresh enterprise is generated daily involving young people, parents, and those in all walks of life, and the work of the Church is gathering force all over the world at once, so much so that it hardly seems possible that it stems from a group heretofore thought of mostly as a reserved people largely concentrated for the past century in the valleys of the Rocky Mountains.

Indeed, to one coming new on the scene, it looks more as if it were some cause freshly projected from a British or German base. To the casual observer in London, Paris, Stockholm, Frankfurt, Mexico City, São Paulo, Sydney, Tokyo or any of the world's great metropolises, the Mormons today seem to have a new look. But to anybody who has known the Mormons for almost a half century, it is not something new. It is more like the explosion—though that is obviously a strong word—of at least the accelerated release of forces that, because of wars, economic upsets, and other worldly affairs, were pent up for a number of years.

The Marque of Integrity

At the outset it is proper to state that the writer, having spent his youth in the Rocky Mountain West, has always known Mormons. One early recollection is of the annual visit to our home in New Mexico of a salesman for the Utah Woolen Mills. We lived in a small mining community, appropriately named Baldy, for it was at an altitude above the limit where trees would grow. The road up the mountain was narrow, rough, and ran dangerously along the bare edge of precipices that dropped off many thousands of feet.

Few automobiles could make it, but the salesman for the woolen mill had one of those early models produced by the Dodge brothers, a car notable for its ruggedness, due (as some thought) to an absence of springs. If you didn't care too much for comfort, the old Dodge would get you almost any place that a horse and wagon would. In such an equipage, the salesman would arrive in the late summer, before the start of school, and the few families in town would gather in the dining room of the small hotel and, under the hissing glare of a gasoline lantern, examine the samples.

For boys, he offered a heavy pullover sweater and the memory comes of how he would ask a couple of the bigger and stronger to take hold of one side while he pulled with all his might on the other. The sweater would stretch out to double its width but when released would immediately spring back to its original shape. A sheet of rubber could have done little better.

When one of the young cynics remarked that the sample did this but that the regular sweater when it arrived would probably fail any such test, one in the room remarked, "No, they're made by the Mormons." That was enough. In the Old West that meant as much as the marque of the Bank of England to the commercial world. The Mormons stood for integrity.

Of course the Mormons represented other things in the minds of the Old West too. One of these things, which raised speculation, was the practice of a small percentage of Mormons of having more than one wife, even though polygamy was outlawed in the nineteenth century. I recall one ancient miner saying, "It wasn't like you think at all. They didn't have harems, those Mormons. Suppose a man died, or was killed. He had a widow and maybe two or three kids and a homestead. Who was to look after them in the old days with a lot of horse thieves and Indians around? Well, suppose there is a well-to-do Mormon farmer nearby, or even in the town. He will marry the lady, make the kids his own, which is to say treat them like a real father and be responsible for them, do the heavy chores around the place and maybe spend half his time there. You might find a man having two or three such families, each living by itself with the old man making visits every few days. I don't say it was the right system, but it did seem the best to them to meet a practical problem, and I used to say, as old Abe Lincoln did, 'Leave 'em alone.'"

Then somebody would say, "Yeah, but how about all those old men marrying the young girls?"

"As to that," replied the old miner, repeating a familiar western joke, "I don't know. But as Jim Young said, 'Probably they found it was trying to get more out of life than there was really in it.'"

As we shall see later in this narrative, there was much more to the polygamy story than this, but in the first decades of the twentieth century that was about as much consideration as the Old West gave to the piquant marital customs of their Mormon neighbors. And elsewhere in the West, outside of Utah, that's probably about all the consideration anybody gave. There were Mormon families around, but you couldn't tell them from anybody else. The boys didn't drink and the girls didn't smoke, and the Mormons tended to keep to themselves; they were friendly, but somewhat apart, that was all.

Choir Tour

Twenty-five years went by, and one weekend in 1955 the writer received a telephone call. The Tabernacle Choir was about to embark on a European tour and the Church authorities were apprehensive that they might sing to half-empty halls because the choir was unknown in Europe. They needed publicity and advertising. Since I had been active in overseas work for some years, the finger had pointed to me.

The next day I was flying to Salt Lake City to meet for the first time with the highest officials of the Church—and to begin pleasant associations and an experience that would prove memorable. It would be immodest, and quite unjust, to take credit for the results of the many hours of prayerful work that members of the choir and others associated with it put into the preparation for the tour, but my Mormon friends were generous enough to say that, at least partly because of the efforts of my company, the tour was a tremendous success.

The great halls were everywhere filled to capacity—Kelvin Hall in Glasgow, Free Trade Hall in Manchester, Albert Hall in London, Odd Fellows Hall in Copenhagen, Concertgebow in Amsterdam—and in Berlin, Berne, even Paris. We had assumed that ticket sales in Paris would be difficult. In that city of sophisticates and intellectual skeptics it seemed unimaginable that great numbers would pay to hear a concert of religious music sung by a chorus of Americans! Moreover, we had a large hall to fill, the Palais de Chaillot, which lies under the Trocodero, near the Eiffel Tower.

To worsen our trepidation, on our initial visit to the hall we ran into a representative of the Philadelphia Orchestra. His group was currently playing there, and he indicated that he was very pleased because that famous orchestra had filled half the seats! Naturally we had hoped to do better. But, as always, my Mormon friends were encouraging—encouraging in their own way; they said they would pray.

I recall reading one time about William Bradford, the first governor of the Plymouth Colony. The Pilgrims had been without rain for a long period and their crops were in danger. Bradford called the group together to pray for rain and he prayed as though expecting results, which in fact soon followed, as a gentle, soaking rain began to fall. Many times during the choir's European tour, and in my relationship with Mormon friends since, I have noticed the same thing: when they pray, they expect results.

But they also assume that help comes to those who help themselves. In any case, we proceeded with our publicity. Soon, the Paris kiosks blossomed with colorful posters picturing the Mormons singing their way across the Great Plains.

Paris Success

A box was reserved for C. Douglas Dillon, then American Ambassador to France and later Under Secretary of State in the Eisenhower Administration, later to become Secretary of the Treasury under Presidents Kennedy and Johnson. When the Ambassador's party arrived they reported that they had required police help to get through the throngs outside the Palais de Chaillot and soon we had word that police had arrested a scalper for selling tickets outside at double the advertised price, all box-office tickets having been sold! Indeed, the interest was so great that the French Radio on the spur of the moment decided to broadcast the entire two-hour program that evening. The reviews in Paris, and elsewhere, were almost ecstatic.

These, of course, were exciting successes, but even at the time I was more struck by a different aspect. This was the wide and deep impact that the Mormons had previously made on Britain and all northwest Europe. Until then, probably like most Americans, I had thought of the Mormons as mostly in and of the state of Utah. I was surprised to find that they had been active overseas, with extensive operations, for more than a hundred years. Their Church was not unknown.

A very urbane and pleasant young missionary, the son of a United States senator, showed me the large home in Glasgow from which a half-dozen young Mormons, mostly from the Salt Lake City area, daily went out to interview people in their homes, set up meetings, and otherwise work for new members for the Church. He also showed me the Cunard docks at Greenock from which thousands of Scots sailed before the turn of the century to start new lives as Mormons in Utah.

In Manchester there were about twenty Mormons set up as an entertainment committee for the six hundred in the choir party! And in London the mission was moving from venerable and rather remote headquarters in Belham to a sumptuous mansion on Exhibition Row. Even then they were breaking ground for a temple on land south of London adjacent to an estate of Sir Winston Churchill. And plans were under consideration for a new chapel in London, the dimensions and design of which were to excite much favorable newspaper comment a few years later.

In a town far out on the Danish archipelago I attended a Sunday evening meeting and found a small but devout band of Mormons busy with a church-building program, glad to have word of activities elsewhere, but quite content to proceed with their own local efforts and concerns.

In a little town in Norway I was entertained in a new building needed to serve the local community of Mormons. In Finland I found that the missionaries had introduced basketball and had formed a very popular league. But my Mormon friends were so intent on the teachings, the theology of their movement, that they brushed aside these external manifestations. They were polite but slightly annoyed that anyone would be more interested in basketball than in their religion.

Berlin Experience

In Berlin I grasped for a moment the Mormon feeling about their Church. The event was heart-touching. It seems that before the war most of the German Mormons lived in what is now the Eastern Zone. Of course the Communists have curtailed all they could of religious activity, and particularly intercourse with outside Church influences, but before the Berlin Wall was erected it was fairly easy for East Germans to visit West Berlin.

The problem was that they had to get back to the Eastern Zone before 9 P.M., when the subway stopped running. So a special concert was scheduled for the late afternoon especially for those still in the Eastern Zone and word was circulated. It was easy to spot them as they arrived—clothes often tattered, shoes quite worn, faces drawn, but some clutched little bouquets of flowers, the only thing they could bring as gifts for the choir members.

As some of the old, favorite hymns began to swell through the auditorium open sobs were heard, and soon, even in the choir, there were few dry eyes. A rapport of sentiment crossed the footlights and for a moment rolled back the curtains of loneliness and fear. Few of us had gone through such an emotional experience.

So it was through this trip I learned that all Mormons did not reside in Utah, that The Church of Jesus Christ of Latter-day Saints was far-flung indeed. And then, ten years later, 1965, I revisited many of the places in which the choir had sung. As I talked with old friends, I saw that in the decade since the tour the Mormons had enjoyed a period of unprecedented forward thrust.

As just one illustration of this, I noted above that when the choir sang in Manchester in 1955 it was hard for the relatively few Church members resident there to help with the concert. Today in Manchester there are 800 members, and their headquarters and chapel are among the showplaces of the city.

Such things may not be startling, but they serve to picture the visible part of the iceberg of activity and interest. In thousands of communities around the globe Mormons are reaching out with the arm of charity, no longer to bring the hungering into the Great Salt Lake basin, but to assist them where they are, to establish new or expanded centers of Mormonism. To the Mormons this present time is among the most exhilarating in their Church history.

Chapter Two

PAGEANT IN PALMYRA

On a warm summer evening you can hear the automobiles whizzing along the wonderful New York Thruway hour after hour at upwards of sixty-five miles an hour with never a slowdown until they approach Exit 43. On the exit road they join other cars, their lights dim in the luxuriant dusk of New York State's beautiful Finger Lakes, pointing in from places with tongue-twisting names, some Indian and some Dutch—Canandaigua, Skaneateles, Niagara, Tonawanda, Schenectady, Oneida. These are the sorts of words Europeans love to roll off their tongues as a mixture of the very strange and the very familiar, an essence of America.

The cars follow asphalt successors to trails that the Mohawks once prowled, and when the sky grows deeper and the car lights seem brighter in vieing with the flashing fireflies, it is clear that the immense traffic is converging on a field just outside the small town of Palmyra. The beams from powerful flashlights dart across the road and onto the field where cars, thousands of cars, are parked in orderly rows. Then the sun finally sinks into the red and pink afterglow of the west, and all eyes are raised to the top of Hill Cumorah, to the east, where suddenly appear four white-robed trumpeters to sound their call.

It is the start of the Hill Cumorah pageant called "America's Witness for Christ," an annual presentation of The Church of Jesus Christ of Latter-day Saints. The New York *Times* has called it the "most elaborate religious pageant in the world." *Time* magazine says it is ". . . put together with the highest professional polish."

Usually held for five or six nights at the end of July and the beginning of August, the pageant draws crowds estimated as high as 200,000 (though the Mormons, with characteristic modesty, never

claim more than 100,000). People come not only from the surrounding countryside and towns and cities, but from almost every state
in the union, and a few foreign countries too.

As the echo of the trumpets fades, we learn that early in the nineteenth century a farm boy named Joseph Smith lived nearby. Students of American history know the atmosphere of the times. A
whole people were free, for one of the first times in human history,
to seek and practice religious experiences as they would. This led
to a lively competition among many church sects and families found
themselves pulled in one direction or another in a way and with a
force hard to imagine today. The Smith family was caught in these
tuggings and it naturally made a deep impression on young Joseph.

The pageant—with a cast of some four hundred, aided by a large
stage crew and possibly the most advanced stereophonic sound equipment to be found anywhere—presents on five major and twenty
minor stages dotted around the slope of Hill Cumorah what Joseph
Smith learned as a result of his prayers for guidance.

The Joseph Smith Story

Most Americans know the Joseph Smith story, for it is now a part
of the national tradition. But sitting in the balmy evening at Palmyra,
one's mind goes back to the story as told in Joseph's own words. It
gives a flavor of his times and of his style. He relates that, when he
was fourteen years old,

> While I was laboring under the extreme difficulties caused by the con-
> tests of the parties of religionists, I was one day reading the Epistle of
> James, first chapter and fifth verse:
>
> > "If any of you lack wisdom, let him ask of
> > God, that giveth to all men liberally and
> > upbraideth not; and it shall be given him."
>
> Never did any passage of scripture come with more power to the heart
> of man that this did to mine. I reflected on it again and again, knowing
> that if any person needed wisdom from God, I did.
>
> So, in accordance with this my determination, I retired to the woods
> to make an attempt. It was on the morning of a beautiful clear day, early
> in the Spring of 1820. It was the first time in my life that I had made

such an attempt, for amidst all my anxieties I had never as yet made the attempt to pray vocally.

I had scarcely done so, when I was immediately seized upon by some power which completely overcame me, and had such an astonishing influence over me as to bind my tongue so that I could not speak. Thick darkness gathered around me, and it seemed for a time as if I were doomed to sudden destruction . . . but just at this moment of great alarm, I saw a pillar of light exactly over my head, and above the brightness of the sun, which descended gradually until it fell on me. . . .

When the light rested upon me I saw two Personages, whose brightness and glory defy all description, standing above me in the air. One of them spake unto me, calling me by name, and said, pointing to the other, "This is my Beloved Son, hear Him"![1]

Joseph then said he inquired about church membership and was advised to join none of them. At some time in the future, he was told, he would be instructed what to do.

A fourteen-year-old boy who claimed to have been spoken to by God and His beloved Son was hardly less a curiosity in 1820 than he would be today. He said that he was derided, that one of the local preachers assured him that such visions were of the devil and that all true revelations had ceased with the Apostles.

"Nevertheless," insisted Joseph, "it was a fact that I had beheld a vision. I have thought since that I felt much like Paul, when he made his defense before King Agrippa, and related the account of the vision he had had when he saw a light and heard a voice; still there were but few who believed him; some said he was dishonest, others said he was mad, and he was ridiculed and reviled. But all this did not destroy the reality of his vision. He had seen a vision, he knew he had, and all the persecution under heaven could not make it otherwise. . . ."

Mormon's Book

The incident remained in the minds of the neighbors, but Joseph said that he did not have another heavenly vision for three years, until he was seventeen years old. At this time his visitant entered his bedroom, "called me by name and said he was a messenger sent from the presence of God and that his name was Moroni; that God had a work for me to do. . . ."[2]

The work, as revealed in this and subsequent visits from Moroni, was to take from the place where it had been deposited on nearby Hill Cumorah a book, inscribed on golden plates, or leaves, that had been buried by Moroni some 1400 years earlier when he walked the earth as a general and prophet and historian. After suitable testing over a period of three years, Joseph was given the plates by Moroni, and at the same time was given means to translate into English the ancient Egyptian-like symbols.

Some of the highlights of what Joseph Smith translated from the plates suggest the principal scenes of the Hill Cumorah Pageant. It would be impossible fully to convey on paper the spirit of the pageant, and of the Book of Mormon, which in part it dramatizes. In brief, however, the story unfolded to Joseph concerned a family which had left Jerusalem in about 600 B.C. The father, Lehi, was a man close to God and had been forewarned of the destruction about to be visited in that city during the reign of Zedekiah. The family, under Lehi, built a ship and sailed westward, ultimately landing somewhere on the American continent. From this family in the New World sprang two nations of peoples, the Nephites and the Lamanites. Although there were occasions of backsliding, the Nephites on the whole were good people, law-abiding and industrious, praying to God and following His guidance. Some Lamanites expressed fine qualities, but others were often in trouble, idolatrous, pagan, and savage.

The Nephites began to prosper in their new environment and built a civilization both of large extent and merit. They had brought with them the history of Israel and certain Old Testament and other accounts available at the time of their departure, and they added their own record of prophecies and progress, wars and disasters. They had no communication, of course, with their former homeland, but they shared in the expectation of the coming of the Messiah. Therefore, it was not a great surprise to them when Jesus appeared to them, following his ascension in Palestine.

Jesus taught the Nephites the same things he had taught in Palestine, and he set up his Church among them, ordaining leaders and conferring the same powers as he had in Palestine. These teachings, and the establishment of the Church, gave impetus for some generations, but as the Nephites prospered, they became indifferent to their religious teachings.

Among the Prophets who exhorted them to greater faith and works was Mormon. He, along with other Prophets, kept a chronicle of the people. From his own words and other accounts he compiled an abridgment which he had engraved on golden plates. These were entrusted by Mormon to his son, Moroni, just before the final destruction of the Nephites by the Lamanites, and these were the plates which Moroni buried on the Hill Cumorah in 421 A.D.

The Restoration

In these and subsequent revelations, Joseph was told that the primitive church which Jesus had established in Palestine had become corrupted and had departed from the true teachings following the death of the Apostles, and that the churches centered in Rome and Constantinople had suffered a "great apostasy." Therefore, since this root was untrue, the Reformation, or Protestant revolt, although sincere, was only an offshoot of an original error. It, too, was an apostasy by the very nature of its origin. The original church of Christ must be restored, he was told.

Among the neighboring farmers and friends and associates of Joseph Smith and his wife, Emma, to whom he had been married just before he received the plates from Moroni, were Oliver Cowdery, Martin Harris, and David Whitmer. They, too, were shown the plates and were instructed by an angel that the plates were authentic and the translation of them true. A statement to this effect, signed by the three, appears in the preface to the Book of Mormon. Eight other qualified witnesses also signed a statement that they had seen and handled the plates. Their testimony to this effect also appears in the forepart of the Book of Mormon.[3]

The Book was printed in March 1830 by a small shop in Palmyra. The printer refused to hand over the volumes until he was paid and Martin Harris sold part of his farm to pay for the first 5000 copies, a suggestion of the faith that motivated these people. Joseph's father and his brothers went out that spring to sell the book from farm to farm in New York State and upper Pennsylvania. And in April, a month after publication of the Book, Joseph Smith and his immediate followers organized the Church.

Naturally, the central question to all who were interested was, "Is all this true? Does this man indeed communicate with angels sent by God? Is his book in fact an actual record of an ancient people who lived on the North American continent?"

These questions obviously raise the age-old debate as to what is faith and what is intellectual reasoning. In Joseph Smith's day this was a lively debate. It is even more so in today's materialistic atmosphere when one hardly dares to contemplate the greeting that would be given a biblical prophet who announced that he saw visions and consciously talked with God. If one such appeared today every rational reason would be advanced for considering his utterances irrational. Religious leaders have agreed that it is not always possible to prove by intellectual processes the truth of religious experience. Religion is an act of faith until proof comes in its own individual way to the individual consciousness.

Joseph Smith lived in a less cynical time. The United States, as a nation, was less than fifty years old. Although its population had doubled since the Revolution, it was still, in 1830, a land of only thirteen million people, and only 5 percent of those people lived in cities. New York was the most populous state, with almost two million, but only 200,000 lived in New York City.

The Age of Opportunity

It was a nation of small farmers, pushing ever westward. Andrew Jackson was President. He was a frontiersman, and the country was moving into Ohio and the country to the west, where it was easy to buy 100 acres for $1.25 an acre, cash or credit, or even just by "squatting," which is to say by moving in. The spirit of the times was hopeful, turbulent, ready for innovation. A religion, keyed to the living present and based in the New World, was in tune with the times.

All this contributed something to the reception accorded Joseph Smith, for the important fact is that Joseph Smith was believed in by a sufficient number to have a ponderable effect. If, as might have happened, his visions had been accepted as the outpourings of a poor, uneducated farm boy, his influence would have extended no farther than his own farm. Within a few weeks, however, the six original members who had organized the Church had grown into hundreds, within months the following had grown into thousands, and in little more than a century they circled the globe.

These members *had* to believe, for in accepting the admittedly quite novel teachings of Joseph Smith they had to cross the bridge of deciding whether the teachings did or did not represent the truth. And if they determined that they were true, they had to go all the way. The teachings allowed for no halfway position. They were either all true or all false. Joseph Smith was either a leader ordained of God or he was not. And having once decided in favor of Joseph Smith, no room was left for doubt; it was, as the Chinese say, Yin or Yang, aye or nay, plus or minus.

Too, if the angel visitants had brought nothing to reveal, if Joseph Smith had only a story to tell of a remarkable experience, if the book he had translated offered nothing unusual, there would be little to tell today of him. But, plainly, he did speak in strikingly different terms from those uttered in other churches by the regular ministry of his time. What was it, then, that he asked others to believe?

Chapter Three

WHAT JOSEPH SMITH TAUGHT

Before going further with the story of the Mormons, it might be well to examine, even cursorily, their beliefs to see what it is that distinguishes them from other Christian sects in the world. The Latter-day Saints do accept the scriptural account of the creation and the fall of man and tend to be literal in their acceptance of the Bible, but there are differences which the Mormons consider crucially important. If this were not so, if their religion simply paralleled others except in detail, the basis for their zeal would not exist.

Mormons today, as of old, tend to live in a religious world apart. Their physical separateness in a Utah, or Zion, of their own is not so great as it once was, but to them Zion is not necessarily a geographical location, it is a state of mind or, as they say, "for the pure in heart."

To some extent, they even have a language of their own. For example, they refer to themselves as Saints, not, as a guide in Temple Square will quickly assure you, because they feel you are "A'ints," but in the biblical sense that all followers of Christ were saints, meaning followers, or believers. Except for Jews, all non-Mormons are referred to as Gentiles, simply meaning one of non-Mormon faith, as to Jews all non-Jews are Gentiles.

Mormons associate themselves with the original tribes of Israel, but not in terms of present-day definitions of race. Indeed, individual Mormons are quite proud of their descent from British, Scandinavian, and other stock, but they believe that all the races represented in their priesthood originally derived from the ancient twelve tribes. Thus, they do have a different view of their background than many Christians.

Just a couple of years before his martyrdom, Joseph Smith was asked by the editor of the Chicago *Democrat* to write a paper on the history of the Church and a statement summarizing or highlighting its beliefs. The response to this included thirteen Articles of Faith, which were subsequently adopted by the Mormons as a standard epitome of belief. It may help to review them here, as indicating both the agreement and disagreement the reader may observe in the similar statements of his own belief:

We believe in God the Eternal Father, and in His Son Jesus Christ, and in the Holy Ghost.

We believe that men will be punished for their own sins, and not for Adam's transgression.

We believe that through the atonement of Christ all mankind may be saved by obedience to the laws and ordinances of the gospel.

We believe that these ordinances are, 1st: Faith in the Lord Jesus Christ; 2nd: Repentance; 3rd: Baptism by immersion for the remission of sins; 4th: Laying on of hands for the gift of the Holy Ghost.

We believe that a man must be called of God by prophecy and by the laying on of hands by those who are in authority, to preach the gospel and administer in the ordinances thereof.

We believe in the same organization that existed in the primitive church, namely, Apostles, Prophets, Pastors, Teachers, Evangelists, etc.

We believe in the gift of tongues, prophecy, revelations, visions, healing, interpretations of tongues, etc.

We believe the Bible to be the word of God so far as it is translated correctly; we also believe the Book of Mormon to be the word of God.

We believe that God has revealed, all that He does now reveal, and we believe that He will reveal many great and important things pertaining to the kingdom of God.

We believe in the literal gathering of Israel and in the restoration of the Ten Tribes; that Zion will be built upon this continent; that Christ will reign personally upon the earth; and that the earth will be renewed and receive its paradisiacal glory.

We claim the privilege of worshiping Almighty God according to the dictates of our own conscience, and allow all men the same privilege, let them worship how, where or what they may.

We believe in being subject to kings, presidents, rulers and magistrates, in obeying, honoring and sustaining the law.

We believe in being honest, true, chaste, benevolent, virtuous, and in doing good to all men; indeed, we may say that we follow the admonition of Paul, "We believe all things, hope all things," we have endured many things, and hope to be able to endure all things. If there is anything virtuous, lovely or of good report, or praiseworthy, we seek after these things.

All Had Been Said

The Articles of Faith are the bare bones of Joseph Smith's statement, but in application he clothed them with examples that were quite novel for his time. Mormons are usually very glad to discuss these religious beliefs with others, and will do so on the agreeable premise that you have the complete option to go along with them or not, as you choose. But if there is this willingness, and sometimes even eagerness, to talk, it is sometimes hard for the non-Mormon to come to grips with what they are saying.

The reason is that questioners frequently do not want to start with simple things. Mormons do their best. They want a subject which Mormons feel may be more complex than atomic physics explained in a word. Indeed, they have long been abjured to start with what they call "first principles" when asked about their religion.

By this they mean to start with the fact that they believe in one God, the eternal Father, that they believe Christ is the Son of God. And thus far they are not likely to lose their auditors.

Then they tell the Joseph Smith story and ask whether it can be accepted that God can communicate with prophets today as readily as thousands of years ago. Joseph Smith taught that God not only exists, but is very much, so to speak, alive at this instant; moreover, that He is not some vague concept or undefinable spirit, but is in solid fact, a being whose presence may not only be felt but seen and heard, and that Joseph Smith did see and hear Him.

Many people, possibly most people in Joseph Smith's time, believed that God no longer spoke to man, that he *had* spoken. All that was required to be said had been said. In the churches it was taught and agreed that there was one God, but there was basic disagreement as to the nature of God. Some pictured Him seated on a golden throne, dispensing grace to those able to get His ear. It was taught that the prophets of the Old Testament had seen God and talked with Him, man to man, so to speak, but that this was not possible in modern times. Something had changed.

Joseph Smith asserted that nothing had changed, that he had seen

God and His Son as personal, glorious beings, and that he had heard their voices, and that they uttered words for this time. This was rather startling news 145 years ago, as it would be today. But Joseph Smith was so sure of his message—as was Moses after the voice spoke to him from the burning bush—that he faced up to the disbelief certain to surround him and once more lead a people out of a wilderness. Even the most cynical cannot dispute that Joseph Smith must have had a special quality in order to present his case and to motivate so many to follow him.

Joseph Smith taught that God maintained a warm, loving kinship with man, that He was not an impersonal force, that the veil between God and man can be penetrated. This is far less revolutionary teaching today than it was a century ago. Today many people of diverse church connections feel that God guides and governs them in their work-a-day affairs. How much the inspiration of Joseph Smith had to do with this may be hard to measure, but Mormons feel that anyone who considers it, even casually, should agree that he had a great deal to do with the concept of God that is entertained today.

Life Before Birth

A second principal teaching of Joseph Smith concerned premortal life, a life before birth. Throughout history men have been intrigued with thoughts of life after death. A century ago, it is fair to say, a very large percentage of the preaching in the churches in America was about heaven or hell—angels with wings and harps or devils with fire and brimstone.

Joseph Smith came along with a perfectly logical but immensely startling question. It was, quite simply: If a man lives after death and if he has, as they say, an immortal soul, did he not live before he was born? He taught that man lived with God as a child, in the spirit world, before coming on earth. The impact of this teaching on a people concerned with the sterner aspects of religion was powerful.

"Why, certainly," they would agree, "if man is to live hereafter, it is reasonable to suppose that he lived heretofore." This was a happy doctrine. It suggested a childlike, exuberant, joy-filled childhood under the care of a loving father, who, when the child was ready, sent him forth into the experience we call our life on earth, like an earthly father sending his boy or girl away to college, and the father stayed at hand, only a veil was drawn softly over the consciousness of the past. In other words, the father says, "Let us see what you can do on your own." In due course, the veil would be lifted.

This leads to a third point. As the Book of Mormon phrased it, "Men are, that they might have joy." Mormons don't necessarily mean "joy" in a frolicsome sense. They mean it in the purposeful sense that, as men are, to use the present-day term, "adjusted," and as they contribute meaningfully to the life about them, they are filled with a feeling of well being, a deep happiness, free from paralyzing fears and anxieties.

Here they probably run into the core of modern man's problem, a different problem from that which confronted Americans of Joseph Smith's time, but a problem even then confronting some parts of the Old World. The industrial revolution had created a class of propertyless people. They were no longer farmers dependent on their own toil and the weather. They were caught in economic forces beyond their control and even beyond their comprehension, a situation requiring immense readjustment on the part of people that is still going on.

The pioneer American of that period, on the other hand, was possibly the most self-reliant individual who ever walked the earth. He either had land or knew where he could get it for the wielding of an ax. His was an active life, full of throbbing experiences. A pulpit that shouted only of misery was not only distasteful, it was foreign to his generous experience. When Joseph Smith announced, "Men are, that they might have joy," it was a clear call of the trumpet. It suggested a life of happiness and progress, of a new and upward looking way to match the opportunities and energies of the opening American West.

The Right of Choice

Many believed in Joseph Smith's time—1830 to 1844 were his teaching years—that man was held helplessly in a destiny that was predestined. Some believed in infant damnation, and sects were divided in arguments on the point. But Joseph Smith said it was obvious to anybody who would think about it for a moment that when we enter this world we have a relatively long period of preparation. First, we are babes, then children. Only gradually do we mature and take on added responsibilities. Yet almost from the first moment of consciousness we are free agents in some measure. We may make a mistake and be corrected for it, but only our own wisdom or ability to learn prevents our repeating the mistake.

Joseph Smith placed great emphasis on this right of choice. It was his doctrine that man had freedom to err as well as to do rightly. He taught that in the life before this present one, a plan of experience was presented to us. You might say that it was like being offered a chance to go to college. The man who accepted the offer left his premortal state and came into this life. The loving father is there to support him, but he must learn on his own. The Mormons will again point to the similarity of the young lad going away to school. The human father will encourage, counsel, but cannot control the lad's rate of learning.

A Mormon poetess, Eliza R. Snow, put it into a hymn which Mormons cherish especially. It is called "O! My Father," and it deserves careful reading:

O! my Father, thou that dwellest
  In the high and glorious place;
When shall I regain thy presence,
  And again behold thy face?

In thy holy habitation,
  Did my spirit once reside?
In my first primeval childhood,
  Was I nurtured by thy side?

For a wise and glorious purpose,
  Thou has placed me here on earth;
And withheld the recollection
  Of my former friends and birth.

Yet oft-times a secret something
  Whispered, "You're a stranger here";
And I felt that I had wandered
  From a more exalted sphere.

I had learned to call thee Father,
  Through thy spirit from on high;
But until the key of knowledge
  Was restored, I knew not why.

In the heavens are parents single?
  No; the thought makes reason stare.
Truth is reason; truth eternal
  Tells me I've a mother there.

When I leave this frail existence—
  When I lay this mortal by,
Father, mother, may I meet you
  In your royal court on high?

Then at length, when I've completed
  All you sent me forth to do,
With your mutual approbation,
  Let me come and dwell with you.[1]

That hymn hints of the spirit of Mormon teaching. A man's eternal Father is at hand to guide and to help but not to do the work for him. The Lord's purpose is one of goodness and joy. As man is obedient, God's purpose unfolds quickly and easily. If man does not cooperate, it may unfold slowly and with difficulty. But God's purpose will in the end prevail, for he has all eternity for His purpose to work out.

This view of life had great appeal for the pioneers of the early nineteenth century. They intuitively felt that there must be some reason for life. Each one of them then—no less than we today—wanted to feel that he had a role to play, some contribution to make. They wanted to participate in God's plan, and Joseph Smith told them that this was possible, in fact, inescapable.

Joseph Smith's teaching that salvation comes to all, but comes in greater degree to some than it does to others, was also popular with those who accepted it because it seemed so reasonable. All in a graduating class are given diplomas or degrees, but some are awarded higher honors than others; some get more out of their classes than others. You might say that those who put most in get most out.

Joseph Smith taught that the meanest sinner will receive a greater gift in heaven than he can imagine, but those whose works here in mortal life have been outstanding will receive a higher place in the mansions of the Lord than others. This is a widely held belief today, but in Joseph Smith's time it was a radical doctrine. Many preachers of that time tried to scare men with threats of eternal fire.

They did not teach "Be loving, virtuous, good, and serve God and thus earn a good reward." Instead, they said, in effect, "Be good, or burn forever." Additionally, they promised a full salvation if only a man would declare his faith and promise repentance.

This could be on the deathbed, after a terrible life, and all would be forgiven. But Joseph Smith emphasized the New Testament doctrine (Galatians 6:7) "Whatsoever a man soweth, that shall he also reap." This appealed to the frontiersman belabored by the old-time preachers, and it appeals to modern man as a normal extension of the laws of cause and effect, which he sees manifested daily all around him.

Unending Progression

This reward of virtue and punishment of error was coupled with Joseph Smith's teaching that there must be unending progression. The power to progress does not end with graduation from high school or college; in a way it just begins there. Joseph Smith taught that man must persistently learn. He is not to neglect his opportunity but should pursue knowledge and development ceaselessly, for, said Smith, "The Glory of God is intelligence." Mormons believe, moreover, that the power to progress does not end with death; in a measure it just begins there. The old-time preachers pictured angels with harps, floating about on clouds. Joseph Smith abruptly stated that forever playing harps near the throne of God was a poor prospect. The young, vibrant Americans building a new nation, and those from the Old World who wanted to help, could not but agree. No harps and fleecy clouds for them.

They looked forward much more to individual improvement and advancement, and that, taught Joseph Smith, was the central idea of existence: unending eternal progression. Throughout endless time man may rise, by his own efforts, to higher levels. What he manifests and proves in the way of useful qualities in this mortal life can be carried forward to a future life.

It is hard, perhaps impossible, for us to imagine how hope-lifting this teaching was. As its logic spread out from Mormon circles to others, it became a principal contributor to that vibrant view of things that opened the American West. Joseph Smith's teachings were a philosophy of building. It suited the times.

Baptism for the Dead

In Salt Lake City, on Main Street, in the heart of the shopping district stands a large building that houses the Genealogical Society. In a mountain canyon a few miles away great rooms have been blasted out of solid granite, and here the Mormons keep the genealogical records. Joseph Smith taught that people come in families and live with their families throughout eternity. When we pass from this mortal experience, he said, we are reunited in full consciousness and memory with our families.

If we, in this life, say the Mormons, have been blessed with the teachings of our Prophet, and design our lives to live forever in these truths, what shall be said of our parents, our forebears, who died before having these truths presented to them?

Joseph Smith cited scriptural authority that for the dead a vicarious service may be rendered, that living persons may be baptized on behalf of the dead. "Else what shall they do which are baptized for the dead, if the dead rise not at all? Why are they then baptized for the dead?" (1 Cor. 15:29). Mormons believe that the departed, being free agents and still fully alert, may accept or reject the ordinances of the Church. Those who accept will engage in the work eternally.

Mormons find this is a hard thing to explain to those not of their faith, but their faith is so free and so full of joy and promise that they can't understand why everybody doesn't enjoy it with them. Most of all, they want those they love, their families, to participate in it.

The Word of Wisdom

Many have noticed that orthodox Mormons do not drink alcoholic beverages, do not smoke tobacco, and many do not use tea or coffee. This is somewhat against the trend of these times. Joseph Smith taught that the body is, in effect, sacred. A century ago bodies were principally a thing that people talked about in terms of pain and suffering, but Joseph Smith taught something similar to the view of the ancient Greeks, that a man's body was a temple, or tabernacle.

In the Mormon view it clothes the immortal spirit. Nobody felt in his time, or now, that alcohol and tobacco were good for the body. Nobody felt that overeating was good, or undereating, for that matter. A normal diet that leaned more toward fruits and vegetables and grains was deemed best, with less emphasis on meat, though not its exclusion. All this was contained in the Prophet's *Word of Wisdom*.[2]

In the years since Joseph Smith gave this word, the world has come more and more to agree with him. Meats are said to contain a high percentage of animal fat in which is found cholesterol, considered by some to be a factor in heart troubles. Smoking tobacco is held by the Surgeon General of the United States and the Royal College of Surgeons to be a causal agent of cancer. Tea and coffee are said to have little food value, but only a certain stimulant effect. In earlier times abstinence from these things was considered an ideal to be achieved as rapidly as possible, but as the harmful effects have become more recognized, we find the Mormons more insistent that the ideal is something to be achieved *right now*.

Brothers and Sisters

There is another point about the Mormons that people comment on: they almost always refer to one another as brother or sister. It is Brother Petersen this, or Sister Evans that. A group is composed of brethren and this word is also applied frequently to the leadership. This, too, evolves from a Joseph Smith teaching. It is one now widely shared. The English historian Toynbee, who spent so many years on his study of civilizations, phrased it: "The Fatherhood of God presupposes the brotherhood of man."

To Mormons there is something of the feeling that we are really the children of God; in a way they think of themselves as children. They feel an obligation to each other to be kindly and helpful. Some have one gift and some another, some may be stronger or more wise than others, but each has a duty to help the other, to work together in harmony and joy and love with him. This is the ideal; it may not always be achieved in this life, but Mormons strive for it and attain as much as they can.

There is nothing negative in this view. If it were to be realized, obviously it would preclude wars and strife. War would be as unimaginable between Russia and the United States as it is today between London and Manchester. It is this feeling of brotherhood, of course, that underlies the work with what they call the Bishop's Storehouses, and of the Women's Relief Society.

Joseph Smith taught that man lives under law. Cause and effect are related, are governed by exact law, and if this is true in the physical world, as great scientists affirm, the Mormons feel sure it is likewise true in the moral or spiritual world. Some have held in ages past, as well as in modern times, that the end justifies the means. Others have felt that a human dispensation could be given to forgive and to place certain individuals above the divine law.

Joseph Smith taught that the first law of life is the recognition of law and the obedient use of it. The highest is the law of God. The universe evidently moves in obedience to law. Everything in the great world of science is governed by law. So it is, he said, with man.

In a work-a-day sense Mormons believe that this law makes it mandatory upon them to express faith in Jesus Christ, to evidence this in Church work and in their other activities. Each is responsive to the Law of God, and as he responds he begins to realize the great blessings of living in harmony with that law. Such is generalization, in "gentile" language, of some of the basic teachings of Joseph Smith. I gathered them from years of discussions with Mormon friends, though there may be a few points that Mormons will not wholly agree with, and of course Mormons feel that a lifetime, and a quite useful lifetime, could be spent in exploring points of doctrine only touched upon here.

The foregoing, however, is intended only as a primer for understanding what it is that motivated the Mormons as they met persecution and brutality and were forced time and again to move like the ancient followers of Moses across the red seas of terror and the deserts of wilted hopes toward their land of promise.

Chapter Four

ORGANIZING A CHURCH

To those who accepted the teachings of Joseph Smith, a whole new way of life opened. And it must be conceded that many unusual things—biblical sorts of things—happened. For one, take the establishment of the Church itself. As noted, it was formed by six members, a requirement of New York law. The members were all young. Joseph Smith, at the time of founding in 1830, was twenty-four years old. This is not an age when men are usually given to the founding of religious organizations.

Joseph Smith has been described at this period as handsome, about six feet in height, a strong farm worker, good at sports, full of good cheer and characterized by some as "jolly." He was sometimes criticized for a lack of the sort of gloomy sobriety expected of men of religion in those times.

One of the first members was Joseph's younger brother, Samuel H. Smith. He was one of several who filled a knapsack with copies of the Book of Mormon and set out to sell them. Among those he called upon was the Reverend John P. Greene, a Methodist minister, who was about to leave home on a journey and was in a hurry. While he said he was not interested in reading the book himself, he agreed to take along a copy and to show it to people as he went around his circuit and to take orders from any who might wish to order it. Samuel was not much encouraged by this, hardly expecting a Methodist minister actively to merchandise the book.

Brigham Young's Conversion

However, the minister's wife saw it, became interested in it, and urged her husband to read it. He did and in time they both joined the Mormons, as the church group soon became known. A few months later this same copy of the book came into the hands of a young carpenter in nearby Mendon, New York, named Brigham Young, and he, too, in time joined the Church, with notable consequences. And Brigham Young introduced the Mormon Gospel to his friend Heber C. Kimball, also with notable results.

The activity of the Mormons was not welcome everywhere. Joseph Smith was arrested several times for holding street-corner meetings which were said to be "disturbing" in Palmyra and neighboring New York towns. There was no universal acclaim for his mission. But for anybody of the time who didn't like it where he was, there was always the beckoning West. In September, following the founding of the Church in the spring of 1830, four of the early Mormons set out for the West on foot. They were dispatched by Joseph Smith as among the first of his missionaries for a special purpose. The Prophet regarded the Indians as descendants of the Lamanites and felt that the Book of Mormon should have compelling appeal to them.

These four were themselves of interest. There was Oliver Cowdery, who had copied off much of the Book of Mormon as Joseph Smith dictated it. There was Peter Whitmer, Jr., brother of David Whitmer, who was one of the witnesses to the Book of Mormon. There was Ziba Peterson, one of the earliest converts, and one whose name was to be featured in much subsequent Mormon history, Parley P. Pratt.

Pratt lived in Ohio, where he was a follower of the Church of the Disciples, or "Campbellites" as they were known. On a visit to New York State he heard of the Book of Mormon, was converted, and soon brought in his younger brother, Orson Pratt, who also became a legendary figure in Mormon history. We will come across the names of Parley Pratt and Orson Pratt frequently in the pages that follow.

These four were eager to carry their message to the Lamanites. Although at that time they enjoyed no more success than establishing reasonably friendly relations with the Indians, which the Mormons cherished and developed from that time forward, it is interesting to note that today, a century and a third later, some of the most fruitful missionary work is being accomplished among the Lamanite-Indians of South America and the South Pacific islands.

Thus it could be fairly said that Joseph Smith's idea about the

Lamanites is bearing a delayed but still completely timely fruit as far as the Mormons are concerned. And even in 1830 this mission of the four brought results that were immediately dramatic and lifted the Church to a new plateau of size, activity, and location.

For as Cowdery, Whitmer, Peterson, and Pratt traveled on they came to a group of the Campbellites that Pratt knew well. They were located in the little town of Kirtland and their leader was Sidney Rigdon, one of the founders of the Campbellite sect. Kirtland was, and indeed is, not far from the northeast corner of Ohio, where it borders Pennsylvania and is near the New York State boundary. It was at that time one of the most important crossroads on the frontier. Traffic following Lake Erie to the north came through Kirtland as did traffic following the road to Cincinnati. The four Mormons presented the story of Joseph Smith and soon a few of the Campbellites were convinced. It was not long before Rigdon himself was converted. So it was that by December a thousand new Mormons had been added to the rolls. The Church had a new center and indeed a new sort of future. It was then a more important city than Cleveland, though that changed with the coming of the railroad.

The Problem in Ohio

News of the conversion of the Rigdon group was dispatched to Joseph Smith, still in New York, and Rigdon went to see Joseph and urged him to move his church and congregation to Kirtland. In January 1831 the Prophet arrived, and in a series of revelations, and with his intelligent and energetic leadership, soon had a thriving community on his hands, and an expanding one as well.

In the meantime the four original missionaries had pushed on westward from Ohio to Missouri. An idea of the zeal that motivated them can be gained from a few lines written by Parley P. Pratt:

We traveled on foot for three hundred miles through vast prairies and through trackless wilds of snow. . . . No beaten road; houses few and far between; and the bleak northwest wind always blowing in our faces with a keenness which would almost take the skin off the face. We traveled for whole days, from morning till night, without a house or a fire, wading in snow to the knees at every step, and the cold so intense that it did not melt on the south side of the houses, even in the mid-day sun, for nearly six weeks. We carried on our backs our changes of clothing, several books, and corn bread and raw pork. We often ate our frozen bread and pork by the way, when the bread would be so frozen that we could not bite or penetrate any part of it but the outside crust.[1]

At Independence, Missouri, near what is now Kansas City, they found friendly Indians who were much interested in the Mormon account of the history of America. The missionaries saw a land which they felt would be suitable for a new colony—good soil, few neighbors to oppose or deride their beliefs, an opportunity to form a new society after their own ideas. This, they knew, was the desire of Joseph Smith.

Their report of a favorable location was brought to Kirtland, where by June 1831 some 2000 Mormons were gathered. By the middle of July, Joseph Smith and twenty-eight of his principal men arrived in Missouri and set about helping to build a new community.

For the next seven years the Mormons were divided between Ohio, and, a thousand miles to the west, Missouri. While both prospered and grew, they had their troubles, primarily in Kirtland.

Jealous of the Mormons

There were reasons for troubles. Foremost, of course, was the fact that a man, young and full of the joy of life, not at all averse to wrestling and other vigorous activity, not at all a sad and dour ascetic, was proclaiming that he was directed by God to establish a new church. This was a newsworthy event. Many people visited Kirtland as curiosity seekers. Some remained as converts. This sometimes divided families and caused friction. Second, as a cause of trouble, was the fact that the Mormons bought more and more land in Kirtland and so tended to dominate the region economically. The Mormons believed in hard work; often their farms were better than those of their neighbors. Perhaps worst of all to some was the fact that Mormons were happy. They sang and danced and seemed to enjoy life. This generated jealousy.

Another reason for resentment of the townspeople was the building of a temple. Hardly were Joseph Smith and his New York congregation settled in Kirtland than he said it was revealed to him that a temple should be built. It was to be no ordinary structure of logs, as most buildings were at that time, but a temple built of quarried stone and finely wrought, with an interior of handsomely crafted wood. Much of this excellent work was done by a young carpenter, the recent convert to the Church, Brigham Young.

It was a building eighty feet long and fifty-nine feet wide, and the tower reached upward 110 feet. For the time it was a remarkably large and fine building in western America. It remains so today, and is an often visited example of good design and frontier workmanship.[2] It took three years to build and represented immense sacrifice of time and resources by those who had to subsist on what they could grow and manufacture with their own hands.

But the temple building itself excited much comment, some of it envious. Talk was one thing—a building which could be seen on a clear day from Lake Erie, twelve miles distant, was something else. It couldn't be scoffed away. Dedication of the temple in March 1836 found Joseph Smith at the height of elation, but he was also aware of troubles brewing, this time in Missouri.

Against Slavery

In addition to the envy and jealousy and general antipathy felt toward any people who profess to enjoy a better grasp on basic religious truths than others, the Mormons in Missouri, who were by this time well established, represented in the eyes of their neighbors an antislave group. And Missouri was a focal point in the slave controversy. For as the nation moved west, settlers from the northern states tended to carry their own "do-it-yourself" enterprise into the wilderness, while the southern plantation people vainly sought to push their slave-based style of life to the Pacific.

To the Mormons, while one human being might be more blessed than another, all were human beings and the children of the one God. Mormon hearts and charity were closed to no one. The idea of buying and selling people, breaking up families, granting no rights whatsoever, treating them as cattle was as abhorrent to the Mormons in the 1830s as it is universally today. While their primary purpose was to build their own community and practice their own religion in it, the Mormons made no secret of their feelings about slavery, and neither did the Southerners, so there was enmity from the start.

Raids were organized against the Mormons. They were harassed and persecuted until at last they were forced out of their settlements in and near Independence and moved to a more hospitable county a few miles to the north. They named their new settlement Far West. Near it they established another town, Adam-ond-Ahman, for Joseph Smith believed that this area was in fact the location of the place where Adam had settled after his expulsion from the Garden of Eden. Life in the new settlement was peaceful and it appeared that progress was being made.

Meanwhile, in Kirtland fresh trouble erupted, largely a money matter. The United States was going through much the same problem that many newly emerged countries confronted in those days toward the end of colonialism. That problem was simply a lack of capital for expansion. President Andrew Jackson was opposed to a national bank. He believed in payment in gold or silver, or notes backed with such values. His policies brought an end to the inflation upon which much of western prosperity had been based. Some land in the Kirtland area, for example, that had been bought originally for $1.25 an acre had been resold at $2000 an acre, but was now reverting to its former price.

The Bank Failure

The Mormons had borrowed heavily to finance the building of the temple, for the establishment of a printing press, and for other requirements. They had attempted to set up their own bank, but a charter had been refused them. Jackson's policies made it easy for the state to refuse new bank charters and difficult for it to grant them. So the Kirtland people went ahead with a local institution which they called a "Safety Society" to avoid use of the word "bank," and it proved to be a disaster.

As the community verged on bankruptcy, along with a great deal of the rest of the nation—800 banks failed in the month of February 1837—Joseph Smith furnished a little noticed but significant testimonial of his faith in the future of his movement by dispatching some of his most trusted assistants to England to carry the Mormon Gospel and seek new members.

He recognized that the new church, no less than the new nation, could increase quickly only by bringing in converts from the outside. These first overseas missionaries started the world-wide Mormon activity.

Chapter Five

THE INTERNATIONAL MORMONS

It is true that there are few spots on earth today where Mormon missionaries have not tried to leave their mark. And on the streets of Salt Lake City, nestled in a Rocky Mountain valley and quite isolated geographically, it is entirely possible to start a conversation in almost any language of the world. This is partly because the Mormon community has been drawn from many countries, but more because Mormon missionaries are going to so many lands.

Today you may chat with a young man in greasy coveralls about the problems of installing a 1966 Olds engine in a '32 Ford chassis to make a hot rod, and a few weeks later you may meet him in a gray flannel suit on the train between Glasgow and Edinburgh where he will point out, with evident intimate knowledge of the details, a hill which is called locally Arthur's Seat, where Orson Pratt, younger brother of Parley, prayed to the Lord more than a century ago "for two hundred souls."

If nothing else—and of course there is much else—the Church has given its people a sense of mission and hence of responsiveness and responsibility about the needs of the world. At some period in his or her life many thousands of Mormons devote a period of time, usually two years, and often overseas, to full-time mission work.

They go out into the world feeling they have a wonderful gift to bestow. Rebuffs sometimes hurt and bewilder them, but Mormon boys and girls have been reared with the stories of the early missionaries ringing in their ears. Disappointments, as well as victories, were the common lot. The stories of the early days are truly noble ones, yet they are often duplicated today.

It sometimes surprises non-Mormons to learn that there were Mormons in England before there were Mormons in Salt Lake City. Indeed, the Mormon Church in England is almost as old as the Church in America. This is because in a time of quite serious troubles Joseph Smith dispatched to England several of his closest, most valued, and most loyal assistants. To the Mormons at the time, and today, this was perfectly understandable: Their Prophet was obeying directions from his heavenly Father. That these directions brought tremendous strength to the Church is deemed by the Mormons to be only a normal result. A hundred thousand British Mormons who emigrated to the Latter-day Saint's Zion gave the Church an infusion of character that continues to be of incalculable value.

The First Missionaries

There were seven that set out in the original party from Kirtland. Several are worthy of special mention and will reappear in our narrative. Heber C. Kimball was their leader. He was from New England, a potter by trade, and he had entered the Church with his friend Brigham Young. He had traveled widely around Ohio and to the west, and was a natural-born missionary.

Orson Hyde, partly of Jewish extraction, was the first to ask to go with Elder Kimball. He had been an apostle for two years. Later he was to be the first missionary to Germany and to Palestine. Then, there were Dr. Willard Richards, a cousin of Brigham Young and also a New Englander, Orson Pratt, and Joseph Fielding, who had been born in Honedon, Bedfordshire, but had emigrated to Canada in 1832 when he was thirty-five years old. He had joined the Church just a year before he returned to England in 1837.

Joseph Fielding had relatives and friends in Canada, and the Church had a number of converts there. Naturally, the Canadians wrote to their home folks in England about their new-found religion. It was believed in Kirtland that there might be a degree of interest in the Mormon Church in Britain—and there was. Joseph Fielding's brother, the Reverend James Fielding, had an active church in Lancashire and he had told his congregation about his brother's religious experience in America. The congregation was expecting the brother to visit them.

When it is said that these Mormons went to England without

purse and without script, it is literally true. Heber C. Kimball had only five dollars. Each made his way from Kirtland to New York on his own. En route, Willard Richards' brother paid off a $40 debt and this helped the small party. Suffice it to say—as they did—that the Lord provided. The passage to England from New York was quite cheap, about $15 per person.

But how different they found things in England! It is hard for us to imagine the condition of the poor, for most of our pictures of England of that time are of great country estates, a merry England of horses and hounds and hunts, and a dining board groaning under the weight of food. The summer of 1837, when these Mormon missionaries arrived, was only twenty-two years after Waterloo.

Victoria Was Queen

And this time was concomitant with the steam engines of Watt and Newcomen, and the mills and the industrial revolution of the early nineteenth century. The ferment and excitement of the British world at that period was enormous. Victoria, a young German girl of eighteen, had just been crowned to reign over people newly emerged as the leaders of Western Christian civilization. It was a time of expansion and prosperity in England, a shift from farms to factories, the rise of urban life, and the creation of new classes of extremely poor factory people. It was a good life for the few, but as some observed, the very few.

In the early years of the British Mormon Mission a novel was published which caused quite a stir. Its author was Benjamin Disraeli, later to become a great Prime Minister. The novel was *Sybil, or The Two Nations.* A passage in it illuminates the times:

"Well, Society may be in its infancy," said Egremont, slightly smiling, "but say what you like, our Queen reigns over the greatest nation that ever existed."

"Which nation?" asked the stranger, "for she reigns over two."

The stranger paused; Egremont was silent but looked inquiringly.

"Yes," resumed the stranger after a moment's interval. "Two nations; between them there is no intercourse and no sympathy; who are ignorant of each other's habits, thoughts and feelings, as if they were dwellers in different zones, or inhabitants of different planets; who are formed by different breeding, are fed by different food, are ordered by different manners and are not governed by the same laws."

"You speak of——," said Egremont, hesitantly.

"The rich and the poor."

This was the thing that impressed the young American Mormons most strongly: the contrast between opulence, silks, and satins on one side and rags and tatters and misery on the other.[1]

They arrived in Liverpool July 20, 1837, strangers in a strange land, upon their own resources, separated from home and home news by a month's travel, with no precedent to follow, no headquarters in Britain with which to communicate.

Heber Kimball described their arrival:

Immediately after we anchored, a small boat came alongside, when several of the passengers, with Brothers Hyde, Richards, Goodson and myself, got in and went to shore. When we were within six or seven feet of the pier, I leaped on shore, followed by Elders Hyde and Richards, and for the first time in my life I stood on British ground, among strangers, whose manners and customs were different from my own.[2]

Liverpool in 1837 was not much of a city. The Mersey River is only a small stream, but at the point where it enters the sea it becomes wide and forms a pool. The tides range quite high, up to about twenty feet, and this pool forms a deep and placid natural harbor suitable for sailing vessels. The Liver Buildings, the Cunard Building, and other structures which came to give the Liverpool quay its architectural distinction were still to be built. Indeed, it would be another five years before Mr. Cunard would establish his North Atlantic service.

The first missionaries did not linger long in Liverpool. It was too big and busy; moreover, they had introductions in a small Lancashire mill town about thirty miles north. They arrived in Preston on Saturday, July 22, and found that it was voting day. Queen Victoria had called for a general election. The town was at its gayest. Bands were playing; flags were flying; men, women and children were parading; streets were bedecked with varicolored streamers and ribbons. And just as the coach bearing the missionaries reached its destination, a large banner was unfurled almost over their heads. Its bold gold letters proclaimed TRUTH WILL PREVAIL. Of course, the missionaries considered it a portent from the Lord.

Preston's Cockpit

The young Mormons soon located Joseph Fielding's brother in Preston, and he invited them to preach in Vauxhall Chapel. It looked as if their work would be serene, but the Mormons, as other religious leaders before them, found that, when the good is stirred up in men, an evil is also unsettled. There is something in mortals that does not give up easily. It is sometimes said of the Christians in Rome and in Greece that they must have been akin to the first labor organizers in the United States in that they were resolute, careless of personal safety, and filled with a zeal that could let them accept beatings and even death. There were few namby-pambys among the early followers of Jesus. And the same could be said for the Mormon missionaries.

It wasn't long before they had stirred up the organized clergy, who could hardly be expected to welcome rival claimants. Among those that came to oppose them was the Reverend Mr. Fielding himself, who could not afford financially to see his congregation leave him for the new dispensation. Some time later Heber C. Kimball related his English experience to Joseph Smith and asked the reason for the hardships. He was told, "The nearer a person approaches the Lord, a greater power will be manifested by the adversary to prevent the accomplishment of his purposes."[3] To which it would be hard to find a religious leader who would not out of personal experience agree.

But while they found churches and even public halls closed to them, the missionaries did find homes where they could stay and where they could preach to a few at a time. Kimball was a tall, thin, sinewy man with a ready smile, wise and tolerant eyes, and a humorous way. He would begin addressing his audience by looking around as if in some question or trepidation and ask, "Am I among Christians?"

Upon receiving an affirmative reply, he would say that this was a happy circumstance because he could safely entrust some news to them. They were, he would say, of course, familiar with such incidents in the Bible as the conversion of Saul of Tarsus, and of the revelations given to him when as Paul he traveled across the world that was known to him, carrying the Christian message to all who would hear, even to Mars Hill in pagan Athens.

While all this was going on in Asia Minor, Greece, and even Rome, Kimball would continue, the same Christian teachings were being practiced in a place Paul's hearers didn't know existed, a New World. There, uncorrupted by the vested interests of the Roman Empire, the pure, undefiled religion had been fostered and preserved. This was now restored in its original purity and in its promise of being "a very present help."

"I assume I am addressing Christians," he would say again, with a smile that embraced all within his fellowship. "Now, I ask whether it is more difficult to believe that Joseph Smith received revelations from God than it is to believe that Paul did? Those who believed in Paul's testimony were saints of God; those who believed Joseph Smith's are just as surely saints, for it is the same gospel!"[4]

On Sunday, July 30, 1837, only a week after they arrived in Preston, they baptized nine persons in the Ribble River, which runs through Preston. As can be imagined, this open-air baptism by missionaries of a new church aroused much interest. Kimball reported that between "seven and nine thousand people" assembled on the banks to watch. That afternoon the missionaries estimated that some five thousand people came to hear them preach in the market place. Before a month was out they had organized a new branch of their Church in Britain, the first one outside of America.

By early autumn the interest in Preston and the increase in Church membership was such that the missionaries rented a building known as the Cockpit, originally built for the purpose the name suggests, but by 1837 transformed into a meeting place for the Preston Temperance Society, and this is a point that has always interested the Mormons. For while the Temperance Society was originally formed in Canada, the first town in England in which men are believed to have taken the "teetotal" pledge was Preston.

Missionary Impressions

The winter of 1837 turned out to be an unusually cold one. Kimball wrote home:

The oldest inhabitants told me that they never experienced such weather before. In consequence of the inclemency . . . several manufacturing establishments were shut up, and several thousands of men, women and children were thrown out of employment, whose sufferings during that time were severe and I was credibly informed, and verily believe, that many perished from starvation.

Such sufferings I never witnessed before. The scenes which I daily beheld were enough to chill the blood in my veins. The streets were crowded with men, women and children who begged from the passengers as they walked along. Numbers of these poor, wretched beings were without shoes or stockings, and scarcely any covering to screen them from the inclemency of the weather. . . .

At the same time there were hundreds and thousands living in wealth and splendor. I felt to exclaim: Oh Lord, how long shall these things exist! How long shall the rich oppress the poor, and have no more care or interest for them than the brutes of the field, nor half so much! When will distress and poverty cease, and peace and plenty abound. . . .[5]

There were others who asked then, or later, the same question; among them, in addition to Disraeli, a young German named Friedrich Engels, whose family owned textile mills in the Lancashire district, and Charles Dickens. Each had his own ideas about solutions, but Kimball told his listeners that peace and plenty would abound. "When the Lord Jesus shall descend in the clouds of heaven, then the rod of the oppressor shall be broken. Hasten the time, O Lord!"

The missionaries had hard times in some places. In Ribchester, for example, a mob gathered to throw rocks at them while baptizing, but in Downham and Chatburn, where they had been warned that church activities were singularly unsuccessful, they met with some of their happiest experiences. In Downham about forty children employed in the mill twelve hours a day ran out to hear the young men from America, and in Chatburn Kimball was invited to a large barn where a crowd gathered to hear him explain his mission. Many parents wept with joy, the missionary said, because their children had been so attracted.

Efforts Successful

The impact of these young Americans, so obviously filled with a conviction that they occupied the same distinctive position, with all its responsibilities, as the original followers of Jesus, can hardly be said to have been less than immense. Although they were careful to express a proper humility and not to claim unusual or supernatural powers for themselves, they did not refuse to lay hands on the sick when asked and certainly no saint of antiquity carried a faith stronger than these missionaries of the nineteenth century. Kimball wrote:

Some days we went from house to house, conversing with the people on the things of the kingdom, and would sometimes be instrumental in convincing many of the truth; and I have known as many as twenty persons baptized in one day, who have been convinced on such occasions. I have had to go into the water to administer the ordinance of baptism six or seven times a day, and frequently after having come out of the water and changed my clothes, I have had to turn back to the water before I reached my lodgings; this too when the weather was extremely cold, the ice being from twelve to fourteen inches thick.

They found that if they preached in a new town or location for two or three days and then went away for a time that when they returned the local people would have forged ahead and made up their own group, but if the missionaries stayed with the group constantly the tendency was for the local people to lean on the missionaries and dispute with one another.

This discovery let Kimball conclude that, with the work well started, it would be proper for him to return to Kirtland. And without question he was strengthened in this decision by the reports he received of serious troubles confronting the Mormons at home. Accordingly, Kimball decided to leave Joseph Fielding in Britain as head of the mission while he went home. In eight months they had accomplished a great deal. On April 8, 1838, representatives from branches in Penwortham, Walkerford, Thornley, Ribchester, Chatburn, Clithero, Barshe Lees, Waddington, Leyland Moss, Leyland Lane, Eccleston, Hunter's Hill, Euxton, Whittle, Dauber's Lane, Bamber Bridge, Longton, Southport, Downham, Burnley, Bedford, Alston, Brampton, Bolton, and Chorley gathered in the Cockpit, Preston, to bid Kimball Godspeed and to arrange their affairs for continued and even accelerated activity. Kimball was comforted in the knowledge that he had hundreds of Brother and Sister Saints "who love me as their own souls. . . ."

After twenty-two days at sea he was put down again in New York, on May 12, 1838.

Chapter Six

LIBERTY JAIL

Heber Kimball hastened to Kirtland only to find that Joseph Smith and Brigham Young had moved to Missouri in the dead of the past winter, for after the bank failure, things had gone from bad to worse in Kirtland.

Recognizing that many of the best Kirtland people were going to the Missouri settlement, as were most of the converts flowing into the Church, and that the Missouri settlement was already at least twice as large as the Kirtland community, Joseph Smith had decided to move west.

He had arrived at Far West in March 1838 after two months' traveling on foot and on horse in the cold, without funds, but not discouraged. He was greeted in Far West by a parade and a brass band, and was told that in Missouri his people believed that God had brought about the failure of the Kirtland bank as a means of forcing him to the new Zion.

When he arrived, there were about 10,000 Mormons in the Missouri settlement, and they continued to pour in all summer, from Ohio, from the East, and some from overseas. Soon they numbered 20,000 and were the largest organized minority group in the state—a political power as well as an economic one. In fact it was the political potential that led to the first outbreak of trouble in the new community not very long after Joseph Smith's arrival.

In August an election was scheduled in the county and the non-Mormons passed out word that no Mormon would be allowed to vote because, clearly, the Mormons could dominate. On the morning of election day about thirty young Mormons arrived at Gallatin, the county seat, to vote. As one of them approached the polls, he was stopped, called a thief and a dupe, and was told that "Mormons don't vote, no more than niggers." The young Mormon persisted on his way to the voting booth and was knocked down.

Immediately his friends jumped into the fray and it wasn't long before the thirty Mormon boys had a hundred of the townspeople fleeing, whereupon they walked into the polls, voted in an orderly way, and departed.[1] In America of that time, and perhaps of the present, to act differently would have been looked down upon.

The Extermination Order

Tempers were hot, and the incorrect rumor spread that two non-Mormons had been killed; tension filled the air. Joseph Smith's own pleas to avoid violence were misunderstood, and he was put under peace bond. Attacks on isolated farms and small Mormon communities continued, forcing many families to abandon valuable property and seek shelter in Far West, where the Mormons were arming. By the end of August the situation was such that the governor ordered out the Missouri militia. The Mormons learned that Governor Boggs had suggested to the military commander their extermination.[2]

Some 10,000 armed men marched on Far West. In desperation Joseph Smith sent an emissary to the governor to ask terms of armistice. The emissary evidently betrayed him, because back came word that Joseph Smith and his principal councillors should come to a meeting with the commanding general. When Joseph arrived he was told that the emissary had agreed that the Mormon leaders would surrender to stand trial for treason, and that all Mormon-owned property would be confiscated; that all Mormon arms would be surrendered and that all Mormons would move from Missouri at once, and peacefully.

The Mormon leaders were naturally struck with amazement and anger, but were immediately thrown into a hastily constructed, roofless stockade, with guards taunting all night in the rain. In the morning they were sentenced to death, but the order to carry out the shooting was given to General Doniphan, who knew the Mormons and had served as their attorney on prior occasions. He returned the order: "It is cold-blooded murder. I will not obey your order. . . . If you execute these men, I will hold you responsible before an early tribunal, so help me God."[3]

This at least gave the militia pause. They held Joseph Smith and most of his councillors and then summoned all the residents of Far West to a meeting held under the muzzles of cannons. The Mormons were told to pack up and get out.

From his imprisonment Joseph sent word placing Brigham Young in charge and directed that he should move the Mormons out, that there was no use in trying to remain, that they would be exterminated. Joseph himself was taken away to jail in nearby Liberty, Missouri.

Haun's Mill

A Mormon family, a husband, wife, and three young sons, lived in a small settlement not far from Far West known as Haun's Mill, which is beside Shoal Creek. As was common practice in the Mormon settlement, they lived in houses grouped together, while they farmed separate fields outside the center. In this way they avoided the isolation of frontier living and could meet in the evening for worship and entertainment.

This family and their neighbors were not really frontier people. They had recently emigrated from the East. They placed emphasis on education, and Mormons today proudly point to the fact that what is believed to be the first school in Missouri was started by their forebears. It was their practice to set up classes wherever they could and their plan of settlement permitted and fostered this.

They knew something of the more gracious world of the theater and arts and books. In the evening they might play at amateur dramatics, or hold a square dance of the sort popular at that time. While they didn't work on Sunday, they held with the teachings of Jesus that the Sabbath was made for man and not vice versa.

They led a happy life, buoyant with good spirits. It was hard for them to understand why all people shouldn't want to join them and be like them. There was deep sadness when they were persecuted and sometimes natural anger and resentment, even emotional desire for revenge, but no hatred or drive to rule by force. Such was the environment of our family in Haun's Mill, where the young father and mother prayed and worked to build a happy home and dreamed of the success and progress that would come to their sons.

On a certain October afternoon in 1838 children romped on the banks of Shoal Creek while their mothers worked around their houses and the fathers were in the fields. All was tranquil, but about four o'clock a troop of some 250 horsemen suddenly charged the Mill shooting indiscriminately at women and children as well as the men who rushed to protect them.

Some of the children ran to the blacksmith shop and the raiders stood at cracks in the logs and shot them. Others in the settlement fared no better. Within a few minutes seventeen of the thirty-eight Mormons were dead, and fourteen seriously wounded. Most of the men were killed, and only a few women and children survived. Amanda Smith found that her husband and oldest boy had been killed. Her youngest son had part of his hip blown away and she relates how she used wood ashes to make lye to go into swabs to clean the wound, and a packing of slippery elm to fill the cavity. She was still taking care of the little boy when a mob of about fifty men returned the next day and demanded why she hadn't left. She later wrote:

I met them at the door. They demanded of me why I was not gone. I bade them enter and see their work. They crowded into the room and I showed them my wounded boy. They came, party after party, until all had seen my excuse. Then they quarreled among themselves and came near fighting. At last they went away, all but two. These I thought were detailed to kill us.

"Madam," said one, "have you any meat in the house?"

"No," was my reply.

"Could you dress a fat hog if one was laid at your door?"

"I think we could," was my answer.[4]

Jail Restored

Visitors to Kansas City, Missouri, today find in the neighboring areas several mementoes of the early Mormon days. One of these is quite unusual. At a cost of $750,000 the Mormon Church has restored the old Liberty Jail and enclosed it in a large monumental rotunda. Since the summer of 1963, when the restoration was completed, thousands of visitors have looked at it, its sides and roof cut away to show the stone and oak walls, four feet thick, the tiny barred windows, the heavy wood and stone roof—constructed more like a shelter for the atomic age than for an early nineteenth-century jail—and have reflected that this is where Joseph Smith, his brother Hyrum, and four others were held for almost five months in the winter of 1838.

It was a time of terror for the Mormons. Many years later Mercy Fielding Thompson, sister of Hyrum Smith's wife, and, like her sister, a recent arrival from England via Canada, described it:

In February 1839, while Joseph and Hyrum Smith, with four other brethren, were incarcerated in Liberty Jail, I accompanied my sister Mary from Far West to visit them. It would be beyond my power to describe my feelings when we were admitted to the jail by the keeper and the door was locked behind us.

We could not help feeling a sense of horror on realizing that we were locked up in that dark and dismal den, fit only for criminals of the deepest dye; but there we beheld Joseph, the Prophet, the man chosen of God, in the dispensation of the fullness of times, to hold the keys of his kingdom on earth with power to bind and loose as God should direct, confined in a loathsome prison, for no other cause or reason than that he claimed to be inspired of God to establish His church among men.

There also we found his noble brother, who, I believe, was not charged with any other crime than that of being a friend to his brother Joseph. There also were four other brethren whose offences were similar to that of Hyrum's. The night was spent in fearful forebodings, owing to a false rumor having gone out that the prisoners contemplated making an attempt to escape, which greatly enraged the jailer and the guards. Under these circumstances we were constrained to bid adieu to the Prophet and his brethren, and hasten our departure from Liberty. My sister was in very delicate health, having with her her babe, only three months old, whom his father then saw for the first time.[5]

That baby was Joseph F. Smith, who survived to become, in 1901, the sixth President of the Church.

There are today in Missouri just about as many Mormons as lived there in the days of the great persecution. Until fairly recent times they still felt, even though more than a century and a quarter has passed, some of the chill of anti-Mormonism.

But when Joseph Fielding Smith, Jr., grandson of Hyrum and son of the first Joseph Fielding Smith, visited Liberty Jail in September 1963, and opened the doors of the museum to the general public, many old prejudices vanished. As the press and radio and television representatives gathered to cover the news event, it was learned that the Mormons had not restored the old jail to honor old and bitter memories, but for quite another reason. Far from memorializing past oppressions, the Mormons were joyfully celebrating the fact that it was during his long winter in this unlikely setting that Joseph Smith received some of the most cherished revelations in the history of the Church.

Not long ago, the Central States Mission of the Church, located in Independence, Missouri, published a booklet in which it was noted:

These revelations should be carefully read by everyone who wants to see the great strength contained in the instructions of the Lord to a persecuted people. Here the Prophet prayed: "How long shall thy hand be stayed and thine eye, yea thy pure eye, behold from the eternal heavens the wrongs of thy people and of thy servants, and thine ear be penetrated with their cries."

The reply that came by revelation was: "My son, peace be unto thy soul; thine adversity and thy afflictions shall be but a small moment; and then, if thou endure it well, God shall exalt thee on high; thou shalt triumph over all thy foes. Thy friends do stand by thee, and they shall hail thee again with warm hearts and friendly hands."[6]

Thoughts Abroad

There was another revelation, which quickly translated itself into a policy and program. Word reached Joseph Smith in jail of the success the missionaries had enjoyed in England. Converts were enthusiastically joining. Many wished to cross the Atlantic to the New World frontier. All during December 1838 and January, February, and March of 1839, while the sad procession of Mormons were leaving Far West and the other settlements, trudging east 250 miles to Quincy, Illinois, Joseph Smith found himself thinking of England. There, he knew, resided people deeply immersed in the wonderful truths of the King James Bible, a people unaffected by the local passions and prejudices of the American frontier, and eager to look forward to fresh unfoldment. But Joseph Smith said that the revelation which came to him mentioned "Islands of the Seas." Britain was an island, but not the only island.

"Escape"

Early in April 1839 Joseph and his brethren were brought before the court. His attorneys asked for a change of venue, pointing out that hatreds were evidently of such a nature as to preclude a fair trial. As a matter of fact, the Missourians had cooled down a great deal. It was rumored that a member of the state legislature had participated in the Haun's Mill massacre, and this was held to be shameful. There was some demand for a federal investigation of the matter; the imprisonment of Joseph had become an embarrassment, and the judge in granting the plea for a change of venue openly hinted to the guards who were to transfer the prisoners that he wouldn't mind if they "escaped."

Brigham Young was with Heber Kimball in Far West and the two were winding up affairs, making certain that the last destitute Mormon was started on the way to Illinois, when they had this news from Liberty. Young and Kimball managed to raise $400, which was duly paid to the guards, ostensibly for the horses which Joseph and Hyrum and the others used to make their way to Quincy.

The imprisonment of Joseph, his revelations while in jail, and the move out of Missouri represent the point at which the teachings of Joseph Smith reached a certain maturity. The organization of his Church, the manner in which it should be governed, and the way in which it should be financially sustained were now clear to him. The principles, the basis, the teachings on which the future could be built were such that a century later the Church could come back and with love in its heart erect a monument and a museum over the site and the remains of the old jail in Liberty.

Chapter Seven

BACK TO ENGLAND!

Certainly the Mormon experience was seldom blessed with peace and tranquillity. Joseph Smith felt he would be more welcome in Ohio than in New York, and in Missouri more welcome than in Ohio. Yet there was clearly something about the situation and circumstances that resulted in conflict.

Was it envy of an industrious people enjoying greater material abundance? Perhaps partly, but only partly, for the Mormons were drawn from the great average. If one had then had available the various intelligence-testing systems of a later time he would no doubt have found that the Mormons were little better and not much worse than the national average.

The Mormons themselves believed that the people simply expressed rejection of their beliefs. More likely, it was the serene and unshakable faith that the Mormons brought to their everyday affairs that roused enmity. The Mormons were taught that this present life experience is at best a passing thing, only preparatory to continued living and progress after what is called death, and that there will be many lives. They had no great fear of death, when they expected to be united with their families under improved circumstances. And this attitude brought a serenity which seemed to annoy some of those who did not have it and was probably a larger cause of the hostility expressed toward them than the more mundane rationalizing about envy, antislave attitudes, or threatened political ascendancy, although, of course, all these played a part in one way or another, and at one time or another.

Welcome in Illinois

After Joseph Smith "escaped" from his captors he made his way
to Quincy, Illinois. Brigham Young had found that the people
of Illinois were shocked by the behavior of the Missourians and
were willing, even eager, to take the Mormons in and attempt in
some way to re-establish the fact that human beings must not act
as the Missourians had. Such men as Young and Kimball advised
the Mormons fleeing from Far West to locate in the vicinity of
Quincy. Joseph Smith had even carried on some correspondence
with a land agent who was willing to take the deeds the Mormons
brought with them from Missouri as payment, or part payment, on
new lands in Iowa and Illinois along the banks of the Mississippi.
When the Prophet arrived in Illinois, he quickly moved forward,
realizing that there must be no delay in offering his people a new
Zion.

The little town of Commerce was on the Illinois side of the
Mississippi and Joseph Smith bought enough land to permit him
to lay out a city of square blocks rising upward from the river
banks to a height of about five hundred feet. It was a commanding
site at a bend in the Mississippi. He changed the name to Nauvoo,
which he said meant "Beautiful Place."

Brigham Young settled his family in an abandoned army barracks
on the Iowa side of the river, a place called Montrose. He was
just in the throes of what must have been influenza, for an epidemic
was then sweeping through the weakened Mormon community,
when Joseph sent for him and the other councillors. He reminded
them of his revelation. The entire Council of the Twelve, he repeated, was to go abroad.

Travel with, and on, Faith

Not one had funds to pay for such a journey. "Go," said Joseph,
"the Lord provides." In this decision Joseph Smith disclosed that
quality so necessary in a leader, an ability to look beyond the
problem of the moment, even while that problem looms at its worst.

The immediate problem, Joseph knew, would be solved; but the longer range answer of building a new and greater Zion required skilled hands and sturdy hearts. From all that Heber Kimball and the others had told him, Joseph Smith concluded that the hands Zion needed were willing and available in England. Go bring them in, said Joseph, and such was their faith that they rose from their sickbeds, wrapped blankets over their shoulders, and set off.

The men who made these early trips to Britain rank among the best known, and most illustrious, in the Church's history. There was John Taylor, later to succeed Brigham Young as President; Wilford Woodruff, also a future Church President; Parley P. Pratt; and Theodore Turley. Taylor and Woodruff arrived in Liverpool in January 1840. To Taylor went assignment in Liverpool. Although a number of Mormon missionaries had been in and out and through Liverpool many times, over many months, none had really attempted to preach there.

But John Taylor had a brother-in-law residing in Liverpool, a member of the Cannon family, destined to play such an important role in Church unfoldment. Indeed, even today the Salt Lake City telephone directory lists many Cannons. Within three months he had a group of some thirty in Liverpool who accepted his teachings and were baptized.

Wilford Woodruff undertook to work in the potteries of Staffordshire. He journeyed there by way of Manchester, where he met for the first time William Clayton, an Englishman who had been brought into the Church previously through the efforts of Heber Kimball.

It was Clayton who, a few years later, during the hard trek across the plains from Illinois to Utah, was to write the popular Mormon hymn, "Come, Come Ye Saints." But in 1840 Clayton was still in Manchester, and filled with unbounded faith. When Woodruff came, Clayton insisted that healing work be undertaken.

Incident of Healing

Although the Mormons have always been conservative in what they claimed for their ability to convey God's power to heal, there are a number of instances in the early records of the Church where such healings are documented. And one of these occasions included Wilford Woodruff who, at the behest of William Clayton, "laid hands" on a "writhing, suffering" woman. The first effort failed because, as Woodruff supposed, there were too many scoffers in the room. Reminded of the story of Jairus' daughter, Woodruff asked all to leave, and then, "the afflicted woman relaxed into a restful sleep. The next day, the Sabbath, she stood before a large audience, healed, and bore witness to the blessing of the Lord in her behalf."[1]

This incident became widely known in Manchester, and attracted a large throng to hear Woodruff; according to all reports it accelerated the missionary work in that area. The Mormons today have turned more to good health care and to doctors and to hospitals for healing, though they still place no limits on the power of God.

But the effect of Woodruff's apparently unlabored and successful effort to heal the sick woman brought much publicity, with the result that he traveled on to the potteries with a favorable reputation. He preached to large and small groups for six weeks, January 22 to March 2, when he suddenly left. He wrote:

March 1st, 1840 was my birthday; I was thirty-three years of age. It being Sunday, I preached twice during the day to a large assembly in the city hall, in the town of Hanley, and administered the Sacrament to the Saints. In the evening I again met with a large assembly of the Saints and Strangers, and while singing the first hymn the Spirit of the Lord rested upon men and the voice of God said to me: "This is the last meeting that you will hold with this people on many days."

I was astonished at this as I had many appointments out in the district. When I arose to speak to the people, I told them that it was the last meeting that I should have with them for many days. They were as much astonished as I was. At the close of the meeting, four persons came forward for baptism; we went down into the water and baptized them.

In the morning I went in secret before the Lord, and asked Him what was His will concerning me. The answer I received was that I should go to the South; for the Lord had a great work for me to perform there, as many souls were waiting for his word. On the 3d of March, 1840, in fulfillment of the directions given me, I took a coach and rode to Wolverhampton, twenty-six miles, spending the night there. On the morning of the 4th I again took coach and rode through Dudley, Stourbridge, Stourport, and Worcester, then walked a number of miles to Mr. John Benbow's Hill Farm, Castle Frome, Ledbury, Herefordshire. This was a farming country in the South of England, a region where no Elder out of the Latter-day Saints had visited.[2]

A Breakthrough

"It is not difficult," another visitor commented, "for any stranger who has tried to find the old Benbow farmstead to believe that Wilford Woodruff would never have reached John Benbow or the United Brethren had not the Lord been his guide!

"Hill Farm just does not happen to be on the road to anywhere in particular. It lies between Worcester and Ledbury by an indirect and circuitous route, about six miles from the latter town; extremely difficult to find!"[3]

It developed that John Benbow was a wealthy farmer and one of a group of six hundred people who had left the Methodist Church and formed a local congregation known as United Brethren, having forty-five preachers as well as numerous meeting places. John and his wife, Jane, were childless and devoted a good deal of their time to work among the Brethren, the spiritual leader of which was Thomas Kington, a licensed preacher.

"I presented myself to Mr. Benbow," Woodruff later wrote, "as a missionary from America, an Elder of the Church of Jesus Christ of Latter Day Saints, who had been sent to him by commandment of God as a messenger of salvation, to preach the gospel of life to him and his household and the inhabitants of the land. He and his wife received me with glad hearts and thanksgiving. . . ."

The next day Benbow circulated word that in the evening Woodruff would preach at the Benbow house. "As the time drew nigh many of the neighbors came, and I preached my first gospel sermon in the house. I also preached at the same place on the following evening, and baptized six persons, including Mr. John Benbow, his wife and four preachers of the United Brethren. I spent most of the following day in cleaning out a pool of water and preparing it for baptizing, as I saw that many would receive the ordinance. I afterwards baptized six hundred persons in that pool of water."

Constable Converted

This was the most dramatic success yet achieved by any of the missionaries, for here were not only large numbers of people, but a man of wealth and substance as well who could lend dignity and finances to the movement. By any standard it was a remarkable achievement and few there will be, regardless of their denomination, who will deny that a superior force was at work. Woodruff reported proudly on his success:

On Sunday, the 8th, I preached at Froome's Hill in the morning, at Standley Hill in the afternoon and at John Benbow's Hill Farm in the evening. The parish church that stood in the neighborhood of Brother Benbow's, presided over by the rector of the parish, was attended during the day only by 15 persons, while I had a large congregation, estimated to number a thousand, attending my meetings through the day and evening.

When I arose to speak at Brother Benbow's house, a man entered the door and informed me that he was a Constable, and had been sent by the Rector with a warrant to arrest me. I asked him: "For what crime?" He said, "for preaching to the people." I told him that I, as well as the Rector, had a license for preaching the Gospel to the people, and that if he would take a chair I would wait upon him after the meeting. He took my chair and sat beside me. For an hour and a quarter I preached the first principles of the everlasting Gospel. The power of God rested upon me, the Spirit filled the house, and the people were convinced.

At the close of the meeting I opened the door for baptism, and seven offered themselves. Among the number were four preachers and the Constable. The latter arose and said: "Mr. Woodruff, I would like to be baptized." I told him I would like to baptize him. I went down into the pool and baptized seven. We then came together. I confirmed thirteen, administered the Sacrament and we all rejoiced together.

The constable went to the Rector and told him if he wanted Mr. Woodruff taken for preaching the Gospel, he must go himself and serve the writ; for he had heard him preach the only true Gospel sermon he had ever listened to in his life. The Rector did not know what to make of it, so he sent two Clerks of the Church of England as spies to attend our meeting and find out what we did preach. They were both pricked in their hearts, received the word of the Lord gladly, and were baptized and confirmed members of the Church of Jesus Christ of Latter Day Saints. The Rector became alarmed and did not venture to send anybody else.

The Ministers and Rectors of the South of England called a convention and sent a petition to the Archbishop of Canterbury to request Parliament to pass a law prohibiting the "Mormons" from preaching in the British dominions. In this petition the Rectors stated that "One Mormon Missionary had baptized fifteen hundred persons, mostly members of the English Church during the past seven months."[4]

Hounds and Hares

But the archbishop and council, knowing well that the laws of England afforded toleration to all religions under the British flag, sent word to the petitioners that if they had the worth of souls at heart as much as they valued ground where hares, foxes, and hounds ran, they would not lose so many of their flock.

I continued to preach and baptize daily. On the 21st day of March I baptized Elder Thomas Kington. He was the superintendent of both preachers and members of the United Brethren. The first thirty days after my arrival in Herefordshire, I had baptized forty-five preachers and one hundred and sixty-five members of the United Brethren. . . . This opened a wide field for labor, and enabled me to bring into the Church, through the blessings of God, over eighteen hundred souls during eight months, including all six hundred United Brethren save one person. In this number there were also some two hundred preachers of various denominations.[5]

This success in Herefordshire, and expanded by Woodruff to Gloucestershire and Worcestershire, was concurrent with the successful work of Taylor, Turley, and the others in the west of England.

Thus was the way prepared for the arrival in Liverpool on April 6 of Heber C. Kimball, Parley P. Pratt, Orson Pratt, Orson Hyde, who was bound for Palestine via Germany, George A. Smith, and Brigham Young. The stage was well set for possibly one of the most dramatically successful forward thrusts of Christian church activity since the first century.

Chapter Eight

BRIGHAM YOUNG IN ENGLAND

When he stepped off the sailing packet *Patrick Henry* in Liverpool April 6, 1840, Brigham Young was thirty-nine years old. The year and fourteen days he was to spend in England became a high point in a life that already had enjoyed enough adventure to satisfy most men. The British experience served as a helpful and broadening prelude to his world-wide recognition as one of the most successful religious leaders and colonizers in history. It might be said, too, in the light of the emigration plans he formulated at this time, that this was one of his most vital years. His plans brought thousands of skilled and resourceful people to the American West and his emigration plans stood for decades as a model for others.

He had been a follower of the Prophet Joseph Smith for eight years, almost every minute of which had been devoted to the interests of The Church of Jesus Christ of Latter-day Saints. Even his best workmanship as a carpenter had been lavished on the temple in Kirtland. And the very circumstances of his getting to England were illustrative of his capacities and his dedication. For if anything can be said of Brigham Young it is that he *believed* in Joseph Smith and his revelations with all his heart.

It took him about two years to become convinced after he had first heard about Prophet Smith, had read the Book of Mormon, and had visited several Mormon groups near his home in upstate New York. He did not claim angel visitants, or any extranatural revelation, but what God willed he *knew*. While many beside him were shaken or diverted, never Brigham Young. And there is no question but that it was wholehearted, without dissimulation. If he was fooled, as some said, he was completely fooled.

One other thing, and obviously the most important, about Young can be stated: he was a heavyweight. Other men instinctively turned to him for the wisdom, leadership, buoyancy they needed in times of trouble. That was why his closest friend, Heber C. Kimball, had asked if "Brother Brigham" could not accompany him on the first Mormon mission to England in 1837.

This had been refused because, as Joseph Smith foresaw, "there were other things for Brother Brigham." One of these, and the most important, was to direct the sorrowful Mormon removal from Missouri to Illinois while the Prophet was held in Liberty Jail. This wrenching away of 15,000 people, under the murderous pressures of mob violence, from hard-won homesteads to the uncertainties of a new and as yet unfounded Zion on the banks of the Mississippi was enough to test the capacities of any man. Brother Brigham stood the test.

But hardly had the Young family found itself shelter in an abandoned army barracks on the Iowa side of the Mississippi, in Montrose just opposite Nauvoo, than the Prophet reminded his chief advisers, his Council of Twelve Apostles, that they were all due in England, for this had been his revelation.

Funds No Problem

Brigham Young, so his account tells us, roused himself from a sickbed, took an old quilt from one of his children's beds, threw it over his shoulders to serve as the overcoat he didn't possess, and with no more scrip or purse than a Galilean Apostle he left his wife and four children—one of them only ten days old—to set out across the frozen fields of Illinois, Ohio, New York, down through New England to New York City. But being without visible means never bothered Brigham Young.

"For me to travel and preach without purse or scrip was never hard," he said. "I never saw the day, I never was in the place . . . but that I could get all I wanted. . . . I was never turned out of doors; I could make the acquaintance of the family, and sit and sing to them and chat with them, and they would feel friendly toward me; and when they learned that I was a 'Mormon Elder' it was after I had gained their good feelings."[1]

A suggestion of his confident, good-humored approach is given

in his report of the last few miles of his journey into New York
City:

Brother George A. Smith [a cousin of the Prophet] accompanied me to
New York City, and we had not enough money to pay the last five miles
fare. We started from New Haven in a steam boat, and when we left the
boat, I hired passage in the stage to New York; the captain of the steam
boat happened to be in the same stage.

When we left the coach, I said to the captain, will you have the kind-
ness to pay this gentleman's passage and mine? I had had no conversation
with him during the day, only in interchanging the common and usual
compliments, but when we left him he greeted us cordially, and said that
he had paid our stagefare with the greatest pleasure, and shook our hands
as heartily as a brother, saying, "May God bless and prosper you in your
labors."

It had taken him four and a half months to make his way from
the Mississippi to the Hudson. Preaching by evening and on Sunday,
Young worked as a carpenter and glazier in New York for two
months, accumulating the $18 required for passage to Liverpool.
A pair of pants was donated to him by one of the New York
Mormon sisters and he and his party were supplied with food for
the voyage along with straw mattresses.

The long sea journey on the packet was uncomfortable. Brigham
was sick most of the time. When he arrived in Liverpool he was
anything but a commanding figure. He was short, about five and
a half feet tall, and thick in a muscular way. If you could have
seen him at the time of his British mission, you would have seen
a man who had mellowed and lost some of the bounce that
people spoke about during his Kirtland days, but the analytical eye,
the good humor plainly showed. He was a firm but understanding
man, a good friend, not a vicious enemy.

Preston Revisited

Young was fortunate in having as his guide Heber C. Kimball,
who noted as they docked in Liverpool that two years to a day
had elapsed since he had himself departed from America as the
leader of the first Mormon missionaries to England. Naturally, he

was eager to lead the way to nearby Preston, the seat of his earlier activities.

Kimball brought his fellow apostles to Preston on April 9, 1840. They held a conference with the other missionaries and Church members active in the area. It was decided that Orson Pratt should go to Scotland and George A. Smith to the potteries, where Kimball, who was himself a potter by trade, had previously enjoyed a good reception. Parley P. Pratt was assigned to Manchester, where he was to explore the problems of printing a periodical; John Taylor was to continue in Liverpool. Heber Kimball was to rove, calling on old friends, supporting those who needed a boost, seeking out new opportunities.

After the conference Brigham Young wrote to Nauvoo:

The work of the Lord is prospering here . . . according to the account the Elders give of their labours. There have been about eight or nine hundred persons baptized [in the previous two years].

The Gospel is spreading, the devils are roaring. As nigh as I can learn the Priests are howling, the tares are binding up, the wheat is gathering, nations are trembling, and kingdoms are tottering, men's hearts are failing them for fear and of looking for those things that are coming on earth.

But despite the grand language, Brigham remained highly practical. To his alert ears the biggest news brought to the Preston conference had been Wilford Woodruff's report that he had baptized an entire former Methodist group, calling themselves the United Brethren and numbering above five hundred. And not unimportant was the word that among the group were one or two of relative wealth, a prosperous farmer and his wife, John and Jane Benbow, and the former minister of the flock, Thomas Kington.

As soon as the conference was ended, Brigham Young and Willard Richards set off with Woodruff for Herefordshire and the Benbow farm at Froome's Hill. Young stayed there for a month, and never asked the Benbows for a cent, but he did suggest that, since they had accepted the truths of the Prophet's teachings, they owed it to others to spread similar blessings and that clearly the best way to do this was to finance the printing in England of the Book of Mormon. Tariffs, and other charges, he explained, and truly so, made it impractical to import the books from America.

John Benbow made a gift, and so did Thomas Kington, but on her part Jane suggested a loan, to be repaid from the profits of the book's sale. Young looked upon her with greater appreciation, and thirty years later, long after Jane had perished on the hard trek across the Plains to Utah, he delighted in telling the story. He ended by saying that he had seen to it that she had been repaid every cent, and repaid out of profits.[2]

On May 20, 1840, Young wrote to Joseph Smith in Nauvoo:

Brothers Woodruff, Richards and myself went on to the top of Herefordshire Beacon where, after prayer, we held a council and agreed that since we had obtained 250 pounds from Brother John Benbow and 100 pounds from Brother Kington towards publishing the Book of Mormon and Hymn Book, I should repair immediately to Manchester and join the brethren appointed with me as a committee and publish 3000 copies of the Hymn Book without delay. It was also voted that the same committee publish 5000 copies of the Book of Mormon.

Already Parley Pratt in Manchester had published the first issue of the *Millennial Star,* which has been regularly issued in Britain ever since, making it the oldest continuous periodical of the Church. Young and Pratt quickly put together the hymnal, Pratt himself composing some fifty hymns for the book.

Emphasis was placed on this hymnal because the missionaries had found that the English people love to sing, but many of them had in recent years left their former country homes to seek work in the factories and very few had brought along hymnals, for these belonged to the churches. The new Hymn Book gave the Mormons a strong tool.

The Emigration Plan

The Hymn Book, but not the Book of Mormon, was ready by July 6, 1840, when the next General Conference of the Church met, no longer in Preston, but in the imposing Carpenter's Hall, Manchester. Eighty branch churches were represented at this conference, with some 2500 members reporting. Brigham Young, as senior member of the Council of Twelve, was formally given charge of the British Mission at this time.

Young was impressed, as had been the other missionaries before him, with the condition of the poor in England. The days of Old County England were closing into a smog-bound dreariness of twelve-hour days in the factory, and a class of workers that stirred the sympathies of social observers was coming into being.

In a letter to his Prophet and friend, Joseph Smith, Brigham displayed a comprehensiveness no less acute than that of Benjamin Disraeli or Friedrich Engels in correctly judging the state of the English people.

The man who has read the histories of the people of England, which we had seen before we left America, is liable to meet with some disappointment, for it is generally the case that what we find in history relates more particularly to the higher classes in the nations. . . . England, unlike America, is divided into classes; many indeed, but they may all be compressed in three—Lords, Tradesmen and mechanics or laborers. Or in other words, the highest, middle and lowest classes, each of which have their particular customs and manners. . . .

A few years since, and almost every family had their garden, their cow on the common and their pig in the sty, which added greatly to the comfort of the household; but now we seldom find either garden, cow or pig.

As we pass around among the country cottages and see the stone walls which are thrown down, but more commonly the hedges in a decaying and mutilated state, it is very natural for us to inquire, "What have you here? What is the cause of this?"

And generally we got this answer: "A few years ago I had a flourishing garden in the spot you now see, and it was surrounded by this hedge which was planted with my own hand; I had a cow of my own which fed on yonder common; I labored on my master's farm and had plenty of time, morning and evening, to till my own garden in which I raised enough for my family, and every year I had a good pig, plenty to eat and we were happy, but my lords and masters have become more avaricious, and are trying to get all they can themselves and will hardly let the poor live.

"You see, my landlord has made my garden into a meadow, and feeds his own cattle upon it; the Lord of the Mansion fenced in the common so I had no place to keep my cow and I was obliged to sell her. I killed my pig to prevent her starving. The small farms are made into large ones, so we could get nothing to do on the land.

"I have been obliged to go into the factory with my wife and children, to get a morsel of bread. . . ."

Manufacturing is the business of England. The cotton mills are the most numerous. The weavers get from six to ten shillings per week; the spinners something more. The hand loom weavers have to work hard to get six shillings a week.

Now, after paying two or three shillings per week for shelter, one shilling for coal, besides taxes of every kind—for smoke must not go up the chimney in England without a tax, light must not come in the window without paying duties, many must pay from one penny to six pence per week for water, and if we should attempt to tell all, we would need a Government list—after paying all taxes, what think you a family will have for breadstuff?

Add to this the tax on corn, which is a great share of the expense of the article, and what is left but starvation, leaving out of account all seasonings, such as pepper, spices, etc. which, by taxation, is four times the value it is in the United States.

The poor are not able to keep dogs, and if they were, they would have to pay from eight shillings to a pound per annum tax.

There are taxes for living and taxes for dying, inasmuch that it is very difficult for the poor to get buried anyhow, and a man may emigrate to America and find a grave for less money than he can get a decent burial in Old England. We scarce recollect anything without a tax, except cats, mice and fleas.

We find the people of this land much more ready to receive the Gospel than those of America, so far as they do receive it, for they do not have the speculative intelligence, prejudice or false learning, call it what you will, which they have there.

Consequently, we do not have to labor with a place month after month to break down their old notions, for their priests have taught them but little and much of that is so foolish as to be detected at a glance.[3]

However, some who joined the Mormons in England found their lot was worsened rather than made better, for they became set apart and frequently found themselves discriminated against in matters affecting their livelihood.

Although England in 1840 was the principal power of the globe, and well on its way to becoming the largest and most prosperous empire the world had ever known, still for many subjects of the Queen America obviously was the "Promised Land." The Mormon missionaries were tremendously proud of the United States and could not refrain from speaking of the relative ease with which a man could rise through his own efforts.

It is remarkable, but easily proved from the record, that thousands of miles away, on the American frontier, Joseph Smith had somehow understood the English mood. For it was his idea and no one else's to dispatch his most trusted councillors, at a time of acute need, to England.

Brigham Young's solution for the problem was to devise a plan and a system that is still regarded as a model for emigrations, and which in the following few decades brought the Mormons more than 100,000 new members, first to Illinois, later to Utah. It is probably fair to say that these English emigrants and their descendants contributed at least 50 percent, and possibly 70 percent, of the Church leadership in the years since.

And if you were to remove all the names of these emigrants and their children from the lists of important persons of the United States, you would remove from the political lists many United States senators, congressmen, governors, and countless lesser officials. From the business world you would remove top executives of great national banks and insurance companies, manufacturing and processing concerns, and the like. The scientific community would lose some of its best-known men and the academic and cultural worlds some of its most respected members. The contribution to America of this emigration is, in fact, incalculable.

One day in 1966, just for the exercise, a list was made up of leading men in Washington whose backgrounds stemmed from the procedures that Brigham Young set up. The list included three senators, Bennett and Moss of Utah and Cannon of Nevada, six congressmen, a member of the President's Cabinet, Secretary Udall, several high-ranking members of the Foreign Service, Milan Smith, head of National Canners Association, one of the largest trade associations in the city, Willard J. Marriott, chairman of an important chain of hotels and restaurants, Mark Evans, an executive of one of the large television and radio systems, and many more.

London Adventures

Another Brigham Young objective in England was to establish the Church in London. In this he was less successful. London was then the greatest city in the world, with a population of 2,000,000, compared with New York's 200,000. For the task of converting London, Young chose Heber Kimball, George A. Smith, and Wilford Woodruff. The three arrived in London on August 18, 1840, and devoted most of their time to calling on established preachers, hoping they might win over an entire congregation, as Woodruff had done with the United Brethren, but the London clergy were not cooperative. This did not dismay the American frontiersmen, any more than did the great buildings and teeming throngs of the big city.

Recalling his success of two years before with the Temperance Society in Preston, Kimball took his two friends to the August 25 meeting of the London Temperance Society in their hall on St. George's Row, "near the Elephant and Castle." George Smith addressed the group as an American opposed to the use of alcohol and was cordially received. They were able to arrange to rent the hall for September 7, 1840, and to have an announcement of that fact made.

Since the seventh was still a few days off, they decided to try some outdoor preaching at Smithfield Market, where they stood on the spot where Queen Mary had ordered the burning of John Rogers, the Protestant martyr. They hoped this association with past persecutions might lead to a more tolerant hearing from the crowd that habitually listened to, and usually taunted, speakers. Before they could speak, however, a constable told them the lord mayor had outlawed street preaching.

"Whereupon," Woodruff reported, "a Mr. Henry Connor stepped forward to say that he would lead us to a place outside the Lord Mayor's jurisdiction."[4] He took them to Tabernacle Square, where a throng of about four hundred was gathered. Kimball worked his way up to the chair on which a preacher stood and told him that there was an American there who would like to be heard. George Smith was then granted use of the chair and spoke for about twenty minutes, starting off on familiar ground from Mark 16:16 ("He that believeth and is baptized shall be saved; but he that believeth not shall be damned").

He was warming up to the Joseph Smith story and the new Zion in America when the preacher jumped up to shout that he had just learned that the American speaker was a Mormon. "I know them, they are a very bad people and have split up many churches, and have done a great deal of hurt . . . we have the Gospel and can save people without infidelity, socialism or the Latter-day Saints."

The preacher demanded his chair and ran off with it, to the amusement of the crowd. Kimball announced that they would return at three o'clock that afternoon with a chair of their own and urged all to come and hear their message. Quite a few did show up and the three missionaries spoke to them for an hour and a half. Even when they were finished several small groups lingered on to pose questions. And Mr. Connor was most interested of all. The Church records show that on the next day, Monday, August 31, 1840, "Elder Kimball baptized Henry Connor, watchmaker, 52 Iron-Monger's Row, London, in Peerless Pool, being the first baptized in London."

For some weeks Connor was the only convert in London, though not for lack of effort. The missionaries had given wide notice to the September 7 meeting in Temperance Hall and had great hopes. Most of their capital had gone into rental, but when the meeting opened only thirty people turned up to hear them.

Slow Progress in London

Wilford Woodruff decided to return to the more rewarding fields of Herefordshire, writing:

We had spent twenty-three days in the great Babylon of modern times and had found it harder to establish the Church there than in any other place we had been. We baptized one man and ordained him a priest; six others had given in their names to be baptized the following Sunday. . . . I therefore left London, feeling that our mission and labors had not been altogether in vain.

Kimball and Smith remained in London and on October 6 reported to Brigham Young in Manchester:

We have baptized eleven only, in the city of London, but through faith and the mercy of God we ere long expect a harvest of souls in that place: but we are willing to acknowledge that in our travels, either in America or Europe, we have never before found a people from whose minds we have had to remove a greater multiplicity of objections or combinations of obstacles, in order to excite an interest in the subject and prepare the heart for the reception of the word of God, than in the city of London.

While conversing with the common people concerning the Gospel we found their highest attainments to be: "Why, I go to church or chapel and get my children christened; what more is necessary?" When we conversed with the learned, we found them too wise to be taught, and too much established in the traditions of their fathers to expect any change in the last days.

While conversing with the ministers of the various orders of the day upon the principles of the Gospel, they would inform us that the ancient order of things was done away, and some of them had preached forty years the good old religion and God was with them, and they needed no more revelation, or healing the sick, or anything as manifest in the days of the Apostles, for we can get along without them in this day of refinement, light and knowledge. . . .

But notwithstanding this, we do not feel discouraged concerning the work being perfected in London, but firmly believe that many souls will embrace the fullness of the Gospel there, though it will be through faith, diligence, perseverance, and prayer.[5]

Among those who were not turned away by this report was Brigham Young, who, almost as soon as he finished reading it, proposed that the publishing offices, which included the British Mission headquarters, be moved to London *as soon as circumstances will permit.* In actual fact, ninety-three years passed before circumstances permitted. But this was only partly due to the resistance of the missionary work in London. More largely it was due to the rapidly growing importance of the emigration to America and the practical need to be near the center of this work, which was Liverpool.

Young in London

On November 30, 1840, Brigham Young made his first visit to London. Heber Kimball, who had played with Brother Brigham when they were boys in Mendon, New York, who had preached with him and for him on numerous missionary journeys, and who had helped in the "escape" of the Prophet from his captors in Missouri, was Brigham's sight-seeing guide. Brigham was not one to pass up any opportunity, whether it was to harangue a crowd, preside over a Church meeting, or fill his eyes and thought with the tourist attractions of London.

In his daily journal Brigham Young noted:

3 Dec. [1840] We visited the Tower of London, the Horse Armory, the Jewel Room, and the Thames Tunnel. . . . 4 Dec. With Brother Woodruff I visited Buckingham Palace and Westminister Abbey. . . . 5 Dec. I walked out with Brother Woodruff to try and find the Book of Mormon, having heard that it was published and for sale by some unknown person,

but could not learn anything about it. . . . 7 Dec. Elders Kimball, Woodruff and I accompanied Dr. Copeland to the College of Surgeons, and went through every department of it. We also visited the National Gallery, Brother Kimball baptized one. . . . 9 Dec. We visited St. Paul's Cathedral, and went through each apartment from the crypt to the hall, which is about 400 feet high. We crossed London Bridge and the Iron Bridge over the Thames, and also visited the British Museum. . . . 10 Dec. We walked over Blackfriar's Bridge and called at Zion's Chapel, to attend a meeting of the Aitkenites, but they refused us admittance, fearing lest we should break up their society. . . .

On the first of December, at Barratt's Academy, Brigham Young preached his first sermon in London. He had learned a little device from Kimball, who had an even easier, more humorous approach than Young. As he stood in the Academy Hall and observed the cynical faces, eager to start their customary heckling, Young was silent for a long moment, pretending to be perplexed about something, and several times he made false starts. The audience couldn't help but find itself keyed up to discover what was bothering the speaker. Finally Young said in a low voice, "London is such a city of diversity and of so many of the learned, but am I correct in assuming that I address those who profess the Christian faith?"

This brought a loud and good-humored response, and a "Yes, yes, we are Christians!"

"Well, I salute you as Christians, and I would refer to Mark 16:16, 'He that believeth and is baptized . . .' "

"Oh, oh, a Baptist! Baptist! You are a Baptist."

"No, I do not come as a Baptist, I come from a church that represents the restored Gospel with Prophets and Apostles—"

"Oh, Irvingite, Irvingite," screamed the audience.

"Not an Irvingite. I speak of the restored prophecy of Jesus Christ—"

Then, from several places at once, "You belong to Johanna Southcote!"

Young shook his head, grinned mysteriously at his audience who by this time were in the spirit of the game. "Our Prophet is come and is with us—"

"Aitkenites," went up the shout.

"And our priesthood—"

"Catholic. Catholic, out with him!"

"In America, a land of great plenty with opportunity for . . ."

And so the speech went with the banter becoming more and more good-natured, and while it cannot be said that Brigham Young converted his audience, he at least charmed it, and afterward a Mormon could be heard there without causing a riot. It was a style that Young first practiced under necessity in London, but which he ever afterward resorted to, sometimes carrying on a two-way conversation with 5000 people in the Salt Lake City Tabernacle.

After ten days in London, Young had some advice for his missionaries there.

"Come to the Water"

Brother Kimball would say, "Come, my friend, sit down; do not be in a hurry"; and he would begin and preach the Gospel in a plain, familiar manner, and make his hearers believe everything he said, and make them testify to the truth, whether they believed or not, asking them, "Now, ain't that so?" and they would say "Yes." And he would make Scripture as he needed it, out of his own Bible, and ask, "Now, ain't that so?" and the reply would be "Yes." He would say "Now, you believe this? You see how plain the Gospel is? Come along now," and he would lead them into the waters of the baptism. The people would want to come to see him early in the morning, and would stay with him until noon, and from that until night; and he would put his arm around their necks and say, "Come, let us go down to the water."[6]

Having made clear his idea about how the work should proceed, and pointing out that there was no dearth of baptismal water, Young left London in the charge of Kimball, with Woodruff assisting.

The balance of his time in England was largely devoted to completing the arrangements for emigration. It was Young's thought that the emigrants should be gathered into sufficiently large companies as to warrant chartering a vessel. In this way the group would gain a unity and friendliness and by sharing their food and supplies they could reduce the cost. As far as he could, Young encouraged those having some means and a trade to emigrate first, so that when they arrived in Nauvoo they might establish businesses that could supply employment for those coming later.

Book of Mormon Copyrighted

Early in 1841 Young was able to send Heber Kimball, in London, twenty copies of the first British edition of the Book of Mormon, and Kimball immediately took the required five copies to Stationer's Hall for copyright in the name of Joseph Smith, Jr. The availability of the Book of Mormon and Hymn Book accelerated the work of the missionaries, who by this time had spread to Scotland, Wales, the Isle of Man, and Ireland.

On April 20, 1841, one year and fourteen days after he had arrived in England, Brigham Young stepped aboard the sailing packet *Rochester* and wrote:

It was with a heart full of thanksgiving and gratitude to God, my Heavenly Father, that I reflected upon His dealings with me and my brethren of the Twelve during the past year of my life, which was spent in England. It truly seemed a miracle to look upon the contrast between our landing and departing from Liverpool. We landed in the Spring of 1840, as strangers in a strange land and penniless, but through the mercy of God we have gained many friends, established churches in almost every noted town and city in the Kingdom of Great Britain, baptized between seven and eight thousand, printed five thousand Books of Mormon, three thousand Hymn Books, two thousand five hundred volumes of the *Millennial Star,* and fifty thousand tracts, and emigrated to Zion one thousand souls, established a permanent shipping agency which will be a great blessing to the Saints, and have left sown in the hearts of many thousands the seeds of eternal truth, which will bring forth fruit to the honor and glory of God, and yet we have lacked nothing to eat, drink or wear; in all these things I acknowledge the hand of God.[7]

Chapter Nine

PLURAL MARRIAGE ON THE SCENE

Brigham Young, Heber Kimball, and the other apostles returned after twenty-two months' absence to a prospering Nauvoo. Joseph Smith, a devotee of city planning, had, as in Kirtland and Far West, laid out a generous city of wide streets and evenly spaced blocks, liberally planted with grass and shrubs and trees. The river marshes had been drained, and the Prophet was encouraging the building of substantial houses.

When Brigham Young pointed out that his own family still lived in a log cabin, Joseph Smith immediately told him to put his family affairs first for the time being. Brigham built himself a red-brick house so well constructed that it was still in use more than a century later.

The results of the Mormon missionary work began to be evident everywhere as skilled artisans and trained workers constructed in Nauvoo a community distinct from the usual frontier collection of crude huts. Within a year it grew from 3000 to 10,000 population. Indeed, the first eighteen months after Brigham's return from England was a time of unprecedented progress and prosperity for the community.

But, as so often happens, there was some trouble. Its name was plural marriage, or polygamy. The usual Mormon attitude today is—if you are friendly—to tell you that polygamy is as distant from their personal experience as it is from yours. When pressed, they will say that polygamy was very limited, never participated in by more than 3 percent of the Church members, completely and utterly outlawed by the Church for longer than they can recall, and that anybody advocating or engaging in it today is cited for immediate excommunication. Polygamy is done, dispensed with, so why not forget it?

Of course the answer is that however small the number who were actually polygamists, the practice deeply affected Mormon history, and is still, today, a factor in the attitude some take toward the Church. Every once in a while a sensational journal gives space to the subject, especially in Europe. A candid examination of the subject is certainly called for.

Three reasons are usually cited for plural marriage. Two of these the Mormons reject for reasons that appear to have the weight of evidence on their side, but they have been so widely repeated that they should not be overlooked here.

The first of these, ascribed by anti-Mormon writers, is that to the early Mormons one wife was simply not enough. The Mormon response to this is that no society in history has held women in such high regard and position as that of the Mormons. Not only do women hold an equality in the Mormon scheme of things but in many matters a superiority. Infidelity is considered a deadly sin and no distinction is made between men and women. This was established by Joseph Smith and constantly upheld since. About the Mormons there may be many things that serious students have disagreed about, but about their teachings, and practice of what the Christian world accepts as high morality, there is no valid disagreement.

The second reason—and this is usually ascribed by non-Mormon apologists—is simply that polygamy met a sociological need: that there were a great many more women than men. They cite such things as the Haun's Mill massacre, in which so many men were lost, the natural inclination for men to care for their brothers' widows (and in the Mormon society they were all "brothers and sisters"), and, finally, the tendency of many churches to attract more women than men to the fold. Further, it is pointed out that, in the pioneer society, children were an economic asset, that the Mormons greatly needed them. It might be convenient for the Mormons now to accept this rationalization, or some variation of it, but they disdain to do so, one reason being that early census figures indicate there were actually more men than women in their pioneer society.

"The Lord Commanded It"

They cite a third reason, and it turns out today to be precisely the same reason they gave a century ago, and for which they—as a society —almost died. It is simply "The Lord commanded it." If you ask, as many do, "How could the Lord command such a thing when it is so clearly contrary to the convictions and beliefs of all the rest of the Western Christian world?" your Mormon friend will very likely reply that his Church rests on the doctrine of a restoration of the Gospel in the latter days, that it has no other reason or explanation for its existence. He will insist that the Mormon Church did not break away from any other church, but that the Mormon religion is truly the original Gospel of Jesus in all its fullness brought back to earth by divine authorization.

Was polygamy a part of that authorization? The Mormons believed that it was. They refer to Jesus' discussion of the woman who married seven brothers, and point to the Mosaic custom of a man caring for his brother's widows. They mention the polygamy known to Abraham, Isaac, and Jacob.

Joseph Smith, who had among other things taken up the study of the ancient Hebrew language, found himself immersed in the Gospel. It was his conviction, brought as he said by revelation, that the gradual changing of the Gospel in the centuries after Jesus had gone so far that nothing less than a full restoration was required. And on July 12, 1843, Joseph Smith said it was revealed to him that full restoration of the Gospel included restoration of the practice of polygamy.

As he reported it, the Lord said to him:

God commanded Abraham and Sarah gave Hagar to Abraham to wife. And why did she do it? Because this was the law, and from Hagar sprang many people. This therefore was fulfilling, among other things, the promises. Was Abraham, therefore, under condemnation? "Verily I say unto you, Nay, for I the Lord commanded it. Go ye therefore, and do the works of Abraham. But if ye enter not into my law ye cannot receive the promise of my Father which he made unto Abraham. I am the Lord thy God, and I gave unto thee, my servant Joseph an appointment and restore all things.[1]

Reluctance

It was not, he said, a popular revelation to Joseph, less so to his wife, Emma.

Brigham Young said, "If any man had asked me what was my choice when Joseph Smith revealed the doctrine I would have said, let me have but one wife. I was not desirous of shrinking from any duty, nor of failing in the least to do what I was commanded, but it was the first time in my life that I desired the grave and I could hardly get over it for a long time."

Young's first wife had died of consumption even before he left Kirtland for Missouri. He had married again and apparently had a complete and happy family life. But with the Prophet leading the way the others followed. Brigham married his first polygamous wife, Lucy Ann Decker, when he moved west. She was twenty; he was forty-one. The next year he married two women, one nineteen, the other forty-one.

John Taylor, who was to succeed Young as President of the Church many years later when polygamy was a national issue said:

I had always entertained strict ideals of virtue and felt as a married man that this [plural marriage] was to me outside the principle of virtue, and an appalling thing to do. The idea of going and asking a young lady to be married to me when I already had a wife! It was a thing calculated to stir up feelings from the innermost depths of the human soul. I had always entertained the strictest of chastity.

Heber Kimball was also deeply troubled, a trouble perhaps compounded by the fact that he was advised to take as his second wife a certain charming young English convert who had come to Nauvoo as part of the company traveling with him from Liverpool. He was so visably disturbed that his wife made inquiries which disclosed the situation. She took the initiative in urging her husband to proceed. Difficult as it may be for us to accept, such evidently was the reaction of a number of the older Mormon wives. It is true—and many Mormons today emphasize this point—that a good many marriages were entered into between men and women of quite disparate ages and were only for the spiritual reason of giving the woman a husband "for Eternity."

Children represented a sacred obligation to provide for their well-being and education. Marriage, plural or otherwise, was not to be entered into unless that obligation was foreseen and provided for. This prevented a multitude of irresponsible marriages to gratify sensual desires. To have more than one wife required that a man be able to provide properly for her and the expected children. This meant, in practice, that only the more mature and established men, and men of property, could undertake plural marriages. And this, of course, limited the number.

In cases of men marrying widows it was believed that the wife would return to her first husband in the next life, and any children resulting from the second marriage would go with the wife and be treated as children of the first husband.

The Mormons recognized that, in an America filled with residuals of Puritanical concepts, any idea of plural marriage, whether based on the traditions of Father Abraham or not, would arouse condemnation and rancor, so they did not publicly divulge the Prophet's revelation. But rumors spread, and were fanned by apostates.

An Island Apart

The Mormons made a conscious effort to get along with their neighbors. After all, the people of Illinois had received them well after their expulsion from Missouri. Stephen Douglas and Abraham Lincoln, both young politicians in Illinois at the time, had assisted in granting the liberal charter to Nauvoo. But as Nauvoo prospered, it became evident that the community was at odds with its neighbors economically, socially, militarily, and politically.

Economically, because it was an island of self-contained prosperity. Envy and criticism were a result. Militarily they were feared because they had their own corps, the Nauvoo Legion, which though nominally a part of the state militia, was nevertheless under the command of Mormons. And politically they got into trouble because they were accused of playing Whig off against Democrat, throwing votes first to one and then the other party. Governor Ford of Illinois said they made their presence in the state a political issue "and in the end suffered the enmity of both major parties."[2]

The general basis of trouble having been laid, it remained only for specific incidents to bring matters to a head. One such incident was the excommunication of John Cook Bennett, who had served briefly as one of the assistants to Joseph Smith. He was excommunicated for licentious and adulterous behavior, and retaliated by writing an abusive article for the newspapers in which he alleged that "it is no obstacle to spiritual marriage if one or both of the parties should happen to have a wife already united to them according to the laws of the land."

Bennett himself was a questionable character. He had been removed from the rolls of the Masons, as well as the Mormons; but his charges were reprinted in all parts of the country and the Mormon cause was not helped. It was not particularly helped either when Joseph Smith became disenchanted with the evasive answers given him by the two leading candidates for the Presidency of the United States, Henry Clay and John C. Calhoun.

The Prophet had written each asking what protection he could assure the Mormons in event of election. Neither would promise anything, and Joseph Smith in disgust announced that he would run for the Presidency himself. There is no reason to suppose that he was lacking in seriousness in his announcement, but neither is there reason to suppose he had any hope of being elected. His aim, presumably, was to bring to public attention the position of the Mormons and to gain for them the sort of protection that experience in Missouri had shown was acutely needed.

But before Joseph Smith's campaign for the Presidency could get under full steam, events suddenly turned against him. Some apostates of the Church had established their own newspaper in Nauvoo and attacked the Mormons for polygamy, political grasping, and financial chicanery. This so aroused the Mormons that they destroyed the press. And it developed that many residents of Illinois were suddenly enthusiastic defenders of the free press.

To the South Seas

While these events were bringing Mormon affairs to a new and more serious phase, Joseph Smith did not in the least abandon his interest in missionary work. He said that his revelations had always included the command that work must go forward in the "islands of the seas." This had been interpreted to mean the British Isles. But in Nauvoo it came to his notice that one of his followers had been in his youth a sailor and had lived for a time in Hawaii. Thus it was that in May, 1843, Addison Pratt was blessed by Brigham Young, Heber Kimball, and Parley Pratt and dispatched to the South Seas. There were three others, Noah Rogers, Benjamin Grouard, and Knowlton

Hanks sent on the same mission at that time, but the Addison Pratt story may better serve to portray the times.

Like many another New Bedford boy, he had gone away to sea on a whaler and had roamed the Pacific for six years. Some of the time he had spent working in Hawaii and he spoke a little of the dialect. On one of his return voyages to New Bedford, he had met a pretty farm girl, Louisa Barnes, and in a short time was married and farming near Ripley, New York. One day they had a visit from Louisa's sister and her husband. They had joined a new church and were on their way to establish a new home in Kirtland, Ohio. Thus were Addison and his wife introduced to Mormonism, and within a short time they, too, were investigating the faith and in due course joined the group at Nauvoo, where Addison was employed on the temple building.

On the day of his departure from Nauvoo, Addison was accompanied to the steamboat landing by his wife and four daughters, one a child of only three years. He was leaving them without visible means of support, though it was expected that the Mormons would take care of any who became destitute. Mrs. Pratt, like the other mothers of Zion, simply wrote in her diary, "I determined to trust in the Lord, and stand bravely before the ills of life, and rejoice that my husband was counted worthy to preach the Gospel."

The journey to New Bedford took from May to October. At New Bedford, he could not find a ship bound for Hawaii so he booked passage for $100 on a whaleship bound for the Society Islands, Tahiti and Papeete, about as remote in the South Seas as one can get.

It was seven months before they sighted land. It turned out to be the island Tubuai, where the *Bounty* mutineers had first stayed before going on to Pitcairn's Island. Pratt tried out his language on the first natives to come aboard, and went ashore with them. The island had been visited by many missionaries before, but Pratt was the first one who could speak to them. They were so impressed that they begged him to stay, and that was the start of the first Mormon mission in the South Seas.[3]

Later, many Mormon missionaries were to play important roles in the history of the Hawaiian Islands, and many others, even Australia and New Zealand, but it began with Addison Pratt on Tubuai.

Chapter Ten

MARTYRDOM

Late in February 1844 Joseph Smith told his twelve apostles that they would probably have to leave Nauvoo. This was sorrowful news, but it was agreed that an exploration party should be sent to seek a suitable location for a new Zion. California was assumed to be the most likely place. Vancouver Island in the Pacific Northwest was also considered, but "somewhere" in the Rocky Mountains was the principal goal.

By June, after the smashing of the printing press, public attitudes in the countryside outside Nauvoo were reaching explosion point. Governor Thomas Ford was brought to the scene by repeated rumors of attacks by Mormons on settlers, first in one place or another, stories which the governor found to be baseless.[1] He asked, however, promising protection, that the Mormon leaders surrender to him.

Joseph Smith, full of premonitions of disaster, actually set forth one night with his brother Hyrum, John Taylor, and Willard Richards for California, but he was persuaded to return the next day by the Mormons who pleaded they would be left without leadership. So Joseph placed himself under the protection of Governor Ford, and the two had a frank discussion about the newspaper.

"It looks to the people like a highhanded disposition on your part to suppress the liberty of speech and of the press," said the governor.

"Could we suffer a set of worthless vagabonds," replied the Prophet, "to come into our city, and right under our own eyes and protection vilify and calumniate not only ourselves but the character of our wives and daughters, as was impudently and unblushingly done in that infamous and dirty sheet? There is not a city in the United States that would have suffered such an indignity for twenty-four hours."[2]

Joseph Smith, along with his brother Hyrum, Apostles John Taylor and Willard Richards (the other apostles being away on missions at the time), and also accompanied by John S. Fullmer and Captain Dan Jones, were at first lodged in a hotel at Carthage, Illinois. Jones was an interesting figure, a dynamic little Welchman who had enjoyed an especially good education—he was a college graduate, which was not common in those days—and had emigrated to the United States to make his fortune. He operated a steamboat on the Mississippi and a good part of his business had been to carry Mormon emigrants from New Orleans up to Nauvoo. This had brought him into friendship and business partnership with the Prophet and he had in time embraced the religion.

For some months before accompanying Joseph Smith to Carthage, Dan Jones had been preparing to leave for Wales, hoping to extend the missionary work that had been started there a few years previously as an off-shoot of the Liverpool effort. This was on his mind as he lay on the floor, Joseph Smith beside him.

"Are you afraid to die?" the Prophet whispered to Jones.

"Has that time come, think you? Engaged in such a cause I do not think that death would have many terrors."

The Prophet whispered to him, "You will yet see Wales and fulfill the mission appointed you before you die"[3]

The Carthage Greys

Early in the morning of June 27, Dan Jones was sent to learn what he could of the situation. Since he was himself not under arrest but simply keeping the Prophet company, he was free to go. Jones talked with an officer of the Carthage Greys whom he knew. This officer said, "We have had too much trouble to bring Old Joe here to let him escape alive, and unless you want to die with him you had better leave before sundown, and you are not a damned bit better than him for taking his part. And you'll see that I can prophesy better than Old Joe, for neither he nor his brother, nor anyone who will remain with them will see the sun set today."

Jones quickly reported this to the Prophet, who asked him to tell Governor Ford immediately what he had been told. On his way,

THE MORMON LEADERS

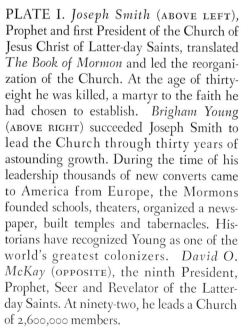

PLATE I. *Joseph Smith* (ABOVE LEFT), Prophet and first President of the Church of Jesus Christ of Latter-day Saints, translated *The Book of Mormon* and led the reorganization of the Church. At the age of thirty-eight he was killed, a martyr to the faith he had chosen to establish. *Brigham Young* (ABOVE RIGHT) succeeded Joseph Smith to lead the Church through thirty years of astounding growth. During the time of his leadership thousands of new converts came to America from Europe, the Mormons founded schools, theaters, organized a newspaper, built temples and tabernacles. Historians have recognized Young as one of the world's greatest colonizers. *David O. McKay* (OPPOSITE), the ninth President, Prophet, Seer and Revelator of the Latter-day Saints. At ninety-two, he leads a Church of 2,600,000 members.

PLATE II. Home of Brigham Young, pioneer President of the Church of Jesus Christ of Latter-day Saints and governor of the territory of Deseret (Utah).

PLATE III. Sea Gull Monument: In commemoration of a great lifesaving event, a fitting monument to the sea gull has been erected in Temple Square. A state law now prohibits the killing of the sea gull, which is the state bird.

PLATE IV. This handcart, located on Temple Square in Salt Lake City, tells the story of those valiant pioneers who walked the 1400 miles to the Valley of the Great Salt Lake, pulling handcarts loaded with their possessions.

Jones heard other ominous words. An officer talking to his men said, "Our troops will be discharged this morning in obedience to orders, and for a sham we will leave the town, but when the governor and the McDonough troops have left for Nauvoo this afternoon, we will return and kill these men, if we have to tear the jail down."

All this sounds a little like the script of a western movie, but it is a plot that has been carefully studied by succeeding generations of historians who can account for almost every minute of the final day of the Prophet. To them it is a tragedy as vivid as Calvary, as indeed it was to many of the players in the drama that day. Governor Ford later said that he would probably go down in history as another Pontius Pilate.[4] But when Dan Jones reached him on the fatal day and reported what he had heard and been told, the governor merely smiled and said:

"You are unnecessarily alarmed for the safety of your friends, sir. The people are not that cruel."

Jones in some heat replied, "The Messrs. Smith are American citizens, and have surrendered themselves to Your Excellency upon your pledging your honor for their safety, and . . . I demand of you protection of their lives. If you do not do this, I have but one more desire, and that is, if you leave their lives in the hands of those men to be sacrificed—"

"What is that, sir?" broke in Governor Ford.

"It is that the Almighty will preserve my life to a proper time and place that I may testify that you have been timely warned of their danger."[5]

When Jones went back to report, he was turned away from the prison gate. The Prophet was left with his brother Hyrum, Willard Richards, and John Taylor. The day was spent, Taylor later reported, in writing letters, and he, Taylor, sang a favorite hymn of the Prophet's, "A Poor Wayfaring Man of Grief."

Death of the Prophet

The guard was changed at four in the afternoon and at five Richards heard a commotion outside. Looking out, he saw a mob of about a hundred men circling the jail. Some had their faces blackened; others scorned disguise. One group separated itself and rushed the guards, who conveniently fired over their heads. They stormed into the jail and up the stairs. Soon the little room in which the four waited was full of men and bullets.

The Mormons were not cowardly. Richards and Taylor had only heavy canes. Joseph Smith had one of the old revolvers in which six barrels turned around to present barrel and bullet to hammer and trigger, an extremely unwieldy weapon and, as it proved, also highly ineffective. He emptied it down the stairs without result. Hyrum had a single shooter. He was the first to fall, pierced by bullets in the head, neck, and legs. "I am a dead man," he exclaimed, even as he fell to the floor. Taylor and Richards were still flailing with their sticks, trying to knock down the guns.

Joseph, apparently hoping to divert attention from his friends, threw down his gun and dashed for the window. Bullets tore into him from both front and back. He slowly fell out the window into the hands of waiting captors, dying as he murmured, "O Lord, my God." And suddenly the mob was subdued. They left quickly while Willard Richards tenderly bound up the wounds of Taylor. He was saved, it appeared, by a heavy watch that deflected what otherwise would surely have been a fatal bullet. Richards suffered only a surface wound.

The reaction in Nauvoo was restrained and Christian, a great and vast sadness at losing their beloved leader of fourteen years, but only passing thoughts of revenge. And through Illinois and the rest of the nation there dawned the realization that in the martyrdom of Joseph Smith the Mormons had been given the final sign of unity between the original and the restored Church of Jesus Christ. Far from spreading dismay, the assassination of Joseph Smith brought a resolution and, after some rivalry, a degree of unity greater than before.

As might have been expected, Brigham Young, as senior member of the Council of Twelve Apostles, emerged as the new leader. He was in New England when first reports of the assassination reached him, and it was not until a full three weeks after the murder that he and Orson Pratt, visiting in Peterboro, New Hampshire, received written confirmation. They hurried to Boston, where they met Heber Kimball and Wilford Woodruff—it was the London group all over again—and came to the conclusion that just as Jesus had named Peter and the apostles to carry on, so it was that the restored

Church should be led by the Twelve Apostles, of which Brigham was the President, or senior member.

They hastened to Nauvoo and, sweeping aside all would-be successors, Brigham Young, in a speech which ranks high in Mormon history, spoke with the authority the Mormons had been accustomed to hearing only from Joseph. Indeed, many reported that they *saw* Brigham's face but *heard* Joseph's voice. They unanimously sustained Brigham and the Twelve. While later there were splinter Mormon groups, from that moment on the main body of the Church was led by Brigham and the Quorum of the Twelve.

This was on August 8, 1844. Joseph Smith had been martyred fifty days before. There was much to be done, and Brigham knew exactly what. First, he dispatched Wilford Woodruff to the vital British Mission to explain events and to keep in motion the missionary and emigration work there. Second, he sent the energetic and effective Parley P. Pratt to New York to keep the Church active there and to represent the cause before the eastern press. To Heber Kimball went the assignment of quietly preparing for the trek westward. To others went orders to hasten completion of the temple; to get in the crops. Over all spread the ascendant, busy, paternal energy of Brigham Young, exhorting, urging, inspiring. Here indeed was a man for all seasons.

Murderers Acquitted

But there were not to be many seasons in Nauvoo. Governor Ford was outraged by the murder of Joseph Smith and asserted his determination to bring the culprits to justice. But when the prime suspects were brought to trial in the spring of 1845 they were acquitted.

Of course this solidified the convictions of the Mormons that they were left "naked to their enemies," subject to harassment, vilification, and even slaughter. At the same time the people outside Nauvoo recognized that the Mormons were growing stronger and more united than ever. In this hateful atmosphere Brigham Young tried to keep community frictions to a minimum while always stressing that the Mormons intended to move westward, hoping the decision to leave Nauvoo would placate the enemies.

Early in the summer of 1845, following the acquittal of those charged with Joseph Smith's assassination, the Nauvoo Temple was completed so that it could be used for the religious rites of sealing, or marriage. A temple marriage meant much more to the Mormons than one performed elsewhere and this was one reason why they expended so much treasure and work on completing a temple that they planned shortly to abandon. But they made full use of it in the time remaining.

All through the summer the noises of unusual activity might be heard, and in November, Brigham Young wrote:

Mechanics are at work in every part of the town preparing timber for making wagons. The timber is cut and brought into the city green; hub, spoke felloe timber boiled in salt water, and other parts kiln dried; shops are established at the Nauvoo House, Masonic Hall, and arsenal, nearly every shop in town is employed making wagons. . . .

Dan Jones in Wales

But while all was bustle and preparation in Nauvoo, the foreign work was not forgotten. In the days following the martyrdom Dan Jones was one of the stalwarts helping to rally the people. Such was the importance, however, to him and to Brigham Young of the mission to Wales that we find him a year after the martyrdom in the little South Wales town of Merthyr Tydfil. He was writing to Wilford Woodruff, president of the British Mission, in Manchester:

The whole place appeared to be in as great an uproar as Mars Hill of old. The first salutation after my arrival was an invitation from the Mayor to defend myself against charges. When I reached his worship, he was in a hasty stew, reading a long catalog of charges which were at the head of a lengthy petition to banish us from the limits of the city; attached were names of the clergy, reverends, doctors, lawyers and deacons, and, following, the names of their deluded followers. After a dozen attempts I succeeded in hearing my own voice, and proceeded to defend myself against their charges, one by one. The first was blasphemy, 2. Infidelity, 3. Saying that the end of the world was at hand, thereby scaring people out of their senses—taking them to a foreign country and selling them as slaves, etc.

You'll be surprised to learn that the chief magistrate had been led to believe these lies so firmly, that he had actually made his arrangements to put me in prison, which he told me to my face! But I had weathered too

many storms to give up the ship so soon. I reasoned with him until he
pledged himself to befriend me.

He summoned the alderman and I had a broadside with each of them
in turn. I was alone amidst all the lions of the city, yet I was uppermost at
every turn, until it was after midnight. Their clergy, my accusers, had
refused to toe the mark.

When I cited them in the treatment which we had received in our
native land, and among the graves of our fathers, for our religion, there
was hardly a dry face in the vast assembly, even the sergeant of police
who had presented, and the big nobs who had signed, the petition wept
like babes. The mayor ordered the police and reporters there, and they
were never in a more suitable place of worship![6]

It began with the hectic atmosphere described in this report, but
within two and a half years, by the end of 1848, he could point to
much progress:

The last Welsh General Conference, which was held last Sunday,
December 31, 1848, and following days, was much the largest and most
interesting of any other; our hall, which will hold two thousand people,
was so crowded before the morning service commenced that we had to
engage another hall nearly as large, which was also soon filled to over-
flowing, and continued for two days with but little intermission. Scores
have come from two hundred miles; all the hotels, taverns and private
lodgings in the town, so far as I have heard, were thronged like an
Egyptian fair; yet order, union, and love were so characteristic of the Saints
throughout, that the Babylonians were astonished.

The statistics of the morning at this conference meeting showed the total
number of branches in Wales to be 55 and 17 new branches organized;
including 156 elders, 180 priests, 147 teachers, 67 deacons. Baptized since
last conference 1,001; total members 3,603; total baptized last year
1,939. . . .

This fills my soul with joy and gladness unspeakable, because the Lord
God of Joseph so abundantly fulfills the predictions of the devoted martyr
on my head; and because I hear my own kin and nation rejoice in the
blessings of heaven, and show forth the wonderful power of God in the
language and the land that gave them birth; and in the prospects of a
heaven on earth in Zion. . . .

All kinds of lying stories that the father of lies and his emissaries can
invent are being told of me; such as that I am going to take this company
over and sell them as slaves. I am called a swindler, thief and everything
but what I really am. . . .[7]

Hard to Leave Nauvoo

While preparations for the Mormons to leave Nauvoo were under-way, efforts were being made by the Mormons to sell their houses in town and their farms in the countryside. But Young reported to England:

Very few sales of property are being made, the citizens of the country around instead of aiding us to sell our property, are using their influence to discourage sales and the authorities constantly haunt us with various writs; efforts are being made to bring us into collision with the authorities of the United States by means of vexations writs from the federal courts. . . .

The exodus was planned for the spring of 1846, but in February word came that Brigham was to be arrested and accused of harboring counterfeiters, indeed that the Mormons had manufactured counter-feit money. Although the charge was proved false, in the middle of February Brigham led an advance group of about two hundred across the frozen Mississippi to Iowa and the establishment of the Old Mormon Trail, perhaps the most traveled and most famous of all the trails that opened the American West.

Holdup Emigration

As can be imagined, these events in far off Illinois were watched with concern by the Saints in England. Brigham never had them far from his mind and to Wilford Woodruff flowed a stream of re-ports. But just before he left Nauvoo he sent the painful message, "Hold up all emigration!"

In Liverpool in a narrow, three-story brick house, next door to a convent, and about a mile up from the quay and Liver House, the message brought dismay. The year before the British Mission had received no missionaries from America, but in 1846 there were nine-teen and they had assisted in the baptizing of some 2500 converts. Emigration had been dwindling for the past couple of years while troubles in Nauvoo grew, but even so several hundred had indi-cated a desire to emigrate. Yet there was no Zion to go to. Zion was in a wagon train.

Notwithstanding, missionary work went on, and far away in Tubuai, the South Pacific isle, Addison Pratt was indeed doing very well. The island abounded not only in fish and fruits, but in pigs and chickens and wild fowl. His Tahitian friends daily brought him food. He even had American company, for in this unlikely spot six Americans were busy building a schooner. Pratt worked tirelessly in improving his language, finding that his Hawaiian was a dialect of the tongue spoken in Tahiti. Soon he was conducting Sunday services in English and in the local dialect. Within three months he had baptized ten new members of the Church, including all six of the Americans!

But in all those months, seven at sea and three in the Islands, not one word from home. How was the family making out? When on the twenty-eighth of June, 1844, a small schooner stopped offshore and the captain came on land, he had two letters for Addison Pratt. But they were from his fellow missionaries on Tahiti.

On that same day, 13,000 miles of sea and land away, Louisa and the four daughters were seized with deepest gloom as they stood in the street in Nauvoo and watched a wagon drive by with the bodies of Joseph and Hyrum. The gloom turned to fear as wild rumors flew through the town: the mobbers were coming because $1000 had been offered for the severed head of the Prophet.

It was just as well that Addison Pratt did not know all this, as he was visited, for the first time, by representatives of an English church that had been sending missionaries to the area for fifty years.

Rival Missionaries

The missionaries visited Tubuai yearly for a few days and were understandably proud that they had translated the Bible into Tahitian and otherwise carried forward good works. They refused to shake hands with Pratt, charging that he had not preached the Bible.

"I preach nothing else," Addison insisted.

"But we understand that you have another book you call a Bible that you teach them from."

"It is a mistake. We have no book that we call a Bible except the Old and New Testament. We have a book we call the Book of Mormon, but it is no use to teach them anything from that till they understand the Bible well."

Addison then talked about Noah. "How was it in the days of Noah? It was thus: The Lord raised up a prophet and told him to go forth and warn the people faithfully, and if they did not repent of their sins and turn from their wicked ways, he would bring upon them a flood that would destroy them all. This people went forth according to command, but the people made light of what he said, notwithstanding he was warning 120 years. Toward the close of the period, God commanded him to build an ark, and set it on dry land. This was another warning before their eyes, but they made sport of it all. And the Lord brought upon them the flood as he promised without Noah ever making a convert that we have any record of.

"Precisely so it is in these last days. The Lord raised up his Prophet whose name is Joseph Smith, and ordered him to establish the Church of Jesus Christ according to its original plan. He has obeyed the command and sent forth his servants, of whom I am one, to warn the People."

Before this blast, which Addison compared with the roaring of lions, the missionaries retreated to their ship. The encounter strengthened Addison's ties with the natives and they voted to build him a house and urged him to send for his family, but not one word came to him from Nauvoo. There were reasons, and perhaps Addison was better off for not knowing.

Chapter Eleven

COME, COME YE SAINTS

In 1846 much that was known and conjectured about the Great American Desert was untrue. As the land gently rose westward from the Mississippi to the Rockies there was dimunition in rainfall until along a line about 99 degrees longitude the forests gave way to a grassland on which vast herds of buffalo roamed. With them roamed tribes of nomadic Indians, the most dreaded of which had obtained horses descended from those originally brought to Mexico by the Spaniards. The young Indian braves had developed the ability to hang on to a horse at full gallop, holding one foot over the rump and sliding along the side of the horse, using the animal as shield while firing an arrow and later a gun from under the horse's neck. It was a fearful method of attack and tended to discourage wholesale travel across the plains. At the same time, the evident lack of moisture discouraged farmers familiar only with the rainfall of Europe and the eastern United States. The development of the Great Plains as a primary source of the world's wheat had to await the discovery of new farming methods.

In 1846 the Great Plains offered little haven for the traveler, and presented dangers and hardships that had to be endured with caution and fortitude. Beyond the Plains were the Rocky Mountains rising, in many places, to 14,000 feet, snow-covered for most of the year and with few charted passes.

Most of the emigration in those days followed a trail to the north, the so-called Oregon Trail; and much travel went by ship from the East around South America to California. Thus, there were developing centers of people in the Pacific Northwest and in California and the reports were designed to attract many more settlers.

Just over the range of the Rockies, 700 miles east of California, was a great basin. The scout Jim Bridger described it as early as 1824, six years before Joseph Smith organized his Church, but apart from the fact that there had once been an enormous lake (Bonneville) which had shrunk to a salt lake in which a man couldn't sink, little was really known of the area. It appealed to few. It was certainly not a prime target for emigration. Just the year before, however, while the Mormons were still in Nauvoo, John C. Frémont had carefully plotted a trail crossing the mountains in southern Wyoming over South Pass. Frémont had then gone on to California, but on his return he followed part of the way an old Spanish trail from Monterey to Santa Fe. This brought him to the Great Basin and to the Great Salt Lake.

His trail blazing, or perhaps it has been better described as trail marking, was very popular and thousands of copies of his report were printed and eagerly read; not a few found their way to Nauvoo. Young and his councillors wanted a place where they could be alone, with no neighbors to cause them trouble. Kirtland, Far West, and Nauvoo had taught their lesson. Vancouver Island might offer such a refuge, but there was no guarantee that the Mormon way of life, including plural marriage, would be safe, and there was even less guarantee against the Mormons being engulfed by new neighbors in California and Oregon.

A Difficult Trek

The westward migration of the Mormons worked out so well that there is some inclination to believe that it was all carefully pre-planned and that it proceeded according to that plan. But this was only partly true. The plan, even the final destination, disclosed itself as they moved along. In the first place, the departure from Nauvoo was hastened by threats that Young and his chief councillors would be arrested. On the day Young's party left Nauvoo the temperature was twelve degrees below zero—hardly a day they would have chosen voluntarily.

While some later experiences of the Mormons in crossing the Plains and the Rockies have had more notice, perhaps this winter-time trek across the length of Iowa was the most difficult of all. It was compounded by the fact that, far from satisfying the anti-Mormons in Illinois, the departure of Young only emboldened them. They immediately redoubled their harassment of those left in Nauvoo, forcing them to accelerate their departure and trade off a house or farm for a wagon and team. Within a short time some 20,000 men, women, and children were struggling across Iowa in the wake of Brigham Young. Many nights they had to shovel away the snow before they could build their campfires and arrange their camp for the night.

Nine children were born one night. Eliza Snow wrote:

As we journeyed onward, mothers gave birth to offspring under almost every variety of circumstances imaginable, except those to which they had been accustomed: some in tents, others in wagons—in rain storm and in snow storm. I heard of one birth which occurred under the rude shelter of a hut, the sides of which were formed of blankets fastened to poles stuck in the ground, with a bark roof through which the rain was dripping.

Kind sisters stood holding dishes to catch the water as it fell, thus protecting the newcomer and its mother from a shower-bath as the little innocent first entered on the stage of human life; and through great faith in the ruler of events, no harm resulted to either.[1]

Young's caravan averaged six miles a day, one hundred miles a month! So it required four months to traverse Iowa and in June reach a place where they could establish a permanent camp which they called Winter Quarters, now a part of Omaha, Nebraska. Many of the Mormons have described the scene. First came the snow and the freezing weather. Then in early spring came the soaking Iowa rains and the famous Iowa mud, a foot deep and sticking to shoes in five-pound gobs. The women learned to let the jolting of the wagons churn the butter. They learned to make prairie roots, even wild onion, palatable, and to feed the cattle bark from young trees. They sewed and knitted while keeping a watchful eye on children playing too near the wagon wheels. Most of the time they did not have enough to eat. They watched as small faces became pinched and many—too many—graves were dug beside the road. But there were schoolrooms in wagons, and at night beside the fire.

In such a wagon rode Louisa Pratt, the wife of Addison, away in the South Seas, and her four daughters. All of them came down with "chills and fever," and while they had plenty of meat there were few vegetables. They suffered from scurvy. Louisa fell and sprained her knee and it became swollen and refused to heal. She limped after the wagon train on crutches, or jolted painfully in the wagon bed. But on she went.

Brigham Young wondered whether anyone had led such a company before—men, women, children, horses, cows, sheep, turkeys, chickens through snow, mud, hot dry flatlands, across rivers, fearful of attack by day and by night. And this was not all. There were apostates to the north in Wisconsin sending messages asking friends to drop out. There was another apostate party heading for Texas. There were even the abandoned farms in Missouri just to the south, open to any who would renounce his faith. Certainly the temptations raged. It was Brigham who more than anyone else had to stand and exhort, ride and exhort, carry the keys to the mysteries of heaven and exhort. Messengers constantly sought him out, bearing news of events along the trail, of reports from Washington, where government help was being sought, and from the British Mission, to which, from the middle of Iowa, Brigham dispatched not only messages but trusted councillors. Franklin Richards bade good-bye to his family in a wagon in mid-Iowa to start for Liverpool!

Come, Come Ye Saints

And constantly Brigham's mind had to range ahead, not to just the next camp, but to the final destination and what should be done on arrival. Too, he had to lead in setting the spirit of the trek. He had the bands play at night, the Nauvoo Brass Band, the English Band, the small groups. William Clayton, one of the earliest converts from Preston, who had come to America with Brigham Young and was now thirty-two years old and a talented man, was in charge of the Church records and served as Brigham's secretary.[2]

One night around the campfire a messenger arrived with word that Clayton's wife had borne a son back in Nauvoo. The day had been disheartening, but Brigham insisted that they pray and that they pray for lightened spirits and cheerful attitudes. Clayton began to scratch out a song which is still today the favorite Mormon hymn, and is always sung with a fervor that literally shakes the walls with its concluding words. Clayton called it "All Is Well," but it is better known as "Come, Come Ye Saints":

Come, come ye Saints, no toil or labor fear;
But with joy wend your way.
Though hard to you this journey may appear,
Grace shall be as your day.
'Tis better far for us to strive
Our useless cares from us to drive;
Do this, and joy your hearts will swell
All is well! All is well!

Why should we mourn or think our lot is hard;
'Tis not so; all is right
Why should we think to earn a great reward
If now we shun the fight?
Gird up your loins, fresh courage take;
Our God will never us forsake;
And soon we'll have this tale to tell—
All is well! All is well!

We'll find the place which God for us prepared,
Far away in the West,
Where none shall come to hurt or make afraid;
There the Saints will be blessed.
We'll make the air with music ring.
Shout praises to our God and King;
Above the rest these words we'll tell—
All is well! All is well!

And should we die before our journey's through,
Happy day! All is well!
We then are free from toil and sorrow, too;
With the just we shall dwell!
But if our lives are spared again
To see the Saints their rest obtain,
O how we'll make this chorus swell—
All is well! All is well!

A Legend

J. Spencer Cornwall, who was for many years conductor of the Tabernacle Choir, tells an old Indian legend heard in the West. It runs:

Many, many moons ago my people were on the warpath. We hated the palefaces. We held council and decided to kill everyone. A band of palefaces was going west. They had almost reached the Rocky Mountains. I was the chief of 1000 young braves. That night, silently, we waited on a mountain pass for these people, who were led by Brigham Young. There were braves with bows and arrows behind every rock and tree, waiting to pounce down upon the palefaces. The pioneers camped for the night and prepared dinner. The big bonfire was burning brightly, and the palefaces danced around the fire. Everyone then sat down and began singing, "Come, Come Ye Saints." I gave signal, but our fingers were like stone—not one arrow was shot. We mounted our horses and rode back to camp. We knew the Great Spirit was watching over the palefaces. This was your song. It was your forefathers' song and it is my song every night before I go to bed. It brings the Great Spirit near to me and makes me and my people happy.

A documented story comes from Hawaii:

On December 7, 1941, the Tabernacle Choir's broadcast was brought to the people of Hawaii through transcription. The broadcast began at 8:30 in the morning. At 8:35 we could hear thunder and a repetition of explosions down Pearl Harbor way. My companion broke into my thoughts saying, "That doesn't sound like maneuvers, that sounds like real war." I laughed and thought it impossible, but the sounds grew alarming in their volume, and finally the broadcast was interrupted halfway through with the announcement that Hawaii was being subjected to an air raid from an unidentified aggressor. Chaos suggested itself to the minds of all of those who heard the announcement, and then the Tabernacle Choir of Salt Lake City was brought back to us, just as it finished singing the last stanza of "Come, Come Ye Saints. . . ." It was a message of courage and hope.

The Mormons naturally felt some restitution was due for the great city and farms they were forced to abandon in Nauvoo. They felt they should appeal to the U. S. Government, and Brigham Young had sent some of the apostles east to see what could be done. Several times in the history of the Mormons they have found friends among non-Mormons who stood up for them. One such was General Doniphan, who rejected orders to "exterminate" them in Missouri. One of them called on John Kane, a noted Philadelphia lawyer soon to be appointed to the federal bench by his friend President Polk.

Kane had a son, Thomas, lately graduated from law school and serving as his clerk. Now it was young Thomas Kane who decided to visit the Mormons and see for himself, and if warranted, carry forward their case.

Nauvoo Revisited

Thomas Kane wrote:

Ascending the upper Mississippi in the autumn, when the waters were low, I was compelled to travel by land past the region of the rapids. . . . My eye wearied to see everywhere sordid, vagabond and idle settlers, a country marred without being improved, by their careless hands. I was descending the last hillside upon my journey when a landscape in delightful contrast broke upon my view. Half encircled by a bend of the river, a beautiful city lay glittering in the fresh morning sun; its bright, new dwellings, set in cool green gardens, ranging up around a stately dome-shaped hill, which was covered by a noble marble edifice, whose high tapering spire was radiant with white and gold. The city appeared to cover several miles; and beyond it in the background there rolled a fair country, chequered by the careful lines of fruitful industry. The unmistakable marks of industry, enterprise and educated wealth everywhere, made the scene of singular and most striking beauty. . . .

As I drew near I was surprised to see in this city no sign of life. No one appeared on the shore of the river—it was a pleasant morning and not nine o'clock yet but not a woman was to be seen in any of the green gardens. . . . After a while I thought I heard the sound of human voices. I listened and after a minute heard it repeat so clearly that I knew it to be distant sound of boisterous laughter. Guided by my ferryman I went to whence it proceeded and found it made by a large number of drunken men who were carousing in the porch of the splendid marble building. . . . They had several jugs of strong waters of various kinds of which they were drinking heavily; inside also which proved to be the Mormon Temple others like them were to be found. . . .

I felt as though I should walk on tiptoe, as if walking down the aisle of a country church, to avoid rousing irreverent echoes. . . .

Nauvoo never prospered again. A French group, the Icarians, practicing a type of communal socialism, settled there for a while, and stones from the temple, which was soon destroyed by vandals and winds and erosion, were used by Catholics in building a girls' school, but the town dwindled in size and importance until the once largest city in Illinois boasted scarcely a thousand people.

Today there is interest in restoring the city. In the mid-1930s a medical student at Northwestern University named J. Leroy Kimball passed through Nauvoo and found the relic of the house that had belonged to his great-grandfather, Heber C. Kimball. He cherished the idea of buying the house and restoring it and this has led to the formation of Nauvoo Restoration, Inc.

If you visit Nauvoo today, you will be shown Heber Kimball's fine old brick home, modeled after the Georgian style, or what is popularly known as New England Colonial; the Wilford Woodruff home, much in the same style; Brigham Young's house, which had no particular style, except perhaps standard American brick farm house; the Ezra Benson house, home of a forebear of Eisenhower's Secretary of Agriculture; and the Joseph Smith house, half log, half clapboard. Nauvoo is often visited by Mormons touring the scenes of the Church's early trials.

Brigham Young and his lead party reached the banks of the Missouri in June and decided to establish camp across the river in Nebraska. His plan was to establish permanent camps along the route. Thus, when they arrived at a likely place, the fields would be plowed, seeds planted, and cabins built to house a few families that would be left behind to tend the place until succeeding wagon trains would arrive to help in harvesting and replanting. It was a system that, again, looked in retrospect like excellent planning, but actually was inspired by the critical need to supply people who had little money and few places to spend it in even if they had. They were very much on their own, and it taught them a lesson, well learned, in what real wealth is. These way stations served not only the move from Nauvoo but succeeding waves of converts from England, Scandinavia, and western Europe for some years.

Lamanites in Nebraska

The most important of these stations was called Winter Quarters. Young's lead party reached the Missouri in June and decided to create their central camp across the river in Nebraska, in Omaha Indian territory. Because of their belief that the Indians were descendants of the Lamanites, a tribe of Israelites that had been a part of the original settlement in America whence the ancient Mormons had sprung, the Mormons always seemed to have a way with Indians. To the Red Men there were "Americrats" and there were Mormons and only the Mormons were to be trusted. So when Brigham Young went to see Big Elk, chief of the Omahas, he spoke as a Brother:

"With your permission we would like to winter here. We can do you good. We will repair your guns and make a farm for you, and aid in any other way that our talents and circumstances will permit. . . . Can you furnish someone who will watch our cattle and keep them safe? Have you any objection to our getting timber and building houses and staying here until next spring or longer? . . . Do you feel disposed to be on amicable terms with us? Are you willing that we should sow wheat here this fall and plant corn next year? . . .

Big Elk replied, "My son, you have spoken well. . . . You may stay on these lands two years or more. I hope we may be friends. . . . Our young men may watch your cattle. We would be glad to have you trade with us. We will warn you of danger with other Indians."[3]

Mormon Battalion

The settlement was begun under fairly auspicious circumstances, but as seemed to be usual in Mormon affairs, trouble was not far behind. One day soon after the main body of Mormons was established in Winter Quarters, building a thousand houses, Captain James Allen of the U. S. Army sought out the leaders. He had a request, almost an ultimatum, for the raising of a battalion of five hundred men to march to the war with Mexico. It meant losing their youngest, strongest, most needed men.

Scarcely could a more unfair demand be imagined. Young heard that it had been sparked by Senator Thomas Hart Benton of Missouri, who insisted that the Mormons prove their loyalty and who was thought by some to be seeking an excuse to organize further persecution of the thousands still creeping across the southern Iowa mud to Winter Quarters. President Polk thought it would be a better idea to have the Mormons for the United States than to have them against, and even better to have a sufficient number of them enlisted in the service.

But, again as seemed common in Mormon affairs, the bad news had a bright side. The Mormons were almost destitute. Young himself said he had only five dollars to his name. Captain Allen offered to pay in advance $21,000, part of the pay that would be coming to the soldiers. The men would be clothed and otherwise provided for and it was agreed they would be discharged in California near where some supposed the Mormons were heading.

To Brigham Young this must have appeared to be a divine bestowal for two reasons: it gave the Mormons opportunity to prove their loyalty to the United States at a time when they sought federal help, and it offered the only way in sight for an inflow of cash that would sustain the migration. So with Heber Kimball and Willard Richards he set off along the trail recruiting the five hundred. But to the young men, their wives, families, and sweethearts it was, of course, a different matter.

After seeing Nauvoo, Thomas Kane went down to St. Louis and then up the Missouri to Winter Quarters in time to witness the farewell party for the first company of the Mormon Battalion, July 15, 1846:

There was no sentimental affectation at their leaving. Light hearts, lithe figures and light feet had it their own way from an early hour till after the sun had dipped behind the sharp sky-line of the Omaha hills. Silence was then called, and a well-cultivated mezzo-soprano voice, belonging to a young lady with a fair face and dark eyes, gave, with quartet accompaniment, a little song, the notes of which I have been unable to obtain—a version of the text touching all earthly wanderers:

"By the Rivers of Babylon we sat down and wept,
We wept when we remembered Zion."[4]

Part Two

THE TIMES OF
BRIGHAM YOUNG

Chapter Twelve

ARRIVAL IN THE GREAT BASIN

Throughout the summer of 1846 the Mormons poured into Winter Quarters. Brigham Young built a mill. Some of the men went out to work for settlers. The women made tents and wagon covers. The children worked in the fields at chores. Everything at Winter Quarters seemed to represent the compressing of a huge spring that in uncoiling would thrust them over the mountains.

Most of the discussion centered on where they should go. Oregon was still favored by a few. Vancouver Island offered its attractions. And even in 1846 the California boosters were in full voice. Maps were studied. Anybody having personal knowledge of the terrain was interviewed. But Brigham Young appeared to be serene in his belief that God would reveal where they should go.[1] He said he had seen the place in a dream and would recognize it when he saw it. And it was evident that he thought *the place* was somewhere in the Great Basin. If only he could talk with Bridger.

One party, eastern Mormons, had sailed from New York at the same time Brigham Young had left Nauvoo. It was a party under Sam Brannon and was headed around South America to California. The Mormon Battalion was marching to California. Certainly when the Nauvoo Mormons arrived at Winter Quarters in the spring of 1846, most of them presumed they were en route to California.

But the summer and winter of 1846 convinced Brigham Young that too many others were headed for California. He wanted his people to be secluded. He thought the Great Basin was the place, so he decided to lead a party to seek out the way. On April 16, 1847, the company left Winter Quarters. It was composed of 143 men, three women, and two children. They had seventy-two wagons, ninety-three horses, fifty-two mules, nineteen cows, seventeen dogs, and some chickens.

This was the "Pioneer Party," chosen to find the Promised Land; but all in Winter Quarters were eager to go, too, so the Pioneer Party was followed at intervals by ten others. All of them followed the usual trail to the West, whether to Oregon or California, except that they broke a new trail along the north bank of the Platte River to Fort Laramie in eastern Wyoming. Most of the emigrant trains up to that time had followed the south bank of the Platte, but the Mormons were fearful not only of Indians but more so of attacks from people in other emigrant trains. They felt few human hands were outstretched to help them.

The Odometer

William Clayton was assigned to keep track of their mileage, but wearied counting the turns of the wagon wheel, 360 to a mile, so Orson Pratt devised an odometer. Appelton Hormas carved wooden gears that would keep a record. Orson Pratt also had surveyor's instruments and he determined latitudes and longitudes and with Clayton compiled a guide which for years was the most accurate one available of the trail. When the time came to build a railroad, the Union Pacific followed closely the Old Mormon Trail. So does U. S. Highway 30. In addition, the Pioneer Party and those that followed put up signposts and even boxes for the exchange of letters, so in following years the Mormon Trail came to be about as well marked as Fifth Avenue or Regent Street.

By the first of June the Pioneer Party reached Fort Laramie, the last center for the repair of equipment, the replenishment of supplies, and the exchange of information about the trail ahead. The odometer had counted 522 miles from Winter Quarters. It had taken forty-five days, and Brigham Young had just turned forty-six years of age. He had expected to be met at Laramie by a group of Mormons coming up from Mississippi and also expected to pick up men from the Mormon Battalion who had been left, because of illness, in Santa Fe, to the south.

He waited four days and when they failed to appear he left a message:

If experience has not already taught you, we would say, keep a sharp lookout for buffalo, Indians and bears, all of which may be met and endanger the life and liberty of men, women and children, beasts and property.

Be wise and watch as well as pray continually, and having done all you possibly can, and exercised all the skill, wisdom and prudence and care and strength that you possess, should you be overtaken with accidents or losses of any kind, take the spoil thereof patiently and cheerfully, and murmur not for Christ's sake.

Near Casper, more than a hundred miles west of Laramie, they had to cross the Platte, and, having secured a leather boat at Laramie, they easily got across and established a ferry. Another train of emigrants, not having the means, asked the Mormons for help, and this was agreed to at $1.50 per wagon, or payable in flour at prices paid in Missouri. This was so lucrative that Brigham left ten men to operate the ferry all summer for the benefit of those who would pay, as well as for the following Mormon groups.

Jim Bridger

On June 27 the Pioneer Party crossed the Continental Divide. Here, in theory at least, if a bucket of water were poured on the ground, half of it would run to the Atlantic and half to the Pacific. Brigham noted that it was three years to the day since the martyrdom of Joseph. But the next day, Monday, June 28, 1847, Apostle George A. Smith came back to the party shortly after noon escorting a weather-beaten gentleman looking much older than his forty-three years, clad in fringed buckskin. He was one of the most famous mountain men in American history, written about in many yellow-backed novels of the West. They called him "Old Gabe," Jim Bridger.

All afternoon they talked, then as dusk came—and it came quite late in the high mountains in late June—President Young invited Mr. Bridger to supper and they sat talking about what Bridger called his "paradise."

Bridger underlined what they already understood, that Salt Lake was a lot nearer Winter Quarters than either California or Oregon. Seven hundred miles of mountains and deserts lay between the lake and the Pacific. True, Bridger was not too encouraging about crops. He advised experimentation before too large a party was brought in. Indeed, many years later Brigham Young was to say that Bridger was certain that corn could not be ripened in the Great Basin:

"Mr. Young, I would give a thousand dollars if I knew an ear of corn could be ripened in the Great Basin. I have been here twenty years and have tried it over and over again."

"Wait eighteen months and I will show you many of them. . . . Did I say this from knowledge? No, it was my faith; but we had not the least encouragement—from natural reasoning, and all we could learn of this country—of its sterility, its cold and frost, to believe that we could ever raise anything. But we traveled on, breaking the road through the mountains and building bridges until we arrived here, and then we did everything we could to sustain ourselves. We had faith that we could raise grain. Was there any harm in this? Not at all. If we had not faith what would have become of us? We should have gone down in unbelief, have closed up every resource for our sustenance and should have never raised anything."[2]

This faith was justified, but in fairness to Jim Bridger it must be said that the Great Basin has never been especially suited to corn. Some varieties do ripen there today, but it is not regarded as prime corn-growing country. Its best agricultural products were unknown to Jim Bridger, who, however, was far more interested in furs than in grains.

Gold in California

Six days farther along the trail the Pioneer Party was met by Sam Brannan, who had come east from San Francisco to try and persuade Brigham to continue to California. He reported that his party had already planted wheat and potatoes and other crops and all was in readiness for the Nauvoo Saints. He also brought news of the Mormon Battalion. It was now in Los Angeles, waiting for the emigrant trains. There is no doubt but that Brigham and his councillors were tempted. They sent letters back to Winter Quarters with the Sam Brannan comments and reports, but Brigham insisted that first they must carefully explore the Great Basin. He believed it was *the place*. Brannan returned to California in great disappointment.

The Pioneer Party followed the thin line drawn on Frémont's map, and Bridger's directions. The trip over the high mountains was difficult and many hours were spent in fording streams and cutting through rough country, with time out for destroying rattlesnakes and crickets "the size of mice." Brigham became ill with a fever which he thought resulted from the cold nights, the heavy dust, and the rigors of the trail. He lagged somewhat behind the advance party and on July 24 was quite ill and riding in Wilford Woodruff's wagon when the party came down Emigration Canyon, and Brigham, according to Mormon legend, pulled himself up to look out on the valley, partly green, partly yellow, with the shimmering lake beyond—not an Eden but grand in the vastness and color and power of the old American West. "Yes," he is reported as saying, as though confirming what his eyes had seen in a dream, "this is *the place!*"

Before the day was ended, several acres had been plowed and planted, and City Creek was being employed in irrigation. It was judicious use of water, of course, that made the desert bloom.

It was already late in the summer and there was much to be done to prepare for the thousands following along the trail and the additional thousands waiting in Winter Quarters. There was plenty of timber in the mountains, but none at hand in the valley, so the first houses were built of mud bricks, or adobe, after the Indian fashion. Even the roofs were modeled after the Indian style, with layers of earth heaped across poles. As winter snows and rains collected and melted, the roofs became sieves, and the first winter was quite damp for the Mormons. Brigham remained in the valley only a month. At the end of August he felt he had to return to Winter Quarters to organize the great migration he planned for the following summer.

There is no dearth of materials concerning this period of Mormon history and among these items are some that were written for immediate use, and which are immensely revealing. One such is a letter written by Brigham Young and sent from a camp on the trail about ten days after he had left Salt Lake City. It discloses both the precision and depth of his guidance, and also what his guidance was, in his own mind, based upon.

Brigham's Counsel

He begins by emphasizing protection and defense:

While with you we used the utmost diligence to erect a fort of sufficient size to contain houses for all who will be at the city the coming winter, and we hope the brethren will not release their exertion until the fortification is completed, and the houses therein with all their necessary fixtures for health and convenience. We would recommend a high and strong fence within the enclosure and about two rods distant from the houses which will form a yard of sufficient extent to contain all your cattle and horses, should any alarm demand their security, otherwise you had better yard your cattle without the walls, so as to keep the fort as clean as possible; also in the corners of this enclosure all your hay may be stacked with safety, for it is wisdom that you cut some hay that your stock may be provided for, in case of deep snow, Indian alarm or any other contingency. . . .

Next he goes into agriculture, and a short excerpt will indicate the care and study that had been given this life-or-death matter:

We would remind the brethren that it does not injure the young and tender corn to be nipped by the frost, and that repeatedly, provided the embryo of the tassel is not destroyed; and the same principle is good in relation to many of the grain and vegetables; and as you are located in a new country and untried climate, and as we know the drouth to be great in the latter part of the summer, we recommend that you begin to plant and sow such seeds as soon as the snow is gone in the spring or even before spring so that we may know by experience whether it is possible to ripen grain in the Valley before the summer drouth shall demand the labor of irrigation; therefore we wish the brethren to begin their farming and gardening as early as possible and continue it so long as they have seed, and keep a record of the time and manner of sowing, planting and cultivating, and also of the weather daily, that we may learn by experience and records the best time and method. . . .

The fall is the time for you to secure your year's stock of salt from the Salt Lake; and we recommend that you procure good timber and erect a substantial bridge over the Western Jordan before the water rises, which will give you easy access to the Lake which is a pleasant place of resort and its water very healthy for bathing, as well as the warm springs on the north of the city. . . .

There were wise words with regard to the Indians, or Lamanites, as they were called in Mormon teachings:

When the Lamanites are about, you will keep your gates closed, and not admit them within the walls; so far as you come in contact with them, treat them kindly; but do not feed them or trade with them, or hold familiar intercourse with them in the city; but if you wish to trade with them go to their camp and deal with them honorably. . . .[3]

Emphasis on Education

Brigham Young had enjoyed only the elementary grade education available in small-town upstate New York early in the nineteenth century—but this was not to be scoffed at, for it was the era of the one-room schoolhouse and emphasis on "readin', writin' and 'rithmetic"—although it was an education completed in one of the early grades. Only a few made it as far as the eighth grade, though that was the ideal. Education always interested Brigham. So, in his letter, education came in for treatment:

As soon as you are located within the fort, let a sufficient number of rooms be appropriated for schools, furnished with the best teachers, or furnish your children with teachers at home, and give every child among you an opportunity of commencing his education anew, and see that he attends to it, and that individual who has the opportunity to educate his children and does not, is not worthy to have children. . . .

When the Mormons arrived in the Great Basin, it was still a part of Mexico. There was no thought of buying land; indeed there was nobody to buy it from. It was there for the first settler to take and use as his own. There was some thought that the entire enterprise should be communal, and obviously the closest cooperation and interdependence were required for survival. They had to stick together, but Young understood that individual initiative must have its rewards.

We have no land to sell to the Saints in the Great Basin, but you are entitled to as much as you can till, or as you need for your support, provided you pay the surveyor for his services, while he is laboring for you. . . .

Some writers have speculated that because of his many great qualities Brigham Young would have risen to the heights in almost any situation. If he had remained in New York State he might have become a business tycoon; if he had stayed in England, he might have been one of the principal colonizers; on the American frontier he might have become an outstanding political leader. But, on second thought, most of those who have examined his life and his works agree that Young's motivation was not personal ambition, at least in the usual sense. He loved the Mormon cause; it was a part of him. He felt that he was ordained as a chosen vessel for these people and spoke with that authority in his conclusion to the letters back from the trail:

Remember at all times, that when we left you to return to Winter Quarters, the oracles of the Church left, and returned with us; and that this our epistle is your oracle and guide until you see us or hear from us again; therefore, let no one undertake to overturn or overrule this letter, but let it be read in the congregation of the Saints every sabbath day; which if ye do, and practice accordingly, ye shall be blest and the spirit of the Lord will rest down upon you, your souls will be filled with light and knowledge; your hearts will rejoice; and the small still voice will be whispering within continually: this is the way, walk ye in it; which voice follow at all times, and you will never go astray; but the riches of heaven and earth will be multiplied unto you, and we bless you with these blessings in the name of Jesus Christ . . . Amen.

The letter covered several pages and proved to be the guide for the establishment of Zion in the Rockies.

As Brigham rode toward Winter Quarters he encountered a stream of wagon trains of emigrants eager to reach the Great Basin before snow closed the mountain passes. One might speculate whether he noticed a seven-year-old pig-tailed girl holding the reins of a team while her mother and sisters walked along beside the wagon in the heavy dust. It was Lois Barnes Pratt. Her father was still far away, a missionary in the South Pacific.

Salt Lake City Grows

Young observed the trudging and sweating emigrants with misgivings. He knew their arrival would tax the food and other resources of the little community in Salt Lake City to the utmost.

Many would surely endure great hardships, yet he had to agree that such rigors were less fearsome than the wrath of the Gentiles. In any case, he could not stay the exodus, and he didn't try very hard. So it was that by the time the first snows fell some 3000 souls were huddled in the temporary shacks and tents of Salt Lake City. A year was to pass before Brigham Young saw the Great Basin, never to leave it again.

On July 1, 1845, two years after he had left his family in Nauvoo, Addison Pratt came into possession of a St. Louis newspaper which told of the martyrdom of the Prophet. There was an account of the persecution of the Mormons.

It was fearsome news for a man halfway around the globe whose family was presumably in the midst of the trouble. Yet as a missionary he had been successful. His little church now numbered sixty members, fully a third of the island's population, and he had the friendship of nearly all who were not members. Drunkenness was a thing of the past as the people, at his instigation, had voted a strict prohibition on liquor imports. If Pratt felt like seeking the quickest way home, he thrust the feelings away. Indeed, he even chose to extend his work in the islands by moving to Tahiti, where the Church was also prospering and greatly in need of his help. But his family was never far from his thoughts. A year and a half later, February 6, 1847, we find him writing in his journal:

This is the birthday of my daughter Ellen Sophronia. This is the fourth birthday that has passed since I saw her last, nor have I had word from her since August, 1844, and whether she or any of the other members of my family are now living is all unknown to me.

Chapter Thirteen

THREE MIRACLES

Visitors to Salt Lake City will hear from their Mormon guides about three miracles which sustained the Saints in their early months in the Valley.

The first is the miracle of the gulls. Obeying the counsel of Brigham Young, the Saints planted their seeds quite early in the spring, augmenting crops already sown the previous fall. The vegetation came up in strong stalks and leaves and the Saints rejoiced that they would have full storehouses for the winter. Then, just as things looked most promising, hordes of the large crickets or locusts that the pioneers had observed on entering the Great Basin swarmed over the tender plants, eating them down to a stub. Rescue parties were formed and the Mormons beat the fields with wet blankets, barrel staves, anything they could lay their hands on to drive off the ravening insects. They even opened the irrigation ditches and drowned millions, but still they came, creeping, leaping, sometimes seeming to fly over their dead to attack new plants. It was clear the Mormons lacked human means to avert starvation not only for themselves, but for the thousands coming over the trail.

There was no question about what the Saints should do. They knelt in the fields and prayed as fervently as ever man did, and then to their horror they saw another disaster approaching. The sky darkened with flights of huge birds—sea gulls from the Great Salt Lake!

But instead of finishing off the crops, as the Mormons expected, the gulls fell upon the locusts, gorging them up by the beakful and disgorging about as many. Nature's balance was restored. A good part of the crop was saved, and by dint of extra effort, fresh planting, and cultivating, and freer use of irrigation, much was regained that had seemed lost. There is a sea-gull monument in the Temple

grounds today, and sea gulls are protected by living Mormon gratitude.[1]

The second miracle came a year later. The winter had been terribly
difficult. Brigham Young had hoped to hold a great many of the
Mormons in Winter Quarters, but the Indian agent had insisted on
their going back across the river, from what is now the Nebraska side
to the Iowa side, and there Young had built a new settlement,
Kanesville, named in honor of their friend Thomas Kane.

But few wanted to remain there. They feared their human neighbors more than they did the cold and the hunger and the savages
which they realized awaited them on the way to the Great Basin.
As a consequence, they poured over the mountains into the valley
and many didn't have time to get in a crop, or build a house before
the intensified chill of the mountain air settled over them. Naturally,
there was grousing and some of the women particularly lamented
the absence in Salt Lake City of items, including finery, found in
the eastern and European markets.

Bargains!

Heber Kimball, given to prophecies that somehow seemed to come
true, asserted that dress goods would be sold in Salt Lake in greater
abundance and at lower price than in New York or St. Louis. This
was a little wild even for the faithful Mormons, but it did come
about, and in this way: One of the Mormon Battalion, working for
Captain Sutter to earn money to take to Salt Lake City, noted in
his diary on January 24, 1848, that he had discovered something that
seemed to be gold. Sam Brannan had returned from Salt Lake and was
visiting this young Mormon, and soon he shouted in the streets in
San Francisco that gold had been found.

This word reached the Saints in Salt Lake and many wanted to
hurry there, but Brigham Young lectured them, "Gold is for the
paving of streets." Meanwhile, the cry of *"Gold"* set off a great
migration from the East. Many of the wagon trains came through
Salt Lake and were pleased to shuck off their heavy burdens before
the final push to the gold fields. Some wagons arrived loaded with
merchandise with which its owners had expected to open stores in
California, but in Salt Lake City the entrepreneurs learned that

swift clipper ships already were carrying great quantities of such things by sea.

So here were the wagonloads 1000 miles from the Missouri markets and 700 miles east of California. Most of the owners were eager to be rid of their merchandise and to hasten to the gold diggings themselves. So they unloaded their stocks in Salt Lake.

One of the Mormon deficiencies had been in iron needed for repairs and for manufacture. But so many wagons were abandoned that the Mormons burned them for the iron and soon had plenty for every variety of purpose. Food was traded for fresh horses. In all, enough merchandise was distributed to lift the level of Mormon morale well above despair. Indeed, the Mormons could not but regard it as a miracle.

And as the sun-dried mud houses began to be replaced with white clapboard produced in the new saw mill Brigham built in the mountains, and modeled after the upstate New York and New England houses, and with the wide streets and square blocks favored by Joseph Smith, Salt Lake City began to take on an appearance of gracious prosperity that has never left it. The Mormons have not been alone in regarding this change of fortune as a miracle.

The Miracle of Reunion

There was a little private miracle in the Pratt family. It is not mentioned on the public tours today because it is long forgotten, but it occurred in Salt Lake City about this time. Addison Pratt had finally made his way to Hawaii and thence to San Francisco, where he had met some of the Mormon Battalion and with them he had trudged over the high Sierras and the flat basin and into the new village of Salt Lake, where his home was pointed out to him. He stepped inside the door and saw his daughter Ellen scrubbing the floor.

"She jumped up as I stepped in and caught hold of my hand with an expression that was wild as a hawk and exclaimed, 'Why, Pa Pratt, you have come home.'

"The next two, Francis and Lois, were soon on hand and looked equally surprised. The youngest, Ann, was out to play. She was soon called in, and when she came in she eyed me with a very suspicious look. When one of her sisters tried to force her to me to shake hands, saying, 'That is Pa,' she jerked her hand away, saying, 'It is not!' and left the room.

"Their mother soon came in. She looked quite natural and quite as young as when I left home, being more fleshy now than then . . . but the children had all grown entirely out of my recollection. . . . I left them June 1, 1843, and now it was the twenty-eighth of September, 1848."

Among the early community projects was the building of a meeting house, at first only a series of posts across the tops of which were strung branches, some with leaves to provide protection from the weather. It was called the Bowery, and it was located near the present Temple. By October 1849 the Saints were ready for their annual Church conference. The fields were ready for an excellent harvest, but fields and streets were deserted while from the Bowery came a strong swell of voices:

> "Come, Come, Ye Saints,
> No toil or labor fear,
> But with joy
> Wend your way . . ."

Overseas Missionaries

There was a docket of Church business to attend to, new settlements to be started in Ogden, Provo, Manti, an express or freight company to be established for regular traffic with Kanesville.

Then came the third miracle. President Young pointed out that one of their primary reasons for moving to the Great Basin had been to establish a place for the gathering of the Saints from all the world. The missionary work, he reminded them, was an ascendant activity of the Church and he quoted a verse from Revelation that the Prophet Joseph had often used:

"And I saw another angel fly in the midst of heaven, having the everlasting gospel to preach unto them that dwell on the earth, and to every nation, and kindred, and tongue and people."

This had been the motivating force behind the establishment of the British Mission and of the sending of missionaries to the South Seas and elsewhere. And so it was that at the first moment he reasonably could, the moment after the movement of the bulk of the Saints to the Great Basin and after the first big harvest, Brigham Young announced a new and more extensive overseas effort than ever before. At the October 1849 conference he gave out the names of those who would go abroad.

The women in the congregation could not help but feel some trepidation, for the tradition was that missionaries left their families while they went off for two years or more to the distant places. Brigham Young's counsel to the men was:

"Don't carry your wives or your children in your hearts or in your affections with you one rod. Dedicate them to the Lord God of Israel, and leave them at home; and when you are in England, or among other nations, no matter where, when you pray for your families, pray for them as being in the Great Salt Lake Valley, and do not bring them close to you, as though they were in your carpetbag. Pray for them where they are. You must feel—if they live, all right; if they die, all right; if I die, all right; if I live, all right; for we are the Lord's, and we shall soon meet again."

And to women:

"I wish to say to you that are left here, whose husbands and fathers are going away for a season—don't cling to them one particle, but let them go as cheerfully as you would give a weary traveler a cup of cold water. . . . Don't send your hearts after them one step, nor suffer your spirits to cling to them one moment. Then you, wives, in very deed will be blessed and be helpmeets to your husbands."[2]

Of course, this was practical counsel, which many a chaplain has given to many a soldier, and which many a soldier's wife has found the best course. His words about dying may seem harsh, but in the Mormon belief there is little fear of death because after this present life experience families are united in happier circumstances in lives to come.

But despite all this good advice there were quite a few whose hearts raced a bit as the names of the new missionaries and their assignments were announced. John Taylor, who had been an early missionary to England, and who subsequently was with Joseph Smith when he was martyred and was himself wounded, was now to go to France. And with him, Curtis E. Bolton and John Pack— from the Great Basin to the Tuilleries, what greater contrast could be pictured!

Erastus Snow and Peter O. Hansen were assigned to Denmark. Lorenzo Snow and Joseph Toronto to Italy. To the vital British Mission, where 30,000 souls were said to be awaiting emigration, went Franklin D. Richards, his second mission there, Joseph W. Johnson, Joseph W. Young, Job Smith, Haden W. Church, George B. Wallace, and John S. Higbee. John E. Forsgren went to Sweden. Others were dispatched to the islands of the Pacific.

Emigration Fund

It was at the October 1849 conference, too, that Brigham Young announced the Perpetual Emigration Fund. They would take some of the money they made from the wagon trains going to the gold fields, and some which they expected to be sent back by the members of the Mormon Battalion working in California, and put it into a revolving fund to help bring the Saints to Zion.

As the emigrants earned money, they could repay the advances and thus revolve and enlarge a fund to help others. But the financial plan was only a part of it. There were still almost 10,000 Saints strung out along the trail as far east as Nauvoo. They must be helped to the Great Basin. Some estimated that as many as 30,000 were waiting in Europe for the opportunity to gather in Zion, but the whole thing must be done in stages. First must come the farmers, to make certain that food was available for later emigrants. These were to be found along the trail. Then, workers of various skills must be brought over: men to build the mills, blacksmiths to repair the implements and wagons, tanners, builders of various skills, shoemakers, weavers, and so on.

The Perpetual Emigration Fund would be used to regulate the volume and the talents admitted to Zion. It was started off with $6000, and in the first summer of its operation, 1850, some 2500 Saints were helped to move from Kanesville and other settlements. In 1851 another 2500 were assisted. And in the summer of 1852 two apostles, Ezra T. Benson and Jedediah M. Grant, were sent to finish up the domestic migration. By summer's end they had brought in virtually all the 10,000, and Salt Lake City was ready to assimilate them.

By October the 1849 missionaries had departed Salt Lake City. They had made their way over the mountains and over the plains, arriving in Kanesville just before Christmas. Some went to New Orleans and sailed from there. Some sailed from New York and Boston, but by one route or another they gathered in Liverpool during late May and early June 1850.

Talents Sought

They knew what they were to look for in Europe—not only people who would accept the restored Gospel and be baptized, but also people of specific talents wishing to emigrate. In the first four years after this enlarged effort of 1850, they dispatched to Salt Lake City ninety-six boot- and shoemakers, ten boilermakers, ten cabinetmakers, forty-six engineers, two ironmongers, 226 miners, seventy-three masons, eight printers, twenty-two spinners, nine weavers, and some three hundred representatives of other special skills.[3]

They offered three different plans for emigrants. The first plan was the Perpetual Emigrants, or PE Companies. These were composed of those unable to pay any part of their way to Salt Lake City.

The second plan was the Ten Pound Companies. They were composed of those who had some means but not enough to cover all their expenses. It was found that by very expert management, the cost for transporting an adult from Liverpool to Salt Lake averaged out at £20, though sometimes it could be done for as little as £10. So emigrants paid their £10 into the Perpetual Emigrating Fund, and PEF did the rest.

Lastly, there were the Cash Companies, whose emigration was handled by the PEF but who paid their own full costs. As it worked out, only about 20 percent of the emigrants came in the fully subsidized PE Companies, while the number who paid their full way was about 35 percent and those who used the £10 plan about 45 percent. As the years went by the £10 rose to £13 and then to £15, but economies helped bring the receipts and the costs closer together.

It is perhaps worth comment that those who came on the PE, or

credit, plan did rather poorly in repayment. This was not from lack
of desire but simply because the same qualities or difficulties that
had kept them poor in Europe were not automatically corrected simply by transport to the New World, while those who had trades and
abilities which had permitted them to amass their own passage
money in the Old World normally prospered with the same equipment in Utah.

In its first three years the PEF expended about $750,000 in helping
some 22,000 from England and Europe to the Great Basin. The total
spent before PEF was discontinued in 1877 was above $8,000,000,
and the total number helped was at least 100,000.[4] Whether the
individuals concerned repaid their personal indebtedness or not really
doesn't matter. For the investment added untold riches in the real
wealth of talents and enterprise to a land that was valueless without
such people. The whole concept of PEF must rank as one of the
world's most rewarding investments, judged by any terms.

Chapter Fourteen

MISSIONARIES TO SCANDINAVIA

To say that the world which the missionaries left in the Great Basin of the Rocky Mountains in 1849 was different from the European world they entered in 1850 would be to indulge in one of those over-simplifications which Napoleon deplored as the enemy of precision. As a matter of fact, though, it was Napoleon's "precision" which was still causing much turmoil in the Old World. The ferments he released and which resulted in a wave of liberalism sweeping over much of the Continent was, by 1850, being followed by the usual wave of reaction.

It was a time of kings. In Vienna, young Franz Joseph had just ascended the ancient throne of the Hapsburgs, where he was to reign until 1916. When crowned, he was first in power among the Germanic princes and dukes—a conglomeration of forty-seven states and free cities. But in Prussia a young giant of a diplomat, Bismarck, was rising to power. Standing six feet four inches, he was all charm and all insolence, depending upon the needs of the moment. To Bismarck, Austria was a "ramshackle empire," a "mongrel nation" of Italians, Croats, Slavs, and whatnots, glued together by their Roman Catholicism, which he felt should be ruled by the pure Prussian spirit, exemplified by the Prussian Army.

So it was a time of nationalism and of religious tension. Any rival of the state religion was an enemy of the state, whether the state was Austria or Prussia, or France. And that was how Mormon missionaries were for the most part treated—as enemies of the state.

John Taylor at first thought this would be no great obstacle in France. He and his companions found rooms at No. 7 Rue de Tournon in Paris, and immediately called at the Hotel de Ville to see the mayor. Taylor reported to his friends in London:

M. le Maire received us very courteously, and wished to know if we had any papers. I showed him a letter I had from the Governor of Deseret, and signed by the Secretary of State, he told me that was sufficient. I gave him to understand that we wished to preach the Gospel, that we had no political object in view, but simply came as Ministers of the Gospel.[1]

The mayor explained that so long as they preached in a consecrated cathedral no formalities would be required. The Mormons knew better than the mayor, however, that established places of worship would hardly be given over to them. So they were required to notify the mayor of each meeting in advance, write out for him the general line they proposed to utter, and receive permission for each meeting separately. And the meetings thus arranged were very poorly attended.

They did a little better in Boulogne, where they stirred up a public debate in which the Mormons appeared opposite a Methodist and a Baptist preacher and one Independent. The argument was of course inconclusive, but brought a little publicity and gave Taylor opportunity to publish a pamphlet which set forth the main points of the debate.

"The French are gay, careless, and volatile, but there are many saints that will yet rejoice in the Gospel of Peace. It is difficult on account of language, etc., to commence, yet the work will roll forth. Meanwhile we shall do what we can and leave the event with God."

The "event" soon proved to be the *coup d'état* of Louis Napoleon, who even then was plotting from London and in the succeeding two years managed to become Emperor, and even the most carefully prearranged meetings were no longer possible. The lid went on.

To a degree this was true in Scandinavia, too. Indeed in Sweden it could be said that the lid was never taken off. Only in Denmark was there a freedom comparable to that experienced in Britain.

The 1849 missionaries to Scandinavia gathered, after following diverse routes, in London in the late spring of 1850. It was their arrival, plus fortuitous developments in Denmark, that marked the really effective start of Mormon development in northwest Europe. For it happened that about the same time the Saints were getting themselves established in the Great Basin, the Danes were adopting a new constitution. This provided more freedom of religion than had prevailed before, or at that time prevailed over much of Europe.

While Erastus Snow, the leader of the Scandinavian group, remained in Britain briefly to confer with the Church people, Peter

Hansen, a native-born Dane, went on to Copenhagen. While he initially met with little success as a missionary, he did learn about the new law and so had this favorable news to report to Snow on arrival in Copenhagen in mid-June. At that time there were four Mormons in Copenhagen—Snow, Hansen, George P. Dykes, an early convert who had learned Norwegian in a Norwegian settlement in Illinois and who was to work in that field, and John E. Forsgren, who was assigned to Sweden.

First Danish Baptisms

The story of how Wilford Woodruff had converted almost the entire membership of the United Brethren in England was already legendary in Mormon circles. Fired with great zeal, the Scandinavian missionaries hoped to do at least as well. They had heard of a Baptist group in Copenhagen and concluded that this might offer likely prospects. So they attended the Sunday services of the Reverend Peter C. Mönster, introducing themselves afterward.

The next day Mönster called on them, and described some of the difficulties he had encountered, despite the new law. The missionaries told of their own trials in the United States and did not miss the opportunity to present some of the principal Mormon beliefs.

Mönster borrowed a copy of the Book of Mormon and promised he would study it. President Snow recorded, "After he left us, we bowed before the Lord and prayed to our Father that he would pour out his spirit upon him and the honest-hearted of his followers and raise up from their midst, friends and fellow-laborers with us in the work of God."[2]

They were disappointed in their prayers concerning Mönster. He decided against joining with the Mormons, and ultimately opposed them. But for a brief period he did introduce them to his congregation and some of these were converted. In fact, they comprised ten of the fifteen who were the first Scandinavians (Danes) to be baptized Tuesday, August 12, 1850, in the clear waters of the Oresund near Copenhagen.

Soon there was activity all over Scandinavia, though Denmark continued to be the base and center. In Sweden, for example, Elder Forsgren went first to his boyhood home in Gefle, high up on the

Baltic shore. Except from his own family, however, he met with little acceptance and could not even persuade the local printer to run off a tract which he had translated into Swedish. He did find a welcome among a group awaiting a ship to take them to America. He scheduled a meeting in a nearby grove and it was well attended by the emigrants, townspeople—and police!

As he was marched into town, the marshals called out to the curious that the arrested man was *"dopparen,"* meaning "the dipper," or baptizer. The crowd, sympathetic to the *"dopparen"* yelled back, "Hurrah for *profeten,"* or "Hurrah for the Prophet." Seldom had the little town enjoyed so much excitement.[3]

The local authorities were baffled by this new experience and decided that they should send him to Stockholm—like Paul to Rome —for judgment. But the authorities there were equally puzzled. His crime was not a religious one in Swedish eyes. It was political in that he sought members for a non-state church. The Lutheran ministers wanted no competitors. They liked their monopoly. All this was argued out publicly in the Stockholm court and was reported in the newspapers, so much so that the American Consul objected to an American citizen being held in jail, and Forsgren was released. Yet the publicity caused many to seek out the Mormon and he could do no less than preach to them as his heart dictated.

The situation daily became more embarrassing to the Swedes, so they decided to buy him a ticket and return him to America. The vessel, under the United States flag, stopped in Denmark and Forsgren was permitted by the American captain to "escape." The Danes arrested him, apparently on notice from the Swedes, but the American Minister to Denmark interceded and Forsgren was allowed to rejoin his brother missionaries in Copenhagen.

Thus the four Americans could review their future activities in the light of this experience. It was clear to them that Norway, Sweden, and Germany offered little welcome, but in Denmark they at least enjoyed a measure of protection and a limited acceptance. The conclusion was clear: they must concentrate on Denmark. It was decided that Forsgren would remain in Copenhagen, Dykes would go to Aalborg, a principal city of Jutland, while Hansen devoted himself to a translation of the Book of Mormon into Danish. Snow was to go to England to seek money to pay for the printing of the Danish edition.

Aalborg Success

These various projects proved to be successful. Forsgren worked with the Danes who were coming into the Church, and the numbers attending public Mormon meetings grew in such size as to attract the notice of the established Danish clergy—and the government, which asked for a written statement concerning Mormon beliefs. This resulted in publicity which called more attention to the Mormons.

Elder Dykes' mission to Aalborg was promising from the start. He arrived there October 10, 1850, and was welcomed by a Baptist congregation. One of the early converts was a wealthy storekeeper, Hans Peter Jensen, who had been president of the Baptists. He soon became the leading Mormon of the community. This was accomplished in hardly more than a month and started Aalborg on the way to becoming a prime source for many Mormon leaders in the years that followed.

This is not to say that things always went smoothly. On Sunday, Jensen, in the full fervor of his recent conversion, announced a public baptismal service in the waters of Limfjord near Aalborg. A number of people gathered to see the event and Jensen could not resist the opportunity to preach to them. He urged them to flee from the "Church of the devil," which the crowd naturally enough took to mean the Lutheran Church. It started a riot, during which the Mormon elders were dragged off to confront the Lutheran officials while others in the crowd went in search of Mormon homes in order to throw rocks through the windows. A combination of a heavy rainstorm and the police finally broke it up.

Before he left for England, Snow dashed off a pamphlet, "En Sandheds Rost" ("A Voice of Truth"), which proved to be the most popular tract used by Mormons in Scandinavia. Indeed, it became a source of wealth for the printer.

Meanwhile, translation of the Book of Mormon progressed, Hansen's literary skills being augmented by those of a talented Danish student. It came off the press in sixteen-page sections and could be purchased in installments. The first sheets were available in January 1851 and at that time there were 135 members of the Church, about a hundred of them in Copenhagen and thirty-five in Aalborg, with a few others in smaller communities. The complete book came off the press in late May 1851. It was the first translation into another tongue of Joseph Smith's original translation.

Three months after the book became available, the membership in Denmark was counted at three hundred. There were Church groups in many parts of the country, and clearly it was time for broader work. Elder Dykes, successful in Aalborg, now wanted to work in Schlesvig, which was then still a part of Denmark, though even at the time, with its sister duchy, Holstein, an object of controversy with the German states. Schlesvig and Holstein were German-speaking. The principal city of the region, Hamburg, as a great Hanseatic trading center, was a "free city," although German in language and sympathy and ultimately a part of the Reich. Elder Dykes' mission was not the first in Germany, having been preceded by some years by Orson Hyde and various other missionaries at sporadic intervals. This attempt was, however, the first concerted effort from a Danish mission to reach northern Germany.

There was an interesting note in this because Hamburg had been the point from which the first Christian missionaries had gone into Scandinavia a thousand years before. Now, said the Mormon missionaries, the restored Gospel was returning. To the Scandinavians and the descendants of the Hanseatic traders, accustomed as they were to great sagas, the Joseph Smith story of the finding of long forgotten plates of a book on a hill in North America did not sound so strange. Strange things were described in their own literature.

Baptism in the Elbe

In September, Dykes baptized two converts in the river Elbe. While police vigilance prevented a rapid spread of the Mormon teachings in Germany, this opposition served to make conversions mean a great deal. Those who joined the Church had to do so wholeheartedly, and with the prospect of suffering. It was not a popular or easy thing to do.

While the missionary efforts were coming from Denmark in the north, John Taylor, based in France, but equally interested in Germany, was issuing a German-language newspaper, *Zion's Panier*, which in its first issue predicted that thousands of Germans would join the Church.

As a matter of fact, while these early attempts of the Mormons to proselytize in Germany were not successful in numbers, quality was another matter. Certainly one of the early converts who contributed incalculably to the Mormon unfoldment was Dr. Karl G. Maeser of Dresden.

He and his wife and other notables of Dresden invited a missionary to talk with them, expecting some intellectual sport. When the missionary from Utah arrived, it was found that he could speak only a few words of German, but his message carried through without words and within a few days Dr. Maeser and his wife were baptized in the Elbe.

Subsequently, he emigrated to Utah, where he introduced Germanic thoroughness in teaching. He became Brigham Young's chief advisor on educational matters and, among other things, founded the academy which in time grew into Brigham Young University. Mormon missionaries make good use of the Maeser experience in their work in Germany today.

North Germany, however, was only one point of attack for the Copenhagen-based Mormons. In Aalborg, Elder Snow met a Norwegian captain who inquired about the Church, of which he had heard. Snow took it as an invitation to try missionary work in Norway and dispatched Hans F. Petersen. The captain tried to be of help and asked the dean of the Lutheran church in Trondheim for permission to hold services in the schoolhouse on the following Sunday.

"Are these Mormons of which I've heard so much really now in Norway?" the Lutheran asked in dismay, and, when assured such was the fact, immediately carried a complaint to the mayor. The mayor questioned Petersen at some length and decided that not only could meetings not be held but that Petersen himself should leave Norway. There was a few days' wait for a ship and Petersen spent them in holding private meetings with those who sought him out.

He returned to Aalborg, but the Captain Larsen who had transported him both ways was now convinced and was himself baptized the night they reached Denmark.

Persistence in Norway

It will seem incredible to any but a Mormon that Elder Petersen did not let his first experience in Norway discourage him, but barely two weeks later he again left Denmark, this time with Johan August Ahmanson as a companion, and entered Norway, once more at Trondheim. On this visit he converted the town blacksmith, John Olsen, and very shortly baptized Olsen and Peter Adamsen, the first two individuals to be baptized in Norway. This set off a sharp reaction. John Olsen's brother objected violently and organized a small mob to seek out Petersen with the thought of running him out of the town, if not out of the country. But Petersen was hidden by Captain Larsen's wife and escaped harm. The incident did, however, recall official attention to him, and Petersen was quizzed about the baptisms, performed without Norwegian sanction.

He was told that only members of the clergy were permitted to perform baptisms, and when he pleaded that he was a member of the clergy he was told that he was not so recognized, and the church he represented was not recognized as a sect authorized to perform such ordinances. A lesser man might have quit, but Petersen decided to move on. The foray of another mob against the Larsen house no doubt speeded his departure, for this time he was forced to hide inside the chimney and needed much soap and water before he could embark for Bergen, arriving in early January 1852.

It was about this time that President Erastus Snow in Copenhagen received a letter from President Franklin D. Richards in England: the Perpetual Emigrating Fund was in operation, would any of the Scandinavian Saints care to join a party of English Saints bound for the Great Basin? Although the subject of emigration to the Rocky Mountains had not been stressed by the missionaries, it turned out that the prospect had not gone unnoticed. Nine Danish members left Copenhagen on January 31, 1852, and arrived in Liverpool on February 7 only to discover they had missed their ship by a matter of hours and faced a wait in Liverpool of more than a month while another company of emigrants was formed.

On March 8 they were joined in Liverpool by President Erastus Snow and nineteen more Danish emigrants. They brought much news. At a conference in Copenhagen February 22 it had been announced that, as a result of this first missionary work, no fewer than seven hundred had been baptized in the year and a half that the restored Gospel had been made known in Scandinavia.

The Book of Mormon had been printed in Danish, and *Doctrines and Covenants* was on the press. An LDS hymnal was already printed and an enlarged version was being edited for printing. Five tracts, including "En Sandheds Rost," were being circulated. It was a work well started. Already a sizable contribution had been made to the Perpetual Emigrating Fund and emigration was rapidly becoming the goal of many of the Scandinavian Church members.

Voyage to the Great Plains

It may be interesting to follow this first group as they emigrated to Zion. They sailed, as a part of a larger English group, on the ship *Italy* from Liverpool on March 11, 1852. Two months later, in early May, they arrived in New Orleans. From there they shipped up the Mississippi and Missouri rivers to Kanesville, which, as we have noted, was across the river from Winter Quarters (now Omaha, Nebraska) and about where Council Bluffs, Iowa, now stands.

In Kanesville they waited through the spring, getting ready for the trek across the Plains. Early in July they set off, a part of a great ox-team caravan. It was during the heat of summer that they crossed the Great Plains, a part of the world so different from the coolish and fog-filled coasts of the North Sea and the Baltic that it is impossible to describe. Years later restaurants in the area were to advertise free meals on any day that the sun didn't shine, and they gave away few meals.

It was a bright, hot sun, unrelieved by trees, and across the flat buffalo grasslands to the stark, high Rockies, the great West, the Old West of so much song and story, they walked with history—and they knew it. Apparently they loved every minute of it, and many of them kept the sort of diary still treasured in many a Utah home. The final press over the mountains was under some urgency, to be certain of being ahead of the first storms of winter. They arrived in Salt Lake City on October 16, 1852, nine months after leaving Copenhagen.

While this first party from Scandinavia was making its way to Zion, a second party was forming in Copenhagen. Indeed, when reading accounts of those early efforts, it is sometimes hard to tell which ranked first in the minds of the missionaries: local conversions or plans for emigration. But this is not to say that efforts were not made to establish the Church more widely.

Several attempts were made in Norway, and although each seemed to be rebuffed, it turned out that a certain amount of seed was sown each time so that the Church always seemed to have some sort of foothold. Much the same could be said for Sweden, but an idea of the progress made can be gleaned from the records of the April 6, 1853, conference in Copenhagen, which showed 1133 members in Denmark, eighty-eight in Norway, and 110 in Sweden, a total of 1331.

Of these, 294 had already left with the second emigration group for the Great Basin. They had sailed from Copenhagen for Kiel on December 20, 1852, had made their way from Kiel to Hamburg and arrived in Hull, England, on Christmas Day. They sailed from Liverpool on January 16, 1853, and arrived in New Orleans March 16. Four deaths and three births had occurred. They sailed up the Mississippi and then prepared for the same trek taken by the first party the previous July, arriving in Salt Lake City on September 30.

With this sort of activity, and because the Mormons themselves sought a greater degree of state recognition, it is not surprising that the "Mormon question" reached the level of the Danish Parliament. The question was whether the Mormons deserved the protection of the laws or whether they were "something fearfully corrupt and false" and therefore outside the law.

Religious Liberty

The arguments ranged from liberal to conservative views. One member of Parliament voiced the opinion that the "Mormons should enjoy perfect religious liberty, as guaranteed under the new Danish constitution, even to taking of additional wives." Others felt that it was all right to guarantee the Mormon converts full rights under the law, but that this right did not include the privilege of going up and down the countryside seeking additional converts.

The principal result of all this talk was a statement from the Minister of Culture that he did not feel justified in interfering with the preaching of the restored Gospel, but felt he must guard against the practice of anything repulsive to the public morals and good. So it was that the Mormons were free to continue in Denmark, but under a more watchful eye.

It was still very rough going, however, in Norway and Sweden. In Sweden missionaries were banished from the land as soon as it was learned that they were baptizing. Nevertheless, as soon as one missionary was sent away, another would take his place and by the end of June 1853 it was possible to find enough Saints in Sweden to hold a conference and establish supervision over branches in Skonaback, Malmo, Lomma, and Lund. But membership was sparse; most meetings had to be held in secret. The pressure on all converts was to emigrate to Zion.

Much the same situation persisted in Norway. In the fall of 1853 the Supreme Court of Norway held that the Mormons were not recognized Christians and therefore were not entitled to protection under Norwegian law. When apprehended, the missionaries were offered the alternative of a small fine or a few days in jail on bread and water. Most of them chose the bread and water.

One of them, Elder Dorius, became a third offender and went on bread and water for nine days, the longest of any Mormon missionary on record. This sort of opposition, of course, forced more thought to be given to emigration. Three hundred left Copenhagen on December 22, 1853, and another two hundred sailed on December 26. There were other groups, so that the total number of Scandinavians arriving in Britain for transshipment to America in December 1853 exceeded six hundred. The attrition by an epidemic of cholera, however, plus the hardships of the journey, were such that only five hundred reached Salt Lake City on October 5, 1854.

Talents Needed

Erastus Snow made increasingly frequent visits to Franklin D. Richards, the president of the mission headquartered in England. The reason soon became clear. Richards was getting requests from Salt Lake City for converts possessing specific talents. One early example was the great need for a paper mill. The Church newspaper, the *Deseret News,* was dependent upon paper hauled at great expense over the plains and mountains. Thus the British Mission and the Scandinavian Mission were asked to try and find an expert paper-maker. This call was answered when Thomas Howard, known as a skilled paperman, joined the Church in Buckinghamshire in 1850. A year later he was in Salt Lake City in charge of building a new paper mill.

Another cry went out for sugar-producing machinery. Brigham Young had read about how the French had developed a sugar-beet industry to offset the British blockade of West Indian sugar during the Napoleonic wars. He wrote Apostle John Taylor in France to look into it. Taylor found that one mill still survived in the northwest of France and after due investigation obtained 1200 pounds of sugar-beet seed and ordered machinery from a Liverpool manufacturer. Converts who knew something of the cultivation, chemistry, and manufacture of sugar were eagerly sought.

In September 1851 the *Millennial Star* in England published a letter from Brigham Young:

If a company of the brethren could be formed in England, Wales, Sweden, or any other country, to come and make iron from ore (magnetic ore of the best quality) and machinery for rolling, slitting and cutting nails, and drawing off wire, it would be one of the greatest auxilaries for advancement in building up the valleys of the mountains; and the presiding elders in those countries are instructed to examine this subject, and forward such a company with the least possible delay.

Presidents Snow and Richards made a quick canvas of the converts and indeed found some who had knowledge of iron works. They also persuaded some of the more well-to-do Mormons to invest and in London they formed the Deseret Iron Company, with a capitaliza-tion of $4,840,000 of which $20,000 was immediately subscribed. This permitted the formation of a company of workers to go to the Great Basin and to take with them much of the required machinery.

This was pretty much the pattern for the first five years of the Scandinavian effort, 1850–55—zealous missionary efforts based in Copenhagen but probing into northern Germany, Sweden, Norway, even Iceland, and aimed often at specific talents. More often than not these probings were rebuffed, but sometimes the missionary was able to leave behind in a community one or two, sometimes a whole family, who had enough instruction to comprehend the idea that this was a religious movement rediscovered in America and restored as the pristine Christan church—and the local group would gradually grow. Evidently the saga of an American youth being led to buried documents which reaffirmed the basic Christ teachings greatly appealed to the Scandinavian mind. During this five-year period Church records indicate more than 5000 baptisms, which can only be regarded as wonderful in view of the forbidding obstacles to missionary endeavors. Of these about 1500 emigrated to the Great Basin.

Dalsgaard's Painting

There hangs from time to time in the State Art Museum in Copenhagen an oil by the noted Danish artist Christen Dalsgaard that was painted about this time, 1855–56. Its title is *Mormon Preachers*. The scene is the interior of a Danish carpenter shop. Two missionaries are calling on the carpenter and his family. The room has the low, beamed ceilings and the whitewashed walls that were later to be found in Utah. There are eight figures, but two are placed and lighted to stand out. One is a missionary, perhaps in his early thirties, with one booted foot propped up on a carpenter's rest, using it as a pulpit to hold an open book, presumably of the Book of Mormon, while he lectures with a sincerity and conviction that glow through the canvas. In the foreground, seated, is the second highlighted figure, a little blind girl, her face lifted up in the beams of light from the casement window as she seems to drink in the words of the missionary. Perhaps he is reminding her that Christ healed the blind and that the Book of Mormon restores the early Christian works. Beside her sits an old man, probably a farmer, with one hand twisted over his cane and dressed in heavy cloth decorated with the brass buttons of the time, while on the floor beside him is his upturned stovepipe hat. Sticking out is a pamphlet, "En Sandheds Rost," the original pamphlet of Erastus Snow, published five years before and reprinted many times thereafter. The carpenter stands beside his bench looking over another tract while a genial but skeptical smile plays over his face. A baby plays under the bench, and beside the door leans a barefooted girl, perhaps the servant girl, impassive, with a certain disinterest. Possibly she has heard gossip of the Mormons. In the background the mother of the house tends a baby.

Before your eyes a hundred years is peeled away and suddenly you glimpse something of the fervor of the missionaries, the great desire to believe on the part of some Danes, and at least a willingness to listen on the part of others.

Chapter Fifteen

ENTERPRISE

To Brigham Young and his councillors the early struggles to build a self-sufficient territory of a certain abundance must have seemed like one disappointment after another. Yet they did have a good many things going for them. First, of course, was the energy and direction of an excellent people. Even the most "citified" of those coming from the Old World—many of them skilled in specific work and long removed from the soil and barnyard—quickly adapted to life on the rugged and vivid frontier. But it was to employ properly these imported talents, and to build a secure and sufficient Church-commonwealth that Young and his councillors extended themselves to establish industries. Before they could do much of that sort of extending they obviously had to go through the always difficult process of forming capital. To do this they had the basic resource of tithing. This underlay—and still underlies—almost all aspects of the Church's economic activity.

Tithing had been introduced in Nauvoo.[1] Church members were expected to contribute one tenth of their possessions and one tenth of their annual increase. Those who had no property or increase were expected to labor one day in ten for the Church. Collections were handled by a tithing office. And a tithing office was one of the first things established in Salt Lake City, and in each settlement as it came into being. About three quarters of the income of the Church was derived from tithing.

Except for two or three years when the Mormons profited from people passing through to California gold fields, there was little opportunity to accumulate cash, so most tithing was paid in kind, which is to say in labor and produce. A tithing account of Ira Allen for 1854 was uncovered by his grandson some years later. He listed as paid:

Oats	$ 1.25
Potatoes	10.50
Vegetables	1.05
Chickens	.25
Pork	7.62
Wheat	28.00
Butter	1.00
Hay	9.60
Wolf Skin	5.25
Labor	29.00
Cash	1.00
	$94.52[2]

In addition, Brother Allen was credited with $25.85 overpayment from the previous year. It was explained that the Mormons were expected to pay tithing as increases occurred, but at the end of the year they met with their bishop and were either credited with overpayment or arranged to make up whatever deficit remained, a "tithing settlement." That this statement for one individual was representative of tithing practices is supported by a general accounting from the General Tithing Office in Salt Lake City. This indicated that out of total receipts valued at $143,372, only $25,000 was in cash and all the rest in farm products, home manufactures, and labor. Naturally, this flow of goods, some of it livestock and much of it perishable, required efficient and complicated organization to turn it to account. Tithing houses, or bishop's storehouses, were set up in every community, with the General Tithing Office in Salt Lake City as the headquarters.

Change, in Chickens

Payment in kind was sometimes amusing to the Mormons as well as to others. An American humorist, Bill Nye, told a story that the Mormons to this day sometimes repeat:

In those days if you wanted to go to the theater you took butter, eggs, chickens, potatoes, wheat, anything like that to a tithing house, and they would give you script for it. Then you took the script to the theater or any store and bought what you wanted with it. On one occasion I took a big fat turkey up to the tithing yard to sell for script and the tithing clerk had gone to supper. I waited and he did not return, so I had to go and get the young lady I had invited to go with me, and I carried the turkey to the window of the box office and asked for two balcony seats.

That clerk at the window handed out the two tickets and two spring chickens for change and I had to sit there all through the performance with a chicken under each arm and the young lady I was with was quite peeved that I paid so little attention to her. . . .[3]

An English visitor to the General Tithing Office in the early days described it:

Here are piles of rawhide, both cow and mustang, or even pig skin; bins of shelled corn, and cribs full of corn in the ear; wheat and rye, oats and barley; cakes of salt provisions; wool, homespun, yarn, and home woven cloth in hanks and bales; indigo; cocoons, and raw silk; butter, cheese and all manner of farm produce; even the most destructible of vegetable growths—not only potatoes, turnips and other root crops, but green peas and beans; fruit and young cabbages; hay, carpenters' work, boys' caps, slop-shop overalls; hemp-rope, preserves, tinware, stogies, confectionery, adobe bricks and tiles, moss and gramma mattresses, buckskin leggins, gloves, moccasins, hunting-shirts, and complete suits. These are but a minute fraction of the contents of the Church Tithing Stores.[4]

All of this was administered by a trustee in trust, who was Brigham Young, as President of the Church. He said that the problem was a complicated one and required "financiering" of a very high order. It also required frequent exhortation to the brethren not to pass off to the Lord the useless and retain the useful.

Walk into the storehouse and examine for yourselves. To be sure there was an old silk dress put in for $40, that had been lying for years rotting in the chest; that is a specimen of the rest. What are such things worth to our workmen? Why, nothing at all. We wish you to put in strong and substantial clothing. Good, strong homemade stuffs make the most suitable clothing for those who are building the public works.[5]

The Hub of the Economy

Because of the lack of cash, the tithing offices came to serve as banks and clearinghouses. They collected taxes in kind and disbursed materials for the construction of roads, bridges, schoolhouses, and other public requirements. Indeed, for the first ten years of the new community the tithing offices were the most important wholesale and retail establishments, the most used employment agencies, weighing stations, warehouses, and communication centers, even post offices, in the region. They regulated prices, issued scrip that was negotiable throughout the territory, and were, in short, the economic hub of the entire Mormon community. One might say that they represented by far the most important centers for the formation of capital.

And when capital in the form of cash, which usually meant gold, was required for investment, the General Tithing Office could issue a call for cattle or wheat and arrange for the sale in some outside market, often California, where cash could be deposited to Church accounts in leading banks. This is how much of the funds were raised to pay for the emigration of Saints from abroad and it is also the principal way in which Church funds were raised for the establishment, or attempted establishment, of important industries.

Frequently, indeed usually, these enterprises drew investment from the state revenues (Brigham Young was governor) and from private Mormon investors as well as the Church treasury. It is perhaps worth noting that this also describes the usual method for the formation and distribution of investment capital in newly emerging states, as observable these days in Africa. The main difference in Utah was that the Church was a more important capital-formation unit than the political entity, and that, for the first years, there was little or no private investment from the outside; indeed it was not welcomed. The Mormons wanted self-sufficiency, which was to bring on difficulties in years to come.

If things went wrong, as they sometimes did, the Church became a proprietor. But this was not the aim. Young wanted the Church to be the beneficiary, to what he regarded as proper degree, of the fruits of increase, but he had no leaning for communal ownership or the socialist approach. When such ownership occurred, it was forced on him against his strong and long-enduring opposition. He understood clearly that it was individual initiative and responsibility, and the goal of individual reward, material as well as spiritual, that accomplished things. He understood that, as a matter of practical necessity, such individual initiative required a banker. Sometimes the banker had to foreclose. Sometimes a man needed a partner. Sometimes the partner had to take over. For the most part, in the early days, that is how the Church got into business. And like a good banker, the Church tried to get its enterprises back on their feet and resume a banking relationship. Apart from a very few well-to-do converts, the Church was the only source of capital. As the territorial government, very much dominated by Church membership, came into effectiveness, it, too, was the source of capital, or grants of property and rights which could be used to forward commercial enterprises, but these were secondary.

The Rag Missionary

Three examples illustrate the manner, the problems, the frustrations of early industrial development. We mentioned previously the urgent desire to make paper in Deseret, as the Mormons at first called Utah. Not only was there a daily newspaper, but the Church required endless quantities of tracts for missionary use and wished to begin the publication of that never ending stream of books by, for, and of Mormons. Paper that had to be freighted in by ox team from either Mississippi or California ports was expensive and the flow uncertain. Thomas Howard, whose conversion, baptism, and speedy emigration has been mentioned, was given the help of a machinist and materials in Salt Lake City and by 1852 a primitive papermaking machine was in operation. The quality of the product was poor, a sort of gray blotting paper actually. The disappointment was high, but Howard pointed out that it was asking too much to build out of homemade designs and bits and pieces of machinery a really workable mill. Therefore, $8500 was invested by the Church in importing from England a complete machine. The big lack then became rags with which to make the paper and Professor Arrington of Utah State University uncovered the amusing story of George Goddard, who was appointed to a "rag mission" by the Church authorities:

. . . after being known in the community for years as a merchant and auctioneer, and to be seen on the streets going from door to door with a basket on one arm and an empty sack on the other, enquiring for rags at every house. Oh, what a change in the aspect of affairs!

But he was a good soldier:

... the humiliating prospect almost stunned me, but a few moments'
reflection reminded me that I came to these valleys of the mountains from
my native country, England, for the purpose of doing the will of my
Heavenly Father, my times and means must be at His disposal. I therefore
answered President Young in the affirmative, and for over three years,
from Franklin, Idaho, in the North and Sanpete in the South, my labors
extended, not only visiting many hundreds of houses during the week
days, but preaching rag sermons on Sunday . . .[6]

The sugar seed sent by Apostle Taylor arrived from France, sealed
in large tin boxes. It was carefully planted with the idea that a
crop would be ready for harvest by the time the machinery arrived
from England. But transporting the machinery was an epic in itself.
The voyage across the ocean and up the Mississippi was normal, but
it required no fewer than forty of the huge Santa Fe wagons with
some four hundred oxen to haul the machinery over the plains and
mountains and took from July 4 to November 10, 1853.

Loss in Sugar

It was the largest and heaviest shipment up to that time and when
finally set up, two seasons after the planned time, it could produce
only a low grade of molasses. All of the $32,000 raised in Europe had
been spent and the Church had invested about $15,000. Creditors were
pressing and the enterprise was bankrupt. At this point Brigham
Young stepped in as trustee in trust and took over the enterprise as a
public works of the Church, sighing, "I for one would have been
glad to have had other men engaged in the manufacture of sugar
from the beet, and not have troubled us with it at all, but so it is in
the all-wise providence of God, and He does all things right."

The Church proved to be no better, and perhaps a bit worse,
manager than the private investors, and although it was proved that
sugar beets could be grown in Utah, it could not be shown that commercial grade sugar could be manufactured in profitable quantities.
The project was dropped in the fall of 1856 with a loss to private
investors and the Church of about $100,000. For the next forty years
the Mormons imported up to $1,000,000 worth of sugar every year,

and every year they lamented their failure to produce beet sugar. In the 1890s they tried again, successfully.

Iron was the third example of frustration about industries. The Deseret Iron Company was formed in London in April 1852. President Snow came from Copenhagen to assist President Richards in England and along with the first company of Scandinavian emigrants went shipments of iron machinery. A party of Welshmen from the coal mines and iron works, augmented by a party of experienced men from Pennsylvania, converged on Salt Lake City in November 1852 and were promptly dispatched to Cedar City in southern Utah, where the iron ore and coal were known to exist. The work proceeded with vim, but first there was an Indian uprising which required diversion of all manpower to the building of a fort and other defensive measures. Then there was a flood, so devastating that it deposited thirty-ton boulders on parts of the new machinery. It was so discouraging that some of the miners and iron workers wanted to go elsewhere and perhaps just be simple farmers, but The First Presidency sent this ringing message:

If you were now on a mission to France or England or any other part of the earth, you would not sit down and counsel together about going to get your families, or about going home till your mission was ended. This is of quite as much importance as preaching the Gospel. The time is now come when it is required of us to make the wilderness blossom as the rose. Our mission is now to build up stakes of Zion and fill these mountains with cities, and when your mission is ended, you are at liberty to go.[7]

One problem followed another for ten years, until in 1858, after the expenditure of more than $150,000 had resulted in little except heartbreak and a few andirons and flat irons, the project was given up. A half century went by before eastern steel interests began to develop Utah coal and iron resources into an important segment of U. S. Steel.

More Troubles

So, in paper, sugar, and iron, three commodities essential for any degree of self-sufficiency, the early Mormon kingdom did not succeed. There were other industrial disappointments too—wool weaving and lead mining could be mentioned as examples—and this naturally led many of the Mormons to question whether they were on the right economic track. Their substance seemed to come from developing their farms and in following individual business pursuits rather than from manufacturing.

By 1855, with completion of the gathering of most American Mormons in Salt Lake City, plus the yearly accession of the Mormons from abroad, the population of the city exceeded 35,000. The harvests had been good. If there was no abundance of manufactures, there was at least a comfortable level of diet. But then, in the summer of 1855, began a series of misfortunes which brought even the supply of food in question.

First came the locusts or grasshoppers. Apparently there was a natural breeding ground in eastern Nevada for these "Rocky Mountain crickets" and in extra dry weather they would head for the mountains. A Mormon pioneer, Joseph Holbrook, wrote:

Everything was literally covered with them by night and from 10 o'clock in the forenoon until the sun was an hour high at night. The air was so full that it appeared like a snow storm even to somewhat obscuring the rays of the sun at times. They destroyed most of the crop taking in one night the heads of oats and the blades of corn, beans, and almost every green thing eating up the grass, etc.[8]

Brother Holbrook later reported that he harvested only five hundred bushels of wheat compared with 1700 bushels the previous year. And this was the usual story, a harvest about two thirds below normal, with population due to expand by almost 5000 with the arrival in late fall of the 1855 immigration! This time even sea gulls didn't prevent the loss.

Next came the most severe winter, 1855–56, the colony had experienced. Farmer Holbrook wrote that he had such a scarcity of feed that he sent his forty-five head of cattle to range in Bear River Valley and that half perished. Before the winter was over Heber C. Kimball estimated that half of all the livestock had been lost. Writing to his son, a missionary in England, he said:

I have been under the necessity of rationing my family, and yours also, to two-thirds of a pound of bread stuff per day each; as the last week is up today, we shall commence on a half-pound each. Brother Brigham told me today that he had put his family on half a pound each. . . . When this drouth came on, I had about 700 bushels of wheat, and it is now reduced to about one hundred and twenty-five bushels, which will not provide for my own family before harvest. . . . Still, we are altogether better off than most of the people in these valleys of the mountains. There are several wards in this city who do not have over two weeks' provisions on hand. . . . Money will not buy flour or meal. Dollars and cents do not count now, in these times, for they are the tightest I have ever seen in the Territory of Utah.[9]

Work Relief

But the prayers that went up were mighty. Brigham Young, Heber Kimball, and the others set the example in assisting as many others as they could. It was estimated that two hundred people were dependent upon Young and one hundred upon Kimball. And when it was observed that too many men were around the court house, idle, Young and his councillors called the men in and sent them on missions—thirty to southern Utah to raise cotton, forty-eight to Green River to make farms and build settlements, thirty to mine lead near Las Vegas, Nevada; eight to the East Indies as missionaries; seven to Australia; and, where twenty-five missionaries had been sent to England in 1854 and thirteen in 1855, in 1856 the number was increased to forty-two, a dramatic increase considering the problems.

Thus was defiance flung in the teeth of adversity. And when the long, cold, hard winter was over, it was found that not one had died of starvation, though there had been plenty of fasting, voluntary as well as involuntary. Even the bad harvest of 1856, another grasshopper year, did not weaken the faith and resolve of the Mormons.

Chapter Sixteen

THE YX COMPANY AND THE HANDCARTS

Economic failures as exemplified by sugar beets and iron, and the terrible infestation of grasshoppers, the drought, the poor harvests, and the hard winters gave many Mormons pause. They had been in the Great Basin nine years, going on ten. Was there enough to show for it? The answer varied, of course, by individuals, but for some the answer—in economic terms—had to be "No."

If Heber Kimball had been shocked by the poverty of Liverpool, where some lacked tatters enough to protect them from the weather, there were a few in Salt Lake in almost similar straits, and the climate was colder. But there was no despair or lack of hope, rather a probing or soul-searching—and unbounded Christian charity to share.

The question naturally arose whether too much attention had been given to seeking wealth. Perhaps the failure of the enterprises was God's way of telling them that such things were not for them. In a way, too, it was the age-old question of whether the Church exists primarily for itself or for its members. Was it too church-centered for the Church to be in business; should the cares of this world be left to "Martha" while the Church concerned itself with helping the individual apply its theology to his daily affairs?

Yet Mormons as individuals, no less than as Church members, recognized that their responsibilities to God did not end with the individual who had already made his way to the Great Basin. Even in the depths of the financial tribulation they thought of those in foreign lands awaiting emigration. "The cry," said Brigham Young, "for our poor brethren in foreign countries for deliverance is great, the hand of the oppressor is heavy upon them, and they have no other prospect on earth through which they can hope for assistance."[1]

The obvious problem was that funds for the Permanent Emigration Fund were quite low and the economic reverses precluded filling the coffers. Young's answer was the famous handcart plan, one of the most talked about episodes in Mormon history. In a letter to the British Mission in the autumn of 1855, Young wrote:

I have been thinking how we should operate another year. We cannot afford to purchase wagons and teams as in times past, I am consequently thrown back upon my old plan—to make handcarts, and let the emigration foot it, and draw upon the carts the necessary supplies, having a cow or two for every ten.

They can come just as quick, if not quicker, and much cheaper—can start earlier and escape the prevailing sickness which annually lays so many of the brethren in the dust. A great majority of them walk now, even with the teams which are provided. . . . They will need 90 days' rations from the time of their leaving the Missouri river, and as the settlements extend up the Platte, not that much. The carts can be made without a particle of iron, with wheels hooped, made strong and light. . . . I think we might as well begin next year as any time, and save this enormous expense of purchasing wagons and teams—indeed, we will be obliged to pursue this course, or suspend operations, for aught that I can see at the present.[2]

Handcarts on the Plains

Descriptions of the handcart idea were published in the Mormon papers in Europe and the cost was figured at only £9, contrasted with £15 the previous year for transit by wagon and team. Almost 2000 European Mormons signed up at once for the trek and sailed early in 1856 from Liverpool to New York, thence by train to Iowa City, where the Church had contracted for the handcarts to be waiting. The carts were similar to those seen in many European markets. They had two large wheels about four feet in diameter with a flat bed box between capable of holding a hundred pounds of food and clothes and utensils. Some were excellently made, but having only wooden bearings and axles lubricated with soap or bacon they tended to wear out and break down in the hubs. They required a healthy tug at the handrail to keep them moving, but they proved true once more the old adage that a man can pull more than he can carry.

As the emigrants arrived and were outfitted they were divided into companies of about five hundred persons with a total of one hundred handcarts and given ox teams and wagons. The wagons carried tents to sleep twenty persons, as well as heavy items unsuitable for the carts.

Some got under way in late May and early June of 1856, and while a walk across the Great Plains and Rocky Mountains was something incredibly different to men and women from the potteries of Staffordshire and the gentle farms of Denmark, the first three parties made it to Salt Lake City without great incident by early September, and were welcomed with brass bands, orations, and assignments to the new communities the Mormons were establishing from the mountain valleys south to Las Vegas and west to San Bernardino, California. But the last two companies ran into trouble. Blame was widely distributed, some to President Franklin D. Richards in Liverpool for permitting so many to emigrate, some to Apostle John Taylor in Missouri for not having enough handcarts ready, but the stern fact is that the weather deserved the blame.

Because of delays in obtaining handcarts and getting them properly outfitted, one company of handcarts did not leave the old Winter Quarters location until August 17 and the last company did not leave until August 27. By the experience of previous winters this still left time, though a close amount of time, to reach Salt Lake City before the snows of winter fell on the Rockies. But that winter of 1856–57 was the earliest and coldest in Mormon records. Snow and freezing weather came even while the handcarts tugged over the plains. Messengers and immigration officials with horses got through to Salt Lake in October, and when Brigham Young learned that more than 1000 men, women, and children were on the plains and headed for the mountains, he immediately grasped the seriousness of the situation and ordered relief parties to carry food and clothing, as well as teams and wagons to hurry to the rescue.

A Mormon with one group later described the ordeal. After relating that his party had set up a mountain camp and decided to wait out a blizzard, expecting relief to come from Salt Lake City, he wrote:

During that time [of a three-day encampment] I visited the sick, the widows whose husbands died in serving them, and the aged who could not help themselves, to know for myself where to dispense the few articles that had been left in my charge for distribution. Such craving hunger I never saw before, and may God in His mercy spare me the sight again. As I was seen giving these things to the most needy, crowds of famished men and women surrounded me and begged for bread. Men whom I had known all the way from Liverpool, who had been true as steel in every stage of the journey, who in their homes in England and Scotland had never known want, men who by honest labor had sustained themselves and their families, and saved enough to cross the Atlantic and traverse the United States, whose hearts were cast in too great a mold to descend to a mean act or brook dishonor; such men as these came to me and begged bread. . . .[3]

Relief did come, but not before some two hundred of the 1000 on the road had perished in one of the great disasters and tragedies of the old American West. The story was widely reported in the eastern United States as well as abroad, and substantially contributed to the array of criticism arising in the East.

The Express Stations

Brigham Young held that the handcart scheme had not failed; it had worked remarkably well, and cheaply, as long as it was planned to get emigrants over the mountains by the end of September. One way to expedite affairs and lessen handcart loads was obviously to provide well-stocked way stations. Why not build a series of settlements along the trail? They would be established about every fifty miles. Each settlement would be laid out over a square mile with ample room for vegetables and other crops to supply travelers. Fresh animals would be available for hauling, repair shops with adequate tools and spare parts would be on hand. Everything would be done to comfort and speed emigrants. This, it will be recalled, was parallel to the plan adopted for the great migration from Nauvoo, first to Winter Quarters and then across the plains.

Coupled with this was a larger plan. A central need of the Mormons was for a better freight and mail service to the East. It was believed also that a well-run express company would attract overland passengers to California, and not least in the Mormon idea was that such a service would facilitate visits from editors, preachers, and politicians who, out of a fund of misinformation, were stirring anti-

Mormon sentiments. And understanding and reliable information was an acute need.

In January 1857 Young chartered the Deseret Express and Road Company, soon to be known as the Brigham Young Express and Carrying Company, or simply as the YX Company. Young realized that the United States government would be loathe to award him, or the Church, a mail contract, so one of Heber Kimball's sons entered a bid at $23,000 a year for carrying one load of mail a month each way between Independence, Missouri, and Salt Lake City. As soon as Kimball was given the contract, he assigned it to YX Company, a fact not greeted with cheers in Washington. But the first mail left Salt Lake in the dead of winter, February 8, 1857, and was delivered in Independence twenty-six days later. Return mail came in twenty-eight days.

Troubles in the Press

Among the letters delivered by the YX Company was one addressed to Brigham Young by Apostle John Taylor. It enclosed newspaper clippings from the eastern press covering the previous six months. The attacks on the Mormons ranged from such items as a demand that a gift of a stone from Utah for the Washington Monument should be declined because it was sent by un-American people to humorous comment in the New York *Herald* about unexpected results of a stay of a detachment of United States soldiers near Salt Lake City. After the soldiers had departed, it was discovered that some of the Mormon girls had been victims of seduction.

The Mormons had received other federal visitors. One was a Judge W. W. Drummond, who, the Mormons were told on good authority, had deserted a wife and child in Illinois and who sat upon the bench in Salt Lake with a mistress beside him while insisting on lecturing the Mormons on the evils of plural marriage. Drummond was finally banished from Salt Lake by the general contempt of the residents and he hurried back East to announce untruthfully that the Mormons were disloyal to the United States, that Brigham Young was setting upon his own independent empire with himself as emperor. All this was in the clippings. So were horror stories of the handcart tragedy. Worst of all were the false stories of the forcing of young girls to cohabit with older men, and of women held as slaves, and subject to torture and even dismemberment for disobedience.

This was not a fortuitous beginning delivery for the fledgling mail service, but the Mormons pushed ahead with their large plans, laying out a mile-square village every fifty miles. Mail and passengers and freight would be speeded through, but all this effort was not for the profit and glory of the Church. It was principally a means to facilitate the emigration of the Saints pouring in from England and Scandinavia, Germany and France.

But here again the preoccupation of the Church with its affairs brought it into conflict with the main stream of United States history. This course was that of individual initiative and private profit. It was an age of personal acquisition. Church enterprises were outside the norm. The Mormons in their ideas for the Brigham Young Express Company were ten years ahead of the Pony Express and the subsequent transcontinental express and stage services. As a matter of fact, the stage services that followed took over many of the settlements that the Mormons began.

But there were a good many, and some of them of the ascendant economic power that can rally public opinion, who felt that it was in the national interest (and no doubt their own) to root out by main force this Mormon obstacle and rival to the westward march of their kind of private enterprise. So in the express company the Mormons were destined to suffer another heartbreaking failure, but not for economic reasons. To the Mormons, Uncle Sam seemed suddenly to don a devil's garb.

Chapter Seventeen

THE "UTAH WAR"

Washington, D.C., Inauguration Day, 1965. In front of the Capitol, along with the nation's leaders—spiritual, political, temporal, and financial—waits the President of the United States. On the inaugural stand with him is the famed band of the United States Marines— and the Salt Lake Mormon Tabernacle Choir. Solemnly Lyndon Baines Johnson takes the oath of office, and the choir immediately fills the immediate area and the world's air waves and television channels with a mighty hymn. President Johnson is soon on the telephone thanking President David O. McKay for sending the choir. Thus honored, and thus was honored, one of the world's great musical organizations.

At a time when The Church of Jesus Christ of Latter-day Saints has a sizable representation of its members serving in the Congress and in a multitude of high federal offices, and in many places of power, as befits its political and economic position, it was a little startling to hear one member of the choir say, "Oh, if only Brigham Young had lived to see this day." To understand the fervent significance of that remark one must recall that there was a time a century ago when it seemed as if Uncle Sam were at "war" with Brigham Young.

One of the first inklings that such might be the fact came in Independence, Missouri, early in July 1857. The Brigham Young Express Company, the YX Company, had been in operation a few months but already more than $100,000 was being spent on establishment of relay stations and dozens of families were moving from Utah to man them. A typical station, by July, had a complement of seventy-five men of various talents, a corral with almost one hundred horses and mules, and dwellings for forty to fifty families. It had a storehouse of several tons of flour, adequate hay, and a garden of fifteen or more acres all in crop. Some stations boasted sawmills, one even had a brickyard.

The key to the success of the whole venture, however, was the contract to carry the United States mail, and on July 1 the post-master in Independence refused to hand over the mail sacks to the waiting YX wagon. Frantic inquiries disclosed the fact that the contract had actually been canceled in Washington on the tenth of June, and that at the same time United States troops had been ordered to take over affairs in Utah. This news, confirmed in bits and pieces, was rushed to Salt Lake City and the messengers arrived on July 23.

They found Brigham Young and several thousand Mormons up in Big Cottonwood Canyon celebrating the tenth anniversary of their arrival in the Great Basin. Brigham Young had pitched a tent and was inside conferring with friends when the messengers rode in.

It was a gala day and four brass bands vied in supplying music, while the people played at games, joined in hymns, and feasted at a true pioneer picnic, food of a quantity and variety to astonish, if not assault, modern-day stomachs. They sought a private word with Brother Brigham and when he knew that his great dream of a regular and effective express line was denied, and that 2500 armed soldiers of the United States were moving against his people, he still had the courage to bottle up the news. The celebration went on, while inside the tent grave decisions were in the making.

It would have been an interesting time to observe Brigham Young. He was fifty-six years old. Twenty-five years had gone by since, as a young carpenter in upstate New York, he had picked up a copy of the newly printed Book of Mormon. In the years intervening he had been a missionary in the eastern part of the United States, particularly in New England. He had worked in New York and had directed the Church's work in England for more than a year. He had stepped into the vacuum left by the martyrdom of Joseph Smith and had led his people on the heartrending move from beautiful Nauvoo to the Great Basin, a migration which stands as one of the memorable episodes in the history of the western United States. For ten years he had served as head of the Church, as governor of of the territory, as the chief financial officer, as the organizer of one of the most successful and largest emigrations of British and North

European peoples to the New World. He had mellowed, grown a little grayer and heavier, but, if possible, stronger in his convictions.

This was the man to whom was brought, in the midst of rejoicing, the word that the U. S. Army was marching to depose him. The reasons as stated by President Buchanan were not complex. The charge was that Brigham Young was setting up a kingdom that did not recognize the federal government as superior authority.

Mobilizing of Forces

In the United States things of important moment are frequently covered by a Presidential message to Congress. The Mormons had achieved that eminence when President Buchanan declared that "The community and, in part, the civil government of Utah Territory are in a state of substantial rebellion against the laws and authority of the United States."[1]

Affidavits from known enemies of the Mormons said that non-Mormon minorities had little rights or protection, and that federal appointees found it impossible to discharge their offices, and that federal records had been destroyed. Behind these charges, of course, were subtle forces. Probably most telling of all was the barrage in the eastern press that the Mormons were licentious religious fanatics, enjoying harems. And, as noted earlier, there was the strong feeling in the national business community that the Mormons were establishing a self-sufficient state athwart the westward march of the nation.

And there were some who felt that leaders from southern states were behind the move on the Shakespearean assumption that it is good "to busy giddy minds with foreign quarrels," which is to say that if the army were engaged in the far reaches of the Rockies, there would be less likelihood of military intervention in the South. Four years before the outbreak of the Civil War, this was not too lightly dismissed. The Mormons themselves, viewing the federal expenditures, which ultimately ran above $15,000,000, thought the action was taken to satisfy the contractors whose profits were in fact the subject of later congressional investigation and resulted in the resignation of a Secretary of War.

That there were negative reactions from a contractor disappointed in the award of the mail contract to the Mormons had been established. And Brigham Young was disappointed by the attitude of non-Mormon businessmen in the Basin. The Mormons felt these businessmen showed enmity and disloyalty by siding with outside interests and this feeling carried forward a half century or more in the business relationships of Mormons with non-Mormons.

How would Brigham Young and the Mormons meet this assault? They felt that it was simply another manifestation of malicious evil. Jesus had stirred up the enmity of entrenched human mores, so had Joseph. This was just more of the same. "If this were not the Kingdom of God upon earth," said Brigham, "do you think that the world would be arrayed against us? No . . . the Kingdom of Heaven is here, and we are in it, they are angry at us solely for that."[2]

But Brigham was not one to turn the other cheek. "Woe, woe to those men who come here to unlawfully meddle with me and this people." An advance party under Captain James Van Vliet arrived in Salt Lake City in September and Brigham received him in the Tabernacle in the presence of several thousand Mormons. The captain naturally wanted to know what welcome the troops would have, whether they would be accepted, whether the Mormons would provide for them and furnish a place for encampment.

Captain Van Vliet observed complete courtesy, and Brigham responded in like manner. He made it plain, however, that the soldiers would not be welcome, would be treated as an invading force, and that rather than surrender, the Mormons would burn their homes, like the Moscovites before Napoleon, and retreat to the mountains. Young went further. He undertook to convince the captain that the charges leveled against the Mormons were unfounded. For one thing, he showed him that the federal records, complete and untouched, had not been burned as had been reported. After the captain had been with him a few days Brigham Young said that he would supply an unquestioned demonstration that the Mormon people were free to leave the kingdom any time they chose. He said that if the federal government would duplicate the offer in the East, he would offer to give every Mormon in the Valley free transportation and ample supplies for a journey wherever he wished to go. He forecast that 1000 would come in for every one that left. And the captain apparently thought Young was correct. Indeed, so convinced became Van Vliet that the reports which had motivated President Buchanan's action were trumped up that he offered to go to Washington and try to straighten things out. The offer was accepted.

In the meantime Brigham Young ordered full mobilization. Missionaries overseas were summoned home. For the first time in twenty years no missionaries went to England. Emigration, which had been above 1000 in the summer of 1857, fell off to a little more than one hundred in the following year. Mormons were called in from San Bernardino in California and from Carson Valley (where a few years later the sensational gold strikes were to be made) in Nevada.

Guerrilla War

The express stations, so painfully and expensively started, were abandoned. Some 3000 men were formed into a militia, still known as the Nauvoo Legion. An advance party was sent out to scout the movement of the federal troops. Their instructions:

On ascertaining the locality or route of the troops, proceed at once to annoy them in every possible way. Use every exertion to stampede their animals, and set fire to their trains. Burn the whole country before them and on their flanks. Keep them from sleeping by night surprises. Blockade the road by felling trees, or destroying the fords when you can. Watch for opportunities to set fire to the grass to the windward, so far as possible, to envelop their trains. . . . Take no life, but destroy their trains, and stampede or drive away their animals at every opportunity.[3]

The sturdy Welsh and Scots, Britons, Danes and Swedes, always thought to be so gentle, were now accounted mountain fighters, and they were pretty good. The Mormon raiders, under Major Lot Smith, burned out three freight trains and captured 2000 head of cattle.

A federal soldier wrote that every night before camping they had to put out fires. And sometimes in the middle of the night the raiders would ride through the camp pretending to be Indians and leaving no horses with which the soldiers could pursue them.

The federal troops had expected to travel over the mountains before the snows, but such delaying tactics made a condition of march which they themselves compared with those of the French before Moscow. The result was that the troops made miserable camp for the winter in the high Rockies while the Mormons rejoiced in the best harvest in their memory.

All this hardened the resolve of Washington and contracts for the spring of 1858 were of unprecedented magnitude, causing the newspapers to refer to it as the "Contractors War." The quartermaster general estimated that the supply trains en route to Utah in the spring of 1858 would make a line about fifty miles long, if bunched together. But before it could even approach the mountains, a mysterious gentleman known as "Dr. Osborne" arrived in Salt Lake City and was immediately ushered in to Brigham Young.

He turned out to be the Mormons' old friend Thomas L. Kane, one in that series of non-Mormon friends who have providentially stepped forward in time of need to defend, mediate, bridge the gulf. He had been to see President Buchanan, following up on the report of Captain Van Vliet that the Mormon question could be peaceably settled, and Buchanan had authorized Kane to see what might be done. Since it had always been insisted in Washington that the principal objective of the troops was to install a new governor, and one awaited in the army camp in the person of Alfred Cumming, Kane suggested that Cumming be permitted peaceful entry and installation. Young and his councillors, after three days and nights of fasting and praying, commissioned Kane to go see Cumming and to "do as the Spirit of the Lord led him."

Move South

But no sooner had Kane left than Young and his councillors were "moved by the Lord" to take themselves and their people away from Salt Lake City. There had been some speculation over this, whether it was a gigantic effort to win public sympathy or whether it was made in fear of the changing political regime and the likely approach of the troops. Whatever the motivation, the fact is that as Thomas Kane escorted Alfred Cumming into the Valley they saw wagonload after wagonload of the Saints moving south. Cumming inquired and with increasing concern saw that furnishings had been removed from houses, along with windows, and that piled against most of them was straw and wood ready for the torch.

Brigham Young had moved forty miles to the south where, in Provo, a new headquarters had been established. By the time he was ready to return to Salt Lake City and talk, Governor Cumming

PLATE V. Inside the Temple: One of the sealing rooms of the Salt Lake Temple where couples are married for time and eternity.

PLATE VI. The World Room of the Salt Lake Temple where temple-goers meet to contemplate man's struggle in the world after Adam and Eve were driven from the Garden of Eden.

PLATE VII. The Council Room at the Salt Lake Temple: Here the President and his four counselors meet regularly with the Latter-day Saints Council of Twelve Apostles.

PLATE VIII. Over a century has passed since the pioneer "Mormon" choir, now the Salt Lake Tabernacle Choir, made its first appearance. Since 1893 it has won national and international acclaim, first in a national competition in Chicago. A 1911 tour took the choir to New York City and the United States capital in Washington, D.C., to sing for United States President William Howard Taft. In 1955 the choir toured Britain and the European Continent, winning praise of critics and public. A reviewer for the *Morgenpost,* Berlin, said, "Extraordinary!" *L'Information,* Paris, reported, "Beautifully pure."

Among the distinguished musicians who have conducted the choir are Leopold Stokowski and Eugene Ormandy. "It's the greatest choir I've ever conducted," said Maestro Ormandy after its first concert with the great Philadelphia orchestra in 1958. On the same tour the choir sang for President and Mrs. Eisenhower.

A pioneer in national radio, the choir is now in its fourth decade of weekly nationwide broadcasts, making it the oldest continuous music series in American radio. Recorded broadcasts of these weekly programs are heard in other nations.

The choir has also been featured on a number of important network television broadcasts and in motion pictures. The recordings of the choir have received wide acceptance both in America and in Europe.

understood that the federal troops might invade Salt Lake City, but that they would find nothing but charred ruins to lord it over. This understanding provided an atmosphere of mutual respect for the meeting, and the two—Young and Cumming—got along reasonably well.

The solution they worked out was for the troops to pass through Salt Lake City but not to occupy it. Instead, they were to make a camp in Cedar Valley, about forty miles southwest of Salt Lake City, not regarded highly as a site by the Mormons. But still the move south continued. Cumming made several attempts, with impassioned appeals, to halt trains, and spoke with urgency to Brigham Young about it. Virtually all the women and children were moved from northern Utah, and Mormon scouts were sent to find oases in the Nevada desert, though few such oases existed. There was talk about moving to Sonora, in Mexico, or to South America, but in practical fact "the move south," as it is known in Mormon history, was essentially a move to the southern part of Utah.

When the troops did march into Salt Lake City, they found it deserted. Some of the soldiers removed their hats, as if attending a funeral. There was no thought of looting or riotous behavior, such as some had talked about on the way. Only a great sadness pervaded.

"It was substantially a city of the dead, and might have been depopulated by a pest or famine,"[4] wrote one correspondent, and suddenly the world's sympathies were on the side of the Mormons. A people who would leave their homes rather than receive conquerors, who preferred life in caves in the mountains to submission, who would die rather than forego their liberty, such people were not to be denied by Americans. And not a few hearts in Wales and England and Scotland, in Scandinavia, Germany, and France were made proud too. President Buchanan declared a "free and full" and unconditional pardon and soon 30,000 Mormons returned to their homes, Brigham Young in the fore. The federal troops remained in their camp. The Mormons took over from the contractors in supplying food at profitable rates. The 3500 soldiers at Camp Floyd in Cedar Valley provided a bonanza for the Mormons until the Civil War erupted three years after their arrival and suddenly they were recalled east, leaving a vast amount of discarded supplies for the Mormons at a fraction of their original cost.

Mountain Meadow

Although Brigham Young and his councillors in Salt Lake City had no way of knowing it, a tragedy had accompanied—indeed preceded—the soldiers into Utah. At the moment Brigham was meeting with Captain Van Vliet, a messenger came in from the area in southern Utah where the Mormons had attempted to produce iron. His word was that a large train of 120 California-bound people had arrived. These emigrants were from Missouri and Arkansas and some among them had boasted to the Mormons that they had been in the party that murdered Joseph Smith. The Arkansas travelers claimed to know something about the fatal shooting of Parley P. Pratt, which had just occurred that year in their state.

There is no reason now to believe there was validity in either story. The "mob" that killed Joseph Smith had been carefully identified, and Parley Pratt was shot by a man who insisted his wife had left him to join the Mormons at Pratt's instigation. But the Mormons of Iron County had no way to evaluate these stories, and the itinerants became increasingly obnoxious: they called the Mormon women whores, they poisoned water holes used by the Indians, and they threatened to join the federal forces in subjugating the Mormons.

Brigham Young, with plenty of troubles of his own, gave wise and conciliatory advice to the Iron County Mormons: use every peaceable means to expedite the travelers through Utah and on to the California road. Protect them if it requires the help of every Mormon in southern Utah. But the advice arrived too late.

The poisoning of the wells had killed Indian cattle, and this, along with the obvious hostility of these white men to their Mormon friends, greatly angered the Indians. They made an attack on the emigrant party and several braves were killed. The Indians then demanded that the Mormons help them punish the emigrants and no doubt many of the Mormons were provoked enough to want to. But they sent a truce party out to the emigrant camp, loaded all the small children on wagons, and started to march the adults back to Cedar City, a distance of about thirty-five miles. On the way the Indians suddenly swooped down and, as it afterward was disclosed, assisted by some of the Mormons, within a few minutes killed all the emigrants. Only the children were saved.

This became notorious in the Old West as the Mountain Meadow Massacre. It was reported to Brigham Young as an Indian massacre, and he accepted it as such. But in succeeding years questions were raised and an investigation indicated that some of the Mormons had acted cruelly and violently and as accomplices of the savages a deep shame fell upon all Mormons, while anti-Mormon elements did their best to heap up shame and blame. Twenty years after the event, and following state and federal investigations, John D. Lee, who had been the government Indian agent for the southern Utah area, and a prominent Mormon, was executed for his participation in the affair.

Even today the Mormons are loathe to think or talk about the Mountain Meadow Massacre and do so only because from time to time the old bones of the affair are exhumed.[5]

Chapter Eighteen

ALL WAS NOT WORK

There has been so much about famine and peril and negative things that one might reasonably carry away the impression that life among the Saints was grim. But as a matter of fact early visitors to Zion often mentioned the spirit of joy that pervaded. Some said that the Mormons seemed to have a song in their hearts, and this was true even in the midst of a sea of troubles. Following in the pattern laid down by Joseph Smith, Brigham Young frequently exhorted them to smile and to be cheerful and agreeable.

To young parents he would say, "A child loves the smiles of its mother, but hates her frowns." He often led the dance and when non-Mormons commented that it was unseemly, he replied:

I want it distinctly understood, that fiddling and dancing are no part of our worship. The question may be asked, What are they for, then? I answer that my body may keep pace with my mind.

My mind labors like a man logging, all the time; and this is the reason why I am fond of these pastimes—they give me a privilege to shake myself, that my body may exercise and my mind rest. What for? To get strength, and be renewed and quickened and enlivened, and animated so that my mind may not wear out. Experience tells us that most of the inhabitants of the earth wear out their bodies without wearing out their minds at all, through the suffering they endure from hard labor, with distress, poverty and want.

While on the other hand, a great portion of mankind wear out their bodies without laboring, only in anxiety. But when men are brought to labor entirely in the field of intelligence, there are few minds to be found possessing strength enough to bear all things; the mind becomes overcharged, and when this is the case, it begins to wear upon the body, which will sink for want of proper exercise. This is the reason I believe in and practice what I do.[1]

The Mormon Theater

His detractors sometimes said that he placed too high a priority on cheerful spirits and cite the circumstance that the Mormons built a theater before they erected a temple. The fact is, of course, that a temple was started, or at least projected, almost as the first act of settlement, but it was felt that the Temple should be for the ages, unhurried and built of the best. In the meantime a make-do "endowment house" was put up to serve for required formalities, on endowment of Mormon teachings.

But to build a theater was entirely in keeping with Joseph Smith's view that "men are that they might have joy." And the western frontier was for the young in heart and not the dour. The West was always throbbing with the cacophony of the fiddle and the guitar and there gradually evolved a style known as "western music," but easily discernible in it are the measured cadences of old Scottish and Irish and Scandinavian dance tunes. The Mormons were a bit more purist in their music in that so many of the emigrant parties had skilled musicians and even choirs among their members, and they were untouched by the folk music of the New World, at least for a time.

The occupation by federal troops, the move south, and the whole traumatic experience of conflict caused Brigham Young and his councillors to feel that something should be done to lighten matters. So although they needed a temple, and although their first tabernacle, holding less than 3000, was long since outmoded, both projects were put on a secondary list while work was speeded on the Salt Lake Theater.

It was started in 1861 and completed in 1862, costing upwards of $100,000. Mormons from London found it oddly familiar, as they might, for it was modeled somewhat after the famous Drury Lane Theatre, the Theatre Royal, originally built in the seventeenth century, though rebuilt several times.

Salt Lake City at the time—1862—boasted a population of not more than 25,000, but only a few larger cities in the United States had anything like its theater. Brigham Young liked to point out that in constructing the theater they had used nails made from iron left behind by the federal soldiers.

Building the theater was a major project. It was designed by architects familiar with such structures in Europe. Three dozen carpenters shaped decorations of Old World quality, while stonecutters and stonemasons added touches. A visitor to Salt Lake City who had previously seen the principal theaters and opera houses in Boston, New York, Philadelphia, and Cincinnati said he was excited "by the remarkable artistic beauty of the gilt and painted decorations on the great arch over the stage, the cornices, and the moulding around the proscenium boxes.

"President Young, with a proper pride, assured me that every particle of the ornamental work was done by indigenous and saintly hands.

"But you don't know yet how independent we are of you in the East. Where do you think we got that central chandelier, and how much do you suppose we paid for it?"

The visitor, F. H. Ludlow, said that it would have been creditable to any New York firm, "apparently a richly carven circle, twined with gilt vines, leaves and tendrils, blossoming all over with flaming gaslights, and suspended by a massive chain of golden lustre. So I replied that he probably paid a thousand dollars for it in New York."

"Capital," exclaimed Brigham, "I made it myself! That circle is a cart wheel, the wheel of one of our common Utah oxcarts. I had it waxed and gilded it with my own hands. It hangs by a pair of ox chains which I also gilded, and the gilt ornaments of candlesticks were all cut after my patterns out of sheet tin."[2]

Brigham Young had a box in the theater equipped with a rocking chair and he often sat in it while his children took turns sitting in his lap. He felt that the theater served a public good and sometimes called upon individuals to serve in the theater, as he might call one to serve in a mission. And young people who wished to have a career in the theater sometimes had his encouragement.

One "requisition" was addressed to "Dear Brother and Sister Colebrook: Would you allow your daughter Nellie to act upon the stage? It would very much please me. Your Brother, Brigham Young."[3]

The theater depended mostly upon local talent for the first few years of its activities. Few of the great performers would come by oxcart or on horseback over mountains and plains, though some did.

But after the opening of the transcontinental railroad, which followed seven years after completion of the theater, Salt Lake City became a regular stop for some of the most important plays and players of the nineteenth century.

Amusing "Echo"

One who came from the East was T. A. Lyne, a noted actor of the period who had appeared in Nauvoo some years before. Learning that Lyne was appearing in Denver, Brigham Young invited him to Salt Lake City to act as coach for the local dramatic group. Lyne soon produced such favorites as *Othello, Richelieu, William Tell,* and *Richard III,* and *Pizzaro.* Lyne sought Brigham Young to play the part of the High Priest in *Pizzaro* noting that he had done so twenty years before in Nauvoo, but Young declined.

One of the local actors, indeed for some years the leading lady, was Annie Adams. On one occasion a super came on stage bearing a baby on a large silver tray, a highlight in the play "The Lost Child." The event went down in theatrical history as the first stage appearance of the noted American actress Maude Adams.

Another who came before the railroad was George Pauncefort, who had acquired considerable fame in both London and New York as the original Armand Duval in *Camille.* He was the first to produce *Hamlet* in the Salt Lake Theater, August 10, 1864.

Brigham Young complained that the drama was getting a bit heavy in Salt Lake, that he wished there could be something a little lighter. Pauncefort gave at least an unpremeditated and unrehearsed lighter moment in answer to this wish a few nights later when he produced *Macbeth.*

He thought that to bring one hundred voices from the Mormon Choir would enhance the witches chorus. The leader of the choir really put his heart and soul into the effort and in addition to producing the weird musical effects expected on stage he added an echo by placing a quartet off in the flies. He was very proud of the quartet, which had just recently arrived from London's cockney district.

As the great chorus sang out, "To the echo, to the echo," there came back from the flies in distinct modulation,

"To the hecho, to the hecho."

The chorus went on, "To the echo of a hollow hill."

And the "echo" responded, "To the hecho of an 'ollow 'ill."[4] The audience roared and there was at least one light moment.

Seven years after completion of the theater, the railroad came to Salt Lake City, and after that the Salt Lake Theater was a regular stopping-off place for the annual tours of the leading artists. Edwin Booth, Charles B. Hanford, Lawrence Barrett, J. H. Stoddard, Joe Jefferson, Denman Thompson, Julia Marlowe, E. H. Sothern, Modjeska, Maurice Barrymore and his daughter Ethel, David Warfield, William Gillette—the names are legion. Maude Adams returned several times with the plays that were winning her international renown: *The Little Minister, What Every Woman Knows, Quality Street,* and others.

The Tabernacle

No sooner was the theater dedicated than work was begun on the Tabernacle, perhaps the most frequented of the attractions that bring hundreds of thousands of tourists yearly to Salt Lake City. It is, as all agree, a remarkable structure, all the more so when one considers that it has been in daily use for a century.

Its principal architect, Henry Grow, had been a bridge builder in Pennsylvania before moving to Salt Lake City. He conceived the idea of building a series of stone piers, like those of a bridge, and spanning them with wooden arches, like those of a bridge. He used gigantic timbers—about a million board feet of lumber went into the Tabernacle—brought down from the mountains, far too thick for nails, so he fitted his timbers together, drilled holes and joined them with strong wooden pegs. The ends and joints were wrapped with rawhide, which as it dried pulled up in a tight union that is today as solid as when the job was done in the years between 1863 and 1867.

Instead of laying a roadway between his arches, Grow hung a beautifully domed ceiling. Thus was made a vast room without interior supports, 250 feet long and 150 feet wide, with seating for 10,000 people. The arches were originally roofed over on the outside with shingles but these have been replaced with a fireproof aluminum covering that is the pride of the Aluminum Company of America.

Visitors to the Tabernacle are usually impressed with three things: first, the acoustical properties, which are excellent. The oft-repeated demonstration has a guide station a group near the rear of the Tabernacle while he mounts the podium in the front and drops a common pin from about shoulder height to the wooden railings. Its arrival can be plainly heard. In a day when many adverse comments are heard about the acoustics of some of the world's most modern and costly auditoriums, it seems all the more remarkable that in the remote Rockies a century ago the problem was so wonderfully solved.

Second, visitors comment on the organ, and the more expert they are in such matters, the more they comment, for it is acknowledged to be one of the world's great instruments. And there is an unusual story behind the organ. It began in Southampton, England, where a young lad named Joseph Ridges lived across the street from an organ factory. Like any boy with such an opportunity, he spent countless hours watching the men at work. One of them took a special interest in the boy and gave him a good education in the theory and practice of organ design and building.

The Organ

Ridges didn't immediately apply his learning but shipped for Australia instead, seeking gold. He didn't find much yellow metal, but he did find some Mormon missionaries established there even in 1855. After joining the Church he began the project of building an organ. Because it was the first organ to be built in Australia, it attracted much attention, and the president of the Mormon Mission suggested that it would be a wonderful gift for Ridges to take to Zion. Ridges consented, and the Australian Mormons put up the money to ship it across the Pacific to California, Ridges in charge. It was carried in fourteen wagons over mountains and desert to Salt Lake City and set up in an adobe building near the present site of the Tabernacle.

It served very well, but when the new Tabernacle was begun, it was generally felt that a greater instrument was required, and Brigham Young consulted Ridges, now settled in Salt Lake, about it. Ridges prepared a sketch and showed it to Young, who said, "Joseph, if you will make that organ, there is nothing you want which you cannot have."

Ridges tells what followed:

We had no material except wood in that early day in Utah, so I went to Boston and New York and purchased what material we had to have, expending about $900—all that could be spared from the Church funds.

That was the start of it. I returned to Salt Lake over the old stage line with the material and erected a shop right within the Tabernacle walls. President Young asked me how much the organ would weigh. I told him between eighty and ninety tons, so he had a platform built capable of supporting that weight. In the shop I put up a small model of the organ, and every pipe that went into the instrument was tested and voiced and tuned from this little instrument.

For a while we were in doubt as to whether the wood in the canyons of Utah would be suitable for the work. I went out into the territory north and south with a teamster, and together we selected and hauled much of the wood that was put into the organ. It was nearly all yellow pine. Over in Grass Creek, I remember my teamster and I had a narrow escape from the Indians who were very hostile in parts of the state.

But finally we had enough timber inside the walls of the Tabernacle and the year following, while they were putting up the roof, the first piece of wood in the frame of the organ was put into place.

Now there was not a man in Utah who knew the first thing about an organ. I had to take each one of the ten assistants they gave me and instruct him in every move. The trees had been sawed at President Young's mill in the canyon and from large timbers about the size of half logs we had to saw out every piece and place them one at a time.

No wonder it took years of toil. We were twelve years building the organ. It had 2,000 pipes when I got through with it, and these pipes were nearly all of wood, ranging in size from two feet to thirty-two feet in length. The biggest, the thirty-two-foot pipe is the one that shakes the seats in the building to this day. It was the most difficult to tune and voice. It took almost a month to get it perfect. At one time I had a visit from fifteen members of Henry Ward Beecher's congregation in New York, and they said that they had recently purchased a new organ supposed to be the greatest in the land, but they had to admit that the Tabernacle organ was its superior. I often received encouragement of this kind, or I never should have accomplished the twelve years' task.[5]

In the past one hundred years, of course, the organ has been enlarged and rebuilt several times and today has upwards of 10,000 pipes, but many of the original pipes of Joseph Ridges are still in the instrument, including the mighty thirty-two-footers that he hollowed out of giant pines.

The Choir

Third among the wonders of the Tabernacle, and indeed a wonder of the world, is the Tabernacle Choir. The Mormons have always had choirs. It was noted that a choir sang at the dedication of the first temple in Kirtland, Ohio, in 1836. And eleven years later, in a rude log structure, roofed over with branches and for that reason called the Bowery, the first conference of the Church in the Great Basin was called to order and the records include the fact that "the choir" sang and even gave the names of the hymns. One of them had also been sung at the Kirtland dedication: "The Spirit of God Is Like a Fire Burning."

The Church conferences are important. They are held semiannually and provide the ordered forum for a review of past business, the sustaining of Church officials, and the projection of affairs ahead. They last two or three days, sometimes longer, and the choir of today stems from the groups that were brought together to add a sacred and joyful note to the conferences.

As with almost every other aspect of life in the West, the influx of people from the Old World added much to the choir. For example, on October 8, 1866, a wagon train of forty-nine wagons rumbled in from Emigration Canyon. There were three hundred people in the group. They were mostly from Norway, and they had a fine choir of twenty-five voices.

The Mormon Choir could be said to date almost from the founding of the Church. This makes it well over a century old, but such has been the policy of continuously recruiting fresh members while older ones drop out that it can at almost any time be called a "new" choir, which is one of the secrets of its sustained success. The choir now has 375 members and at almost any given moment about half will be found to have been in the choir five years or less. Thus, the traditions are continuous but the membership is ever refreshed.

As the visitor sits in the Tabernacle and looks at the faces in the choir he may wonder what power has taken such a cross section of western American men and women and made them into what is acknowledged, even hailed, by leading music critics of the world as possibly the foremost choir on earth. The choir consists of bankers, policemen, telephone linemen, barbers, doctors, teachers, nurses, a good many housewives—indeed almost the gamut of professions and trades of this work-a-day world.

For these singers who make up this notable choir are, with only a few exceptions, not trained musicians. They come together every Thursday evening for a practice session and every Sunday morning for a nationwide, even worldwide, radio broadcast. Yet it is common-place for them to sing with the Philadelphia Orchestra or the New York Philharmonic under great conductors in the most difficult of selections.

Noted Conductors

The Church, and the choir, have been fortunate in always having available conductors of extraordinary abilities. In recent years, since the advent of radio and the great popularity of the choir, there have been two conductors: J. Spencer Cornwall, who led the group for twenty-two years, from 1935 to 1957, and became widely and favorably known in the world of music; and Richard P. Condie, who succeeded Cornwall and had served as assistant director for twenty years. Professor Condie enjoyed a fine and cosmopolitan musical training. He was graduated from the New England Con-servatory in Boston and from the Fontainbleau school in France. He sang in opera in Europe and the United States and has been a professor of music at the University of Utah for many years.

That the Mormons had a great choir became known early, but it was not until about 1890 that it blossomed as a sort of national institution. In that year Professor Evan Stephens was named con-ductor. He expanded membership from two hundred to three hun-dred, and soon was accepting invitations for appearances outside of Utah. The first such major trip came in the late summer of 1893 when the choir entrained for the Columbian Exposition, otherwise known as the Chicago World's Fair. Several stops were made along the way, perhaps the most interesting of which was in Independence, Missouri, the seat of Jackson County, whence fifty years before the Mormons had fled from the hostile mobs. On this occasion the mayor and chief officials participated in a welcome that caused one of the Kansas City papers to call it a "friendly mob."

A Good Image

This trip, followed by others to the east coast and to California, indicated to the Mormon authorities that in the choir the Church possessed an unusual public relations asset. For the choir's repertory could bridge the seeming gap between the unknown mysteries of a theology that seemed strange and apart to non-Mormon persons and the familiar world of hymns, oratorios, and even operatic selections, while the obvious dedication of the people who made up the choir membership also provided an understandable communication.

Certainly the choir is best known in America because of its weekly radio broadcasts. These were begun when the first station came on the air in Salt Lake City in the early 1920s. When this station, KSL, became a member of the National Broadcasting Company's network, the choir began its singing to a nationwide audience. The first network program was given July 15, 1929.

The program was an instant success and was hailed by many critics. It continued on NBC until September 1932 when KSL changed its affiliation to the Columbia Broadcasting System and the choir was also transferred and continued its Sunday morning broadcasts.

Thus with three decades of broadcasting it is no wonder that the choir has become both popular and famous, and not only in the United States. Every week a tape of the choir broadcasts goes to the Voice of America, where duplicates, with translations, are made for use over the powerful transmitters of the "Voice" as well as other networks around the world that ask for tapes.

It was this sort of background and acceptance at home which led the Church authorities to decide to send the choir to Europe in the summer of 1955, at a time when they wished to respark their overseas missionary work. The logistics of transporting almost six hundred people, including singers, soloists, organists, electronic engineers, property men, and other staff people can be pictured. But the job was done, and the choir did the Church proud.

As television became more popular, the choir was called upon for many appearances. Hardly a Christmas or Easter season passes without seeing the choir featured on one or more important programs. The United States Information Agency has made two filmed productions for use of overseas television; the choir was a feature of the first Telstar international broadcast. The Tabernacle has been equipped with the latest video tape, lighting, and sound equipment for such telecasts.

Additionally, the choir has become a favorite on Columbia records. One of its selections, "The Battle Hymn of the Republic," recorded with the Philadelphia Symphony, Eugene Ormandy conducting, was a top favorite with the teen-age set for a season, while its more serious works, such as *The Messiah,* also with the Philadelphia Orchestra, rank with some of the most notable recordings.

That there have been innumerable items of praise from the press goes without saying. To merely list them would fill a volume, but if one had to choose just one as representative of the mass, it might well be this editorial in *Life* magazine of July 26, 1954:

Before the H-Bomb, before the atomic age, before World War II, before "the long Presidency," before Hitler, before the Japanese seized Manchuria, before the Great Depression and even before the Wall Street crash, long, long ago on July 15, 1929, a great 375-voice choir began broadcasting coast-to-coast from the Salt Lake City Tabernacle. Every Sunday morning in the intervening years, winter and summer, war or peace, rain or shine, it has broadcast its half hour of hymns old and new, of Bach and Handel and of all sweet and stately and spine-tingling sounds from the whole library of Christendom's sacred music. Behind the 375 voices swells an organ of 10,000 pipes.

Like the vast house of worship in which they sing, the Tabernacle Choir was founded over a century ago by Brigham Young. On the national air, it is the oldest coast-to-coast sustaining program in existence. Those who know this program need no arguments for listening to it, or no introduction . . . to the disciplined voices of the farmers, grandmothers, businessmen, high school girls and other devoted Mormons who make its enormous sound.

Millions have heard them, and more millions, we hope, will hear them in the years to come.

A feature of the broadcast almost from its inception has been "The Spoken Word," a brief sermonette, sometimes topical but characteristically aimed at some common phase of human experience —raising children, growing old, being kind, being truthful and the like—gracefully handled for the general audience, but from the Mormon point of view. While no attempt is made to proselytize in these talks, the appealing wisdom of the speaker, Richard L. Evans, has caused many to make further inquiry. So wide has been the response that several volumes of his talks have been published.

With this sort of acceptance, the choir is today, better than ever before, in a position to assist in projecting an attractive and inviting image to the world.

Chapter Nineteen

THE RAILROAD AGE

Abraham Lincoln succeeded James Buchanan as President of the United States and as soon as possible Brigham Young sent an emissary to sound out his attitude on the "Mormon question." Lincoln was no stranger to it. As a young legislator in Illinois he had cooperated in granting the unusually broad charter to Nauvoo and, of course, he was familiar with the main events of Mormon history. But the South had seceded, the war between the states had begun, and Lincoln had more vivid matters at hand to concern him. Moreover, Brigham Young had used the opportunity of the recent opening of the transcontinental telegraph to flash word to Lincoln: "Utah has not seceded, but is firm for the Constitution of our once happy country."

So Lincoln thought for a while, and then turning to the Mormon questioner said, "When I was a boy on the farm in Illinois there was a great deal of timber on the farm which we had to clear away. Occasionally we would come to a log which had fallen down. It was too hard to split, too wet to burn, and too heavy to move, so we plowed around it. That's what I intend to do with the Mormons. You go back and tell Brigham Young that if he will let me alone, I will let him alone."[1]

It soon appeared that Lincoln's attitude was to be pretty much that of the whole country. The Mormons were granted a respite in which to shape their course and as they looked back over the decade they saw that, despite the famine years and the years of Buchanan's "war," they had grown. Indeed the records indicate that the years between 1850 and 1860 were the best up to that time. The largest number had actually come in the handcart years when drought and grasshoppers were at their worst. Church records indicate that

43,304 were baptized in Britain during that decade, and 12,355 had emigrated to Utah!

One reason for this was the fact that Brigham Young, Heber Kimball, John Taylor, Wilford Woodruff, and, indeed, virtually all the principal Mormon leaders had served in the British or European missions and constantly encouraged emigration. Except when terribly harassed at home, they always tried to send twenty-five to fifty missionaries every year to England and the Perpetual Emigration Fund had supplied money. Thus it was that every autumn saw the Mormon colonies enriched by a fresh arrival of dedicated emigrants, many of them—the largest number of them—from England.

The peak years for such arrivals were 1854, when 2100 came, 1855 when 2686 set foot in Utah, and 1856 when the number was 2434. Lowest years were 1858 and 1859, when the "war" inhibited emigration. But in the decade 1860 to 1869 emigration continued at a high level, and despite the Civil War in the United States averaged out at above 1000 a year.

A Model Emigration

It was a time of great movement, of course, for many who were not Mormons and conditions of travel were sometimes, indeed often, the subject of much criticism. But the Mormon plan of emigration was held up as a model. A committee of the House of Commons investigated the Mormon system in 1854 and concluded that ". . . no ships under the provisions of the Passenger's Act could be depended upon for comfort and security in the same degree as those under his [the Mormon agent's] administration. The Mormon ship is a family under strong and accepted discipline, with provision for comfort, decorum, and internal peace."[2]

In his book *The Uncommercial Traveler* Charles Dickens recounts visiting the Thames Wharfs to have a look at a Mormon ship. "I went on board their ship to bear testimony against them if they deserved it, as I fully believed they would; to my great astonishment they did not deserve it; and my predispositions and tendencies must not affect me as an honest witness. I went over the *Amazon*'s side, feeling it impossible to deny that, so far, some remarkable influence had produced a remarkable result, which better known influences have often missed."

Dickens reported that in addition to eight hundred on the *Amazon*, the Mormon Agent told him that 1000 had sailed the day previously from Liverpool. Such was the tide of Mormon emigration. This was the spring that kept refreshing the Utah desert. Once arrived in Salt Lake City they found their presence was needed in the new Utah colonies. During the decade of the 1860s at least 150 new towns were started. All along the edge of the mountains, wherever a valley suitable for irrigation could be found, new colonies were begun. Some extended into Wyoming, Colorado, and Nevada.

When they arrived in Zion, they found a society considerably different from the one they had left, or indeed of any other in the Christian world. It was sufficiently different to cause wide interest not only in the United States but abroad, so it was natural that a procession of writers made the long trek. One of the most interesting accounts was written by the noted French botanist, Jules Remy. As a man of science he approached any new social development with a certain detachment. Moreover, he came to Utah from the Hawaiian Islands so he was prepared for relationships between the sexes that did not necessarily adhere to the Puritan ethics.

Remy's trip from Sacramento had taken fifty-eight days and he had been subjected to unusual hardships even for those days; he arrived looking more like a destitute wanderer than the distinguished academician that he was. Some days passed before his true identity was established, and during those days he was regarded with some suspicion; but once he was known, the people of Salt Lake City hastened to make amends.

Even the doors of Brigham Young's house were opened to him and everything was done to put the Mormon cause before him in the frankest light, in hopes that he would fairly present their case in France. He did his best, subsequently putting down one of the most extensive and unprejudiced descriptions of the Mormon case for polygamy, circa 1855, that is extant.

Remy's Interview

Remy realized that a large part of the outside world's condemnation of polygamy was based on the assumption that the system was forced on unwilling women. There was condemnation for the Mormon men, pity for the Mormon women. He knew that if he could present the woman's side of the matter, he would have the heart of the story and the kernel of interest. He had supposed that talking with Mormon women would be as difficult as conducting an interview in a seraglio. But to his amazement he found that once his identity was established and he was accepted, it was as easy to talk with Mormon women as with women in any other Christian society.

He was even more amazed when he found that the greatest approval for plural marriage came from the Mormon women. He was fortunate in finding a wife of a prominent Mormon—some thought it was a wife of Brigham Young, though this is not disclosed—who was educated, very much aware of the world, and who freely talked things over with the visitor.

"Why, then," she said to me one evening when the conversation had recurred to this subject, "why should I blush to accept this dogma of our faith which the majority of Christians reject with so much contempt and disdain. Have I not the Bible on my side? That Bible, which I have been accustomed to consider sacred from my childhood, does it not sanction polygamy? I there see, in that very Bible, that a man unquestionably holy, the friend of God—a man faithful in all things, and a man obeying God's commandments, who is called in the New Testament the *Father of the Faithful*—in a word that Abraham was a polygamist. That some of his wives were called concubines matters not; they were not for this the less his wives, and the difference in name does not alter the thing. And Jacob, his grandson, was he also a man according to God? Did not the Lord bless him? Was he not commanded to become a stem and to multiply? Now, Jacob, unless I am mistaken, had four wives who gave him a dozen sons and one daughter. Who will dare to say that God ever condemned these several marriages, and the fruits that came from them? The twelve sons which Jacob had by his four wives became princes, heads of tribes, patriarchs; and their names have been preserved throughout all generations. . . . At a later period I find plurality of wives perpetuated, sanctified by the laws of Moses, and everything ordered in conformity with it. David the Psalmist not only had several wives, but as the Lord himself, speaking through the mouth of the Prophet Nathan, told him that since he had been guilty of adultery with the wife of Uriah, and had committed murder, he would take away all the wives he had bestowed upon him, and give them to one of his neighbors. . . .

"Consider if this fact be not conclusive: in this instance God blames and punishes adultery and murder, while he authorizes and approves polygamy."

Remy confessed that, while his faith in what he regarded as the Christian ethic of monogamy was not set aside by this onslaught, he found his teacher to be a very convinced and doubtless sincere zealot "whose natural beauty was enhanced by the fervor of her argument." And hardly pausing for breath, she continued:

"The Polygamous law of God throws open a door to all vigorous, healthy, virtuous women by which they may become the honored brides of virtuous men, and the mothers of dutiful, virtuous, healthy and vigorous children. Let me ask you, Sir, what woman is there in the whole of France who would be inclined to marry a drunkard, a debauchee, a spendthrift, an idler, a man tainted with hereditary disease—what woman would ever consent to become a prostitute, or to pass all her life unmarried and in the deprivation of all natural affection, if the polygamy of Abraham, or in other words the patriarchal word of God, were adopted in your country and accounted by everyone honorable and sacred?

"Behold the result of abandoning the sacred laws of marriage [polygamy] appointed by God; behold the consequences of the adoption of the laws of Rome which forbid marriage to Priests and Nuns, and do not allow others to marry more than one wife. This law compels a number of women to pass their lives in *single blessedness*, without husband, without children, without a friend to protect and comfort them; or still more, it condemns them to a life of poverty and loneliness, in which they are exposed to temptations, to culpable connections, to the necessity of selling themselves. Man, on the other hand, rich in means, is tempted to squander them in secret with his mistress in an unlawful way, while the law of God would have given her to him as an honorable bride. All this engenders murder, infanticide, suicide, remorse, despair, wretchedness, premature death, and at the same time their inevitable accompaniments—jealousies, broken hearts, dissensions in the bosom of families. . . ."[3]

Remy was impressed by this torrent but questioned whether polygamy would in the end prove to be successful.

Sir Richard Burton

Remy and other visitors to Utah indicated that this young matron expressed the attitude of most of the Mormon women, while the polygamous husbands considered themselves to be lawfully and religiously bound to their wives and completely responsible for the children. As one of them remarked to a federal governor: "I married my wives in good faith. We have lived together for years, believing it was the will of God. The same is true of the Mormon people generally. Before I will abandon my wives as concubines, and cast off my children as bastards, I will fight the United States government down to my boots. What would you do, Governor, in like case?" The governor is quoted as replying, "I would do the same!"[4]

Another visitor of international fame followed a few years after Remy. This was Sir Richard Burton, one of the best known of the British explorers and adventurers of the nineteenth century. Today he is best remembered for his translation of the *Arabian Nights,* but when he visited Salt Lake City in 1859 he was famous for his recent pilgrimage to Mecca. With complete command of the Arabic language, and dressed in robes, he had passed as a Mohammedan and was admitted to the circle of the most blessed. He had also lived in India for a number of years, and his experience, combined with his Near East adventures, had made the practice of having plural wives seem not only familiar but quite usual. So he carried a worldly background with him when he met Brigham Young, whom he disarmed immediately by proposing that he be baptized, outfitted in robes, and taken into the sanctum. Young, who, of course, had heard of Burton's Arabian exploits, took it as the joke intended and remarked that Burton was getting experienced in such things. Burton was attracted to Young, comparing him with other leaders in the world. "The first impression left upon my mind . . . was that the Prophet is no common man, and that he has none of the weaknesses and vanity which characterize the common uncommon man."

At the same time, Burton's researches for his book *The City of the Saints* led him to look into the character of Joseph Smith. There were many in Salt Lake City, including Young, who could give firsthand information about the founding Prophet. "In America," Burton wrote, "Mr. Joseph Smith has by the general suffrage of the anti-Mormons been pronounced to be a knave, while his successor, Mr. Brigham Young, has been declared by the same high authority—vox diabolic, the Mormons term it—to be a self-deluded but true man."

Burton, with perhaps unconscious reference to his own special talents, commented:

I can scarcely persuade myself that great events are brought about by mere imposture, whose very realm is feebleness. Zeal, enthusiasm, fanaticism, which are of their nature strong and aggressive, better explain the abnormal action of man on man. On the other hand, it is impossible to ignore the dear delights of fraud and deception, the hourly pleasure taken by some minds in finessing through life, in concealing their real selves from the eyes of others, and in playing a part 'til by habit it becomes a nature. In the estimation of unprejudiced persons Mr. Joseph Smith is a man of real genius, of high courage, of invincible perseverance, fired by zeal, of great tact, of religious fervour, of extraordinary firmness, and of remarkable talent in governing men. It is conceded that had he not possessed strong and invincible faith in his own pretentions and "Divine Mission" he probably would have renounced the unprofitable task of prophet and sought refuge from persecution and misery in private life and honorable industry. Be that as it may, he has certainly taken a place among the notabilities of the world—he has left a footprint in the sands of time.[5]

Burton, a man of the great outside world, whom nothing could shock but everything interest, projected the Mormons of the nineteenth century against the vast screen of the religious past in an effort to identify and place them, but it was futile. The Mormons were unique!

Women Not Secondary

Mormons did not consider the status of women to be secondary— and Burton did at least differentiate the Mormons from the society that was bearing in upon them from the East and West, and which had little to do with any philosophy except that of "get rich quick."

Brigham Young was fifty-eight years old when interviewed by Burton, and although Burton's appreciation of Joseph Smith won Young's approbation, he was quite uncommunicative about polygamy and his own marital situation, which reputedly included at that time seventeen wives. It was said that nine children had been born to him the previous spring and he had enough to require his own private schoolhouse.

Possibly some of his reserve about discussing his marriages resulted from the fact that he was to take another wife. Many were amused, and perhaps secretly pleased, when he fell in love with a twenty-five-year-old woman, Amelia Folsom. The famous beard was trimmed, new clothes were worn. Soon Amelia had her own fine house and carriage. No living in the house with the stone lions in front, the Lion House, where many of Brigham's wives lived in a community. It was said that Brother Brigham had taken most of his wives in Nauvoo immediately after the martyrdom and the trek following. In the years in Salt Lake City it was said he had taken but two wives—Eliza Snow, a poetess and sister of Lorenzo, and an English serving girl who had worked in the household seven years and insisted that in biblical terms she deserved better. Brigham evidently felt she had a good case.

But the marriage to Amelia in 1863 stirred up the forces of opposition to polygamy. Up to this point many of the prominent visitors to Utah had felt that it was economically as well as socially unsound and would in time disappear. The Mormons themselves recognized that to many of their countrymen the idea of a "kingdom" in the enclave of the American commonwealth was unthinkable, even though the kingdom was that of Zion.

They recognized, too, that plural marriage was probably the largest single obstacle in the way of Utah's being admitted to the union as a state. As a state it could elect its own governor and carry forward in a high degree of autonomy; as a territory its governor was appointed by the President of the United States and autonomy was limited.

Railroad Route

In 1862, the year before Brigham and Amelia were married, Congress passed the first of a series of laws aimed at plural marriage. Brigham Young thought it was unconstitutional, and some speculated that the marriage to Amelia was deliberately provocative. But once the Civil War was ended, Brigham Young and the Mormons understood that they would confront fresh assaults. And as the North triumphed, it was realized that a tremendous American industrialization had been accelerated. It was inevitable that a world that had been too busy to intrude upon the Utah Zion would not remain too busy for long and that the Iron Horse would shortly follow the telegraph across plains and mountains, and surely the institution of polygamy would be a point of contention.

Some of the Mormons hoped the railroad might pass north or

south of them, that is, follow the Oregon or the Santa Fe trail and thus leave them alone, but as the promoters sought the shortest routes, it was seen that the Union Pacific would closely follow the Old Mormon Trail, which the Central Pacific pushed eastward from California across the Nevada dry lands and met in northern Utah. Then the Mormons began to worry that Salt Lake City would be by-passed, as it was. So the approach of the railroad was viewed with mixed feelings. Unlike many dreamy or otherworldly religionists, the Mormons were sharp realists. They knew that the railroad would bring them closer to their overseas missions, that it would facilitate the emigration they so highly prized, and that it would bring into closer reach many of the items they needed to import. But at the same time they realized that emigration by train would be costly and would require cash; no more sending of Church wagons and teams out of tithing supplies and labor. Also, the availability of imports that had to be paid for in cash would cut into much-needed capital formation of the community.

Over and above these considerations was the fear that their way of life would be subject to the impact of the thrusting, boisterous, hard-drinking, profit-minded people who were hammering across the American West in the "rootin', tootin', pistol-shootin'" fashion, today over-glamorized in literature, motion pictures, and television. To the Mormons the saloons and dance-hall girls of the railroad towns were anything but attractive, while to the non-Mormon Westerners, the sight of prim little communities in which polygamy flourished was at least disconcerting.

Like many societies before them, the Mormons, when confronted by the assault of different mores, faced the choice of resisting or joining. And like most other societies in history, they did a little of both. They accelerated their attempts to be apart. Groups of women vowed not to spend money for fancy imported dress goods, to say nothing of tea and coffee.

The weight of progress was, nevertheless, on the side of the rail-roads, and the solution worked out, after much debate in the Mormon ranks, was for the Church, in the name of Brigham Young, to take the contract to build the railroad from the mouth of Echo Canyon to Ogden. This was a distance of only ninety miles, but it had two important effects: it kept the rowdy railroad construction elements out of Utah and it gave the Church cash with which to pay the fares of emigrants.

The Mormons worked so well that before long Leland Stanford, head of the Central Pacific Railroad, signed a contract with the Church, in the name of Ezra Taft Benson, to construct two hundred miles of track from Humboldt Wells, Nevada, to the juncture with the Union Pacific just west of Ogden, Utah, at Promontory Point. The job was completed and East and West were united by rail on May 10, 1869.

Good Builders

Brigham Young was proud of the fact that his men knew how to use nitroglycerine, and this, combined with the respected Mormon willingness to work, caused their parts of the contract to be completed on schedule. But the railroads were slow in paying. The Central Pacific paid in cash in time but the Union Pacific was involved in the infamous credit mobilier, a device under which the Boston and Philadelphia promoters took the government bonds issued to help the railroad and used them to a personal advantage that became a principal congressional scandal of the period.

The Mormons were paid, ultimately, in iron tracks and rolling stock, plus some cash, and while many individual Mormons suffered greatly (the death of Ezra Benson, for one, was attributed to worry over his financial position) the Mormons ultimately found that this delayed settlement gave them the means with which to build the thirty-seven-mile connection between Ogden and Salt Lake City. By giving the Union Pacific and Central Pacific land for stations and warehouses they were able to induce the two roads to make Ogden their junction point, and thereby the Mormons assured the doom of Corinne, a "hell on wheels" town of nineteen saloons, located twenty-five miles northwest of Ogden and originally selected as the junction. But the delay in payment by the railroads, plus a national postwar recession, combined to give the Mormons a bad economic period. It drove them into even greater efforts to supply their wants from within their own facilities.

Chapter Twenty

BRIGHAM YOUNG'S FAREWELL

In the years immediately following the coming of the railroad it began
to appear that the primary economic problem of the Mormons in
Utah was a kind of overpopulation. It was not, as some inferred, a
result of the plurality of wives. The problem was that the great
influx of emigrants took up the arable lands. The paucity of annual
rainfall in the Great Basin was a well-known fact. The Mormons had
been the first, or among the first, pioneers to apply irrigation in the
American West, but irrigation is limited in the area it can serve. By
1870 the Mormons had exhausted the valleys of Utah, and even
many of those in neighboring and available areas in Wyoming, Colorado, New Mexico, and Idaho. Unlimited land was no longer available. Emigrants coming from abroad could not be sent to establish
new Mormon colonies within three hundred miles of Salt Lake City.
Young people getting married and ready to establish families of
their own no longer could easily obtain farms.

The early Mormons, as we have seen, had been disappointed in
their attempts at industry. Iron and sugar were examples cited earlier.
In more homely industrial pursuits—weaving, shoemaking, and the
like—they were more successful, but these, unfortunately, were not
high-earning, large-employment industries. So the emphasis remained
on agriculture, and this served Brigham Young's purpose.

Some have commented that it was ironic that Brigham Young
lived within sight of what is now the world's largest known deposit
of copper, and never exploited it. But it required methods for han-
dling not available to him. And while uranium was identified
as an element even a half century before his time, only a very few
chemists—and most of them were in Europe—had an interest in it.
Some silver was found in Utah and small deposits of gold, but the

great fortunes in minerals were to come a half century or more after
Brigham Young.

If sparse land was the main economic problem, there was no question what the political problem was. The limitations on land arose
about the time that the reformers in the United States, having outlawed slavery, were looking for new causes to embrace, and rediscovered polygamy. Few, if any, of them took the trouble to look
into it from the social and economic viewpoint of a Burton or Remy.

The human, social, economic needs of an embattled society in the
Great American Desert in the nineteenth century might indeed have
been different from those normal in another society in another land
in another age, but not many were inclined to think about that.
Ulysses S. Grant became President in the year of the railroad, 1869,
and when his soldier friends told him that the people in Utah were
an uncooperative lot, living in sin, the old general sent a message
to Congress calling Mormon marriages "licensed prostitution" and an
old war suddenly took on a new look.

Economic Pressure

Washington's idea of how to bring the Mormon affair to a satis-
factory conclusion always was to use specialized legislation, aimed
largely at Church finances. For example, the Wade Bill of 1866 would
have, if passed, taxed all Church property over $20,000 in value;
in addition, it would have prohibited officials of the Church from
solemnizing marriages.

A somewhat similar measure was introduced by Senator Cragin,
but having the additional feature of abolishing trial by jury in cases
involving polygamy. This also failed, but was succeeded by the Cullom Bill, which would have placed selection of jurors solely in the
hands of United States marshals and confined polygamy cases to the
exclusive jurisdiction of federal judges. Additionally, it deprived
plural wives of immunity from testifying against their husbands. The
Cullom measure also provided that Mormons leaving Utah because
of it would forfeit their property, which would be used by non-Mormons for the benefit of Mormon families. This passed the House but
was turned down in the Senate.

The Ashley Bill proposed transferring large parts of Utah to neighboring states, having the effect of dismembering the territory. It was not passed, but the Poland Act of 1874 was. This gave federal judges jurisdiction over criminal, civil, and chancery cases and otherwise greatly increased the authority of federal officials.

The attitude of the federal judges is illustrated by the statement of Utah's Chief Justice James B. McKean, one of Grant's appointees:

The mission which God has called upon me to perform in Utah is as much above the duties of other courts and judges as the heavens are above the earth, and whenever or wherever I may find the local or federal laws obstructing or interfering therewith, by God's blessing I shall trample them under my feet.[1]

McKean had been a Methodist preacher before coming to Utah, and he ran into trouble from the start when the Mormon-controlled legislature decided that, if all the courts were under federal jurisdiction, as McKean insisted they were, there really was no reason for the territory to appropriate funds to support them or pay the jurors. McKean found some money in the United States marshal's account and with his usual venom promptly had Brigham Young arrested for "lewd and lascivious cohabitation."

This was in the early autumn of 1871. Brigham Young was seventy-one and his health had been poor. Indeed, he was on his way to his winter home in St. George, Utah, about three hundred miles south of Salt Lake City, where the winter climate was warmer. Judge McKean's minions pursued him there and Brigham Young ordered out a special train to hasten back to Salt Lake City just before Christmas. McKean refused him bail and kept him under house arrest for five months, until the United States Supreme Court ruled that McKean's ways were unconstitutional. Young was automatically released.

Marital Troubles

But these troubles with McKean came about the same time as did Young's best-known marital disaster. Three years earlier Young had married Ann Eliza Webb, a divorcee of twenty-six with three children. Around Salt Lake City it was said that the marriage was requested by her family in order to provide for the children and to bring them honor. Ann Eliza had a different story: Brigham Young, even in his late sixties, she said, was an ardent suitor.

Whatever the facts, Ann Eliza is hard to describe as anything but the source of trouble for Brigham. Finally she decided to divorce him and the case came before Judge McKean. Ann Eliza charged "neglect, cruelty and desertion," and told the court that her husband had an income of $ 40,000 a month. She asked for $1,000 a month while the divorce pended, and a settlement of $200,000. The judge decided on $500 a month, pending final action, and when Young refused, the judge fined him $25 and ordered him to spend one day in jail. But by thus ordering Young to pay alimony, McKean in effect recognized the legality of a plural marriage and this posed a difficult question for those opposing polygamy.

As it worked out, McKean was removed from office five days after this ruling and his successor, Judge David B. Lowe, ruled that there had been no legal marriage; therefore, there could be no divorce and no alimony. This turned out to be the final decision, though it dragged through appeals until just a few months before Brigham Young died in 1877.

Eliza made a living by writing and lecturing on life as a wife of Brigham Young. She called her book *Wife Number 19*, though others said she was actually number twenty-seven. Brigham Young said nothing. She did her best to make Brother Brigham's last years unhappy, but there is no record that she succeeded, for, judged against the frame of the earlier hardships, the persecutions of the 1870s, and the economic troubles, his latter days were rather tame.

Even the overpopulation was not without its blessings, for if it is sometimes commented that Mormons still predominate in the best parts of Utah and some of the neighboring states, the reason is clear: the Mormons filled up many of the best valleys. And while in Brigham Young's last days it was necessary to discourage emigration, still the Church, boasting some 150,000 members, was well supported. Revenues were estimated at about $1,000,000 a year, half of which came from tithing and the balance from extra donations, and from income on Church-owned properties, including railroads. Brigham Young was not too harassed by Eliza or anything else as he dictated rather full directions for a simple and sensible funeral.

A Typical Appearance

He was in sporadically poor health for several years before his passing, but he is remembered for his vigor of mind and body, a benign patriarch in his last years. The picture of him that is perhaps the best to hold in one's memory is set in the Tabernacle, and the occasion is the spring conference of the Church in 1872. On April 28 Brother Brigham came out of his five-month, court-imposed solitude to stand before his people. He was a national figure. The famed American circus impresario P. T. Barnum had recently visited him and offered $200,000 a year for appearing in New York. "I consider you," he said, "the best show in America." At this time in his life Brother Brigham was a man of such complete and commanding dignity that he could decline the offer in the same generous spirit in which it was intended. Possibly it pleased him to be such a recognized celebrity.

In any case a contemporary observer described him as entering the Tabernacle wearing a suit of gray homespun and a tall, steeple-crowned hat with a black ribbon, which he removed as he sat down in a chair in the middle of the rostrum. He was short, robust, cheerful, and his near white beard was closely trimmed. All eyes centered on him and the air of expectancy increased noticeably as wives nudged husbands awake and the realization came that Brigham Young was about to speak, for he was a great speaker.

Slowly, but without dramatic effort, he advanced to the rostrum. He took a drink of water. Slowly he looked about the room, seeming to have a glance of recognition for all the thousands present. Then, gripping the desk with both hands he leaned forward. A bit of the old technique used in London thirty-two years before came into play. He hesitated as if not certain who his audience was. Then he smiled:

"A word to the Latter-day Saints. Good morning!"

"Good morning," the audience responded in a cheerful, almost exuberant, glad-to-be-alive way that Mormon missionaries still greet each other with after prayers in the morning.

"How do you do?"

"Very well!" cheered every voice in the Tabernacle, fully awake now and enjoying the fun.

"How's your faith in the Lord?"

"Strong!"

"How do you think I look after my long confinement?"

"Very good!"

There followed a usual Brigham Young lecture. A selection from his talks to his people runs something like this:

The Lord reveals a little here and a little there, line upon line, and he will continue so to do until we can reach into eternity and embrace a fullness of his glory, excellency and power. Where is your code, your particular creed? asks one. It fills eternity; it is all truth in heaven, or earth or in hell. This is "Mormonism." It embraces every true science; all true philosophy. The philosophy of the heavens and the earth of the worlds that are, that were, and that are yet to come into existence, is all the Gospel that we have embraced. Every true philosopher, so far as he understands the principles of truth, has so much of the Gospel and so far he is a Latter-day Saint, whether he knows it or not. Our Father, the great God, is the author of the sciences, he is the great mechanic, he is the systemizer of all things, he plans and devises all things, and every particle of knowledge which man has in his possession is the gift of God, whether they consider it divine, or whether it is the wisdom of man; it belongs to God, and he has bestowed it upon us, his children dwelling here upon the earth.

In a conversation not long since with a visitor who was returning to the eastern states, said he, "You, as a people, consider that you are perfect?"

"Oh no," said I, "Not by any means. Let me define it to you. The doctrine that we have embraced is perfect; but when we come to the people, we have just as many imperfections as you can ask for. We were not perfect; but the Gospel that we preach is calculated to perfect the people so that they can obtain a glorious resurrection and enter into the presence of the Father and the Son." I am decidedly in favor of practical religion—of everyday useful life. And if today I attend to that which devolves upon me to do, and then do that which presents itself tomorrow, and so on, when eternity comes I will be prepared to enter on the things of eternity. . . . My religion must be with me from one Monday morning to the next, the year around, or it will not answer me.

There is a power that has organized all things from the crude matter that floats in the immensity of space. He has given form, motion and life to this material world; has made the great and small lights that bespangle the firmament above; has allotted to them their times and seasons, and has marked out their spheres. He is our heavenly Father; he is also our God, and the Maker and upholder of all things in heaven and on earth. He sends forth his counsels and extends his providences to all living. He is the

Supreme Controller of the Universe. At his rebuke the sea is dried up, and the rivers become a wilderness. He measures the waters in the hollow of his hand, and meteth out heaven with a span, and comprehendeth the dust of the earth in a measure, and weigheth the mountains in scales, and the hills in a balance; the nations are to him as a drop in a bucket, and he taketh up the isles as a very little thing; the hairs of our head are numbered by him, and not a sparrow falleth to the ground without our Father; and he knoweth every thought and intent of the hearts of all living for he is everywhere present by the power of his Spirit—his minister the Holy Ghost. He is the Father of all, is above all, through all, and in you all; he knoweth all things pertaining to this earth, and he knows all things pertaining to millions of earths like this.

Now, my friends, brethren and sisters, ladies and gentlemen, how do you know anything? Can you be deceived by the eye? You can, you have proved this; you all know that there are men who can deceive the sight of the eye, no matter how closely you observe their movements. Can you be deceived in hearing? You may hear sounds but not understand their import or whence they came. Can you be deceived by the touch of the fingers? You can. The nervous system will not detect everything. What will? The revelations of the Lord Jesus Christ, the spirit of truth will detect everything, and enable all who possess it to understand truth from error, light from darkness, the things of God from the things not of God. It is the only thing that will enable us to understand the Gospel of the Son of God, the will of God and how we can be saved. Follow it, and it will lead to God, the Fountain of light, where the gate will be open, and the mind will be enlightened so that we shall see and know things as they are.

Some of the brethren come to me and say, "Brother Brigham, is it my duty to pray when I have not one particle of the spirit of prayer in me?" True, at times, men are perplexed and full of care and trouble, their ploughs and other implements are out of order, their animals have strayed and a thousand things perplex them; yet our judgment teaches us that it is our duty to pray, whether we are particularly in the spirit of praying or not. . . . If I could not master my mouth, I would my knees, and make them bend until my mouth would speak.

Shall we deny the existence of that which we do not understand? If we do, we would want to keep an iron bedstead to measure every person according to our own measurements, and dimensions; and if persons were too long we would cut them off, or if too short draw them out. But we should discard this principle, and our motto should be, we will let everyone believe as he pleases and follow out the convictions of his own mind; for all are free to choose or refuse; they are free to serve God or deny him.

Who owns the earth? Does the Devil? No, he does not, he pretended to own it when the Savior was here, and promised it all to him if he would fall down and worship him; but he did not own a foot of the land, he only had possession of it. He was an intruder, and is still; this earth belongs to Him that framed and organized it, and it is expressly for his glory and the possession of those who love and serve him and keep his commandments. . . . The power of the Devil is limited; the power of God is unlimited.[2]

Thus spake Brigham Young, whose funeral was held in the Tabernacle, September 2, 1877, and 25,000 filed past his body. He was not the Prophet Joseph, he was "Brother Brigham" and he was loved as a brother. For more than forty years he had led and directed. His final instruction was typical and typically meaningful: ". . . No crying or mourning with anyone as I have done my work faithfully and in good faith."[3]

Part Three

THE TWENTIETH CENTURY

Chapter Twenty-one

THE MANIFESTO AND TEMPLES

Leland Stanford had assured Mark Hopkins that the Mormon Church would not last very long once Brigham Young passed away, and this was the widely held belief outside Utah. Young's great powers as a colonizer and leader were recognized, but, like Abe Lincoln, the men in power judged that Brigham Young, and not the Mormon people, was the log that had to be plowed around.

In this judgment they had little understanding that however powerful he appeared to be, Brigham Young was only as strong as the support his people gave him. Several of his top counselors—men like Heber C. Kimball, who was perhaps closest to him, and the popular George A. Smith died a few years before Young. But there was little doubt as to who the immediate successor to Young would be. Brother Brigham had furnished the answer to that himself when he had pointed out in Nauvoo that the senior member of the Quorum of Twelve, which is to say, the apostle with the longest service record, should advance to the presidency. The senior apostle after Young was John Taylor, who without delay was given the reins laid down by Brother Brigham.

Taylor had been baptized by Parley P. Pratt in Canada, had helped build Kirtland, had moved to Missouri with Joseph Smith, and had gone to England with Pratt and Brigham Young. It was Taylor who established the first missionary effort in Liverpool, where he had converted the first of the Cannon family. He was with Joseph Smith when the Prophet was murdered, and he, himself, was saved from death only by the fact that a bullet lodged in his heavy gold watch. As it was, he was severely injured. Later he had established the French mission. A highly gifted speaker and writer, Taylor took over at a moment of peril for the Church.

The Edmunds Act, passed by Congress in March 1882, left little to the imagination of federal judges, no matter how authoritarian they might be. The main thrust took away the privilege of voting from the Mormons. This was done by a commission appointed by the President of the United States, empowered to supervise elections in Utah, decide on who could be registered to vote, and to count the ballots.

The commission interpreted the Edmunds Act to mean that persons professing belief in polygamy or cohabitation as a religious principle, whether or not proved guilty of the practice, could not vote or hold office. This, of course, excluded the Latter-day Saints. The act provided fines up to $300 and six months in jail for those found guilty of polygamy or cohabitation, and as arrests were made and as convictions were upheld in the higher courts, even the United States Supreme Court, federal officials began vigorous pursuit of what they called "Polygs and Cohabs."

It was soon evident, however, that even if Uncle Sam were to incarcerate every adult Mormon, he still could not win. They were a resolute people, certain that God was on their side. Clearly something further was called for, and this turned out to be a revised Edmunds Act, called the Edmunds-Tucker Act, adopted in 1887.

In addition to the previous penalities, this new act returned to the old plan of attack and virtually destroyed the Church economically. It dissolved the Church as a corporate entity; it seized the property of the Church and ordered it sold for the benefit of public schools in the state; it dissolved the Perpetual Emigrating Fund; it disinherited children of plural marriages, abolished the right of women to vote, and placed all the schools under federal officials.

Supreme Court Rules

Interminable legal actions followed, but in almost every lower court they lost. This left the Mormons hoping that the Constitution of the United States, which they believed was divinely inspired, would in the end rescue them. Their hopes, in a material sense, thus rested in the United States Supreme Court.

This hope sustained John Taylor through ten years, the last of it spent in hiding, irregular communications with his followers, and long periods of separation from his family. But in 1887, when Taylor was seventy-nine years old, and while he was still in hiding, he died. His successor was chosen, again the senior member of the Twelve, but was not publicly announced.

It was Wilford Woodruff, next in seniority as an apostle. He will be remembered as one of those who went with Heber Kimball on the first mission to England and who converted the United Brethren in the first big breakthrough in British missionary work.

Finally, three years after President Taylor's death, the Supreme Court handed down its ruling—disastrous for the Mormons. The Edmunds-Tucker Act was declared Constitutional!

A Church conference was called for Salt Lake City, and Woodruff was publicly "sustained" as President. The persecution, or "raid" as it is known in western history, had raged for too many years. Everybody was weary of it, and the Church was almost exhausted financially. President Woodruff had seen it all—Kirtland, Far West, Nauvoo, the martyrdom of Joesph Smith, the great trek west, the struggles and the heartbreaks and the progress. He could ask his people for no more. On September 25, 1890, he wrote: "I have arrived at a point in the history of my life as President of the Church where I am under the necessity of acting to the temporal salvation of the Church."[1]

A little later in the day he penned the famous manifesto:

Inasmuch as laws have been enacted by Congress forbidding plural marriages, which laws have been pronounced constitutional by the court of last resort, I hereby declare my intention to submit to those laws, and to use my influence with the members of the Church over which I preside to have them do likewise.[2]

Manifesto Supported

A few days later, October 6, the general conference of the Church unanimously supported President Woodruff's statement. Clearly, the Saints were weary of the strife, and their Revelator, President Woodruff, had the power to release them from previous doctrine. The mighty forces of the nation had been arrayed against them and even the Constitution had denied them. Some considered moving on to the islands of the South Seas, or to Canada, and a few did leave the Great Basin for Mexico, but the majority had no desire to abandon what they had wrested from one of the least abundant corners of the world. No doubt some of them felt that in human affairs all things are temporary and that if polygamy had been proper and right for them in a certain season, they had always realized the practice was not universally acceptable. So, as they may have reasoned, the world had moved in on them, and they must do, for a season, as the world did. The Lord was willing that eternal things—if polygamy was an eternal thing—should take care of themselves.

And if the Mormons were weary, the nation was tired of the chase too. For more than forty years certain reform groups had cried out against plural wives and intermittently they had stirred the federal officials. Now there were more important things to look after. In victory, the United States government began to show a magnanimity not previously evident. Prosecutions became less numerous and less violent. It seemed to be understood that old families were not to be broken up. Rather, the practice was to end insofar as new marriages were concerned, but time was to be allowed to take its course in dissolving outstanding arrangements.

Possibly one added pressure on President Woodruff to issue the manifesto was his desire to complete the Temple, a hope which appeared to mount as the years advanced. Brigham Young, as we recall, had driven a stake into the earth as the site of the future temple as almost his first act after arriving in the Great Basin. He had sent an architect to Europe to study cathedral design, even though Young said he had seen how it should look in a dream and had described it. Immense amounts of labor had been expended in Young's lifetime in laying solid granite foundations; a road, and later a rail line, had been built to a granite quarry and the work had gone forward, though was never hurried, and sometimes it was set aside to build a theater or a tabernacle. Indeed, several outlying communities had temples long before Salt Lake City did. Brigham Young said they had a greater need. Salt Lake City had the Endowment House, which he said would suffice until a proper temple could be completed.

Temple Baptism for the Dead

It is impossible for one who is not a Mormon to appreciate the special distinction that temples have for Mormons. Mormon temples are not meeting places, or churches in the ordinary sense. They are not open to the public, as are Mormon chapels and the Tabernacle in Salt Lake City, and other such buildings. Temples are, so to speak, schools where the highest doctrines are taught, and are taught only to those deemed acceptable to receive the mysteries. The buildings themselves are not secret, but they are held to be sacred and only Mormons having proper credentials are admitted, except, as will be noted later, for brief periods of public inspection prior to dedication.

The privilege of visiting and being taught in a temple is highly regarded by a devout Mormon, who feels that repeated visits are required to bring within his full grasp the temple teachings. Moreover, not to be minimized is the role that temples play in the Mormon beliefs regarding the dead.

In Little Cottonwood Canyon, twelve miles in the mountains from downtown Salt Lake City, there is a solid face of granite from which was taken much of the stone used in the Temple. A narrow mountain road leads to a leveled-off place where one confronts six large concrete portals resembling entrances to a railroad tunnel. If you walk into the main portal and proceed about 150 feet, by which time you are under 800 feet of solid granite, you come upon a cross tunnel, or room, some 402 feet long and fifty feet wide. This is lined in curved corrugated steel, something like the interior of a Quonset hut. Between the rough-hewn granite and the exterior of these ten-gauge steel linings has been pumped waterproofed concrete. The floor is laid with a pleasant, neutral-colored asphalt tile, and the steel walls and ceilings are painted in pastel shades. Generous fluorescent lighting provides almost daylight brilliance. This vast room is the central office for the genealogy records.

You see three huge banklike vault doors. One, you are told, weighs fifteen tons and could withstand almost any known blast. Each of these vault doors leads to a 350-foot long room, extending even farther back into the granite mountain. These immense rooms, also lined with softly painted steel, and floored and lighted like the most modern offices, are connected with three cross extensions of similar design. Beyond these rooms is still another, left in its rough-hewn form, and this houses a large, concrete water reservoir, fed by underground springs.

The vaults have their own self-contained power plant, their own emergency supplies, fresh air filters, and other equipment to endure even a severe atomic attack, which one can only suppose was at least at the back of the minds of designers and builders. But the vaults are not reserved for emergency use; they are in daily service as the principal storage area for the 250 million or more feet of microfilm in the Church's genealogical library. The temperature and moisture are controlled for the benefit of the film. Here are the master records of as much of humanity as can be garnered from the vital statistics of some twenty nations around the world. The most recent acquisition, for example, are microfilms of every birth and death in New Zealand since records were kept.

It may surprise some to learn that probably the best records of their family are not in some quiet vestry in the Old World. It is possible that the most complete and certainly the most usable set of such records now reposes in the granite fastness of Little Cottonwood Canyon.

Since the development of microfilming, representatives of the Church have roamed the world, and particularly those parts from which came the larger part of the Mormon migration, interviewing the local authorities, including in many instances the custodians of old church records. They have offered to make two sets of microfilm records—one to be left with the local people for their use and safe-keeping; the other to be filed in the vaults at Little Cottonwood, where they can always be available for duplication in case of need. This is a generous offer which few refuse. It is said to be the world's most extensive recording effort.

Vicarious Ordinances

Why do the Mormons expend great amounts of time and energy and money on such a project? The answer, as we said, relates to the special position of temples in their belief. It goes back to the early days in Kirtland and Nauvoo, where members of the Church often pressed their Prophet for some view of what happens after death to those who knew nothing of the true Gospel.[3] They might say that their fathers and mothers were righteous people. Could they not be united with true believers in the spirit world?

Smith's answer was that the living may be baptized for the dead, that a son may be baptized for his father or a daughter for her mother, and that the Gospel principles would be taught to the dead in the spirit world.

Joseph Smith taught that Jesus preached to the spirits of the dead as indicated by Peter in his epistle (1 Peter 3:18–20) and that Paul mentioned vicarious baptism of living persons for the dead (1 Cor. 15:29).

But Joseph Smith made it clear that all such work must be done in good order. Gospel ordinances could be performed for dead ancestors only as the living provided adequate identification of those persons by the use of vital statistics. This set off the vast genealogical research program for which the Saints are now famous. They feel it is the personal responsibility of each member of the Church to "seek out his dead" and to perform ordinances of salvation for them.

The Prophet also taught his people that such vicarious work could be done only in specially prepared buildings, temples, and that there they could enter baptismal fonts, making available this sacred ordinance for their dead in the hope that it would be accepted by them in the spirit world. So temple building and genealogical work became major activities of the Church.

Temples also provide eternal marriage, both for the living and the dead. It is not believed by the Saints that families should be broken up by death, or that marriage should come to an end at the demise of either party. In the temple marriages are "sealed" for all eternity.

The second temple of the Church was built at Nauvoo, but it was finished only a short time before the move of the Saints to the West. This prevented their using the building as fully as had been hoped. They abandoned it, and enemies later burned it. But this did not end temple building with the Saints. As soon as they reached the Great Basin Brigham Young designated the spot for the erection of the world-famous Salt Lake Temple, and began construction also on three others in Utah, one in St. George, one in Manti, and a third in Logan.

Today genealogical work is a favorite occupation with many of the Church members. On a normal business day in Salt Lake City you will find perhaps one hundred men and women entering the centrally located genealogical headquarters and peering into the big reading machines on which microfilms are projected. Others will be consulting Church experts, furnishing the family names and other material that can be fed into the information retrieval computers.[4] The im-

mediate objective is much the same as that of any other person having an interest in his forebears, but the motivation for the Mormons
is vastly stronger, for as family group sheets are prepared, they are
taken to the Temple for the ordinance work.

Most of those visiting the genealogical library are of mature years.
It is evident that they are deriving a satisfaction out of what they are
doing. If you stop a kindly faced, white-haired gentleman at random
and ask what it is all about, he will explain that his family name is
Jones. His grandfather joined the Church in Pennsylvania sometime
around the time of the Civil War, and came West a few years afterward to Salt Lake City. They settled first in Cache Valley, which is
on the Utah-Idaho border. They were farmers but our Mr. Jones
sold his interest in the farm to one of his brothers and went into
railroad work. Now he is retired and it came to him that it was time
to find out what he could about the Jones family and see to it that
all was in order.

"You see," he explains, "we are all descended, all of us human
beings, from Father Adam, so we are in actual fact all one family, as
the Bible says. Perfect genealogical work would trace each one of us
back to Father Adam but, of course, few things are perfect. I am
tracing my family back as far as I can. From Pennsylvania I think
we can go back to Wales. I am getting a great deal out of giving
these good people who went before this opportunity to belong to the
Church, and isn't it wonderful that our faith has made this provision?"

In the hereafter that person will know that he has been offered
the salvation of the Gospel and will be free to accept or reject. On
this basis, Saints living in the present can express their love and consideration for their families and friends who have departed. It is
their feeling that they are extending into the lives and times to
come the fellowship and gentle guidance and protection of the Christian Gospel, restored as it was in the time of Jesus. While to the
worldly of this world this procedure may seem a little other-worldly
—and Saints usually speak of it only to those they know and like
and hope will be with them after this life—it is very comforting to
them to feel that they will not simply leap into a black unknown but
will experience a continuation with their families and friends. And
this thought of eternity, and continuation, of course, is central to all
Christian teaching.

Temple Marriage

Certainly not to be omitted in any list of temple blessings is that of the marriage ceremony. Mormons consider marriage the most sacred human relationship and only the temple marriage ceremony, in their belief, properly instructs in the obligations of marriage; only temple rites, lived up to by the contracting parties, assure an eternal union.

But, despite this importance of temples, the fact remains that until 1900 there were only four temples in all the world available to the Mormons and they were all in Utah. The Kirtland Temple had been lost, the Nauvoo Temple destroyed, and the temples in Far West and Independence, Missouri, had not been built. It was obvious that if the benefits of temple work were to be offered to those outside Utah—and this was clearly the need because of the limitations on emigration—there must be a wider dispersion of temples. Yet in this the Mormons were long delayed.

The first overseas temple, and indeed the first outside Utah except for Kirtland and Nauvoo, was in the Hawaiian Islands. On June 1, 1915, President Smith was visiting in Hawaii and noted that it was an anniversary of Brigham Young's birth. He decided that a temple should be built there for the convenience of the Hawaiian Mormons and those of the South Sea Islands as far away as New Zealand. This decision was supported by the Church membership the following October, but World War I, and problems in construction, delayed dedication until November 1919. This was followed by dedication of the temple in Alberta, Canada, in 1923; in Mesa, Arizona, in 1927; and Idaho Falls, Idaho, in 1945. It wasn't, however, until 1955 that the long-cherished aspiration to have a temple in Europe was realized.

The Tabernacle Choir was in Europe that summer and President David O. McKay had chosen the time to break ground for a new temple in Surrey, twenty-five miles south of London, and to dedicate the completed temple at Berne, Switzerland. Some of the Swiss press had published outlandish stories about the purposes of the temple. For after all, without explanation, the idea of baptism for the dead and eternal marriages can be subject to misinterpretation. But the

Swiss-American Friendship League stepped into the picture and at a luncheon, with the United States Ambassador as guest of honor, the role and importance of temples was explained. It was also explained that Mormons in Europe had prayed for a temple for more than a hundred years. Its construction meant that Church members from Switzerland, Austria, Germany, France, Holland, Denmark, Sweden, Norway, and Finland would have much more readily available to them than ever before the sacred ordinances. To allay fears and answer questions, the temple was opened several days before dedication and Swiss from the neighboring towns were invited to come and see for themselves what was "sacred but not secret."

What they saw was a rather plain, gray, rectangular building with a single spire, not too unlike many church edifices of other denominations. Inside they walked on deep broadloom carpeting into a small, tastefully decorated room with folding seats that seemed much like those in a new motion picture theater. Indeed, the whole ordinance room resembled a small, deluxe theater, complete with screen. Except for the obvious quality of decorations and furnishings, the visitors might have seen its duplicate in almost any Swiss village. Films and slides and tapes were to be used in teaching.

Presence Felt

When he dedicated the Berne Temple on September 11, 1955, President McKay indicated some of the motivations and feelings of the Mormons:

"We welcome all who are present at the opening session of the dedication service of the first Temple completed in Europe by The Church of Jesus Christ of Latter-day Saints. It is a memorable event, and each one present this morning is favored by having the opportunity of attending. I welcome also an unseen but, I believe, a real audience among whom are former presidents and apostles of the Church, headed by the Prophet Joseph to whom was revealed the essential ordinance of baptism for those who have died without hearing the gospel, President Young, President Taylor, President Woodruff, President Snow, President Joseph F. Smith, who forty-nine years ago last month in the city of Berne prophesied that 'Temples would be built in diverse countries of the world,' President Heber J. Grant, President George Albert Smith. Among them, too, I fancy would be Elder Stayner Richards who was so active in helping to select the two Temple sites already chosen in Europe. With these distinguished leaders, we welcome departed loved ones, whom we cannot see, but whose presence we feel."[5]

The Los Angeles Temple, largest and most costly yet erected, was dedicated by President McKay a year later. It is a four-story structure, with a center spire that rises 258 feet above the ground, topped with a golden statue symbolizing the Angel Moroni blowing a trumpet. Situated on a high point on Santa Monica Boulevard, the temple, beautifully illuminated at night, easily dominates a large part of the Los Angeles skyline and reports have been received that it has been seen twenty-five miles out at sea.

The New Zealand Temple was dedicated by President McKay in April 1958, and the London Temple in September of that year. A temple in Oakland, California, and one in Innsbruck, Austria, have been completed since that time, and others are in prospect and even on the drawing boards, for the LDS Church is rapidly expanding and temples are, in a way, measurements of the acceleration.

Inside the Temple

The Salt Lake Temple has a great baptismal bowl in its lower level, a tank of copper resting on the back of twelve oxen, each symbolic of a tribe of Israel. The water is warmed, and much of the lower level area is devoted to dressing rooms, for no longer are baptisms left to the chilling water of seas and rivers.

The first floor is divided into several rooms, one a sealing room for marriage ceremonies, and others are classrooms, for temples are primarily used for religious teaching. One large room represents the primeval world, or world as it was in the formless and vague beginning, another the Eden of Adam and Eve; another represents the world as we now know it, with its imperfections; while still another represents the celestial world, or life as it is to be for those who learn and properly execute the lessons of this world. Murals carry out these teachings.

There is a meeting place for the First Presidency and the Council of the Twelve, a beautiful room in pale yellow and gold and white, with large comfortable chairs in which the apostles sit with the President and consult on affairs of the Church.

The Salt Lake Temple was finished in 1893; the cost was above $4,000,000. There is nothing else quite like it in the world. There is a strong hint of Middle West, American Gothic, a suggestion of the East in its six spires and its golden Angel Moroni blowing his trumpet to the east. And with Rocky Mountain granite several feet thick, it is built for the ages. A simulation of the east façade, complete with golden Moroni, was a feature attraction of the 1964–65 New York World's Fair. Approximately six million people visited it.

Economic Troubles

But to return to our story, the Edmunds-Tucker Act had chimed the end of the Perpetual Emigration Fund. The seizure of funds had been accompanied by a determined effort on the part of the U. S. Department of State to discourage emigration from England and Europe. But these efforts only magnified the more central difficulty, which was that, as we noted, the free-land frontier had passed.

The last big year for emigration had been 1883. That year from England alone nearly 1500 had come. Ten years later the number was down to eighty-six, and only a few times did it go over 150 a year until the end of the century. Without the Emigration Fund the Church had no formal means to assist emigration. Steamships were constantly raising their rates, railroads were expensive and had to be paid in cash. The end of the Perpetual Emigration Fund was the end of an era, but in its thirty-eight years it was credited with assisting some 100,000 persons to emigrate, mostly from England and Scandinavia, to Utah. The Fund possibly represented the most important enterprise undertaken by the Saints. Its consequences were of a value and importance that are still unfolding today.

Acceptance of the manifesto by United States authorities signaled the gradual return of seized Church property. As this was done, it became evident that the non-Mormon receivers had followed a general program of turning assets into cash, a policy aimed at getting the Church out of business. By 1896, when the bulk of the return was completed, saddened Church officials could see that legal and receivers' fees and other such charges had greatly diminished the wealth and the economic position of the Church.

The Church would never yield its social consciousness or shirk its responsibility to its members; nor would the members lose sight of their great obligations to the Church, but no longer would Utah be a separate kingdom. Signifying this, the boon of statehood was granted to Utah, also in 1896. The Latter-day Saints divided themselves up into Republicans and Democrats. The Gentiles began to remark how "just like everybody else" the Mormons really were.

But in this they miss a vital point, for the Mormons have a continuing serious purpose in life, one in which they feel they are expressing the deepest love and sympathy for all mankind in pursuing, and one from which they are not likely to be diverted by either tolerant humor, popularity, or antipathy. Theirs is still the task of carrying the option of redemption and salvation to all men. Today, as a century ago, they are prepared to make any sacrifice, and to count all trials as blessings of the Lord. Their work, as we shall see, is still unfolding in many marvelous ways.

As with temporal kingdoms, historians have had a way of writing about the Saints in terms of the periods of various presidencies, just as they divide up the history of England into reigns of the kings, and the history of the United States into terms of the succeeding presidencies. But this method of partitioning history leaves out of account a circumstance of organization within the Church: the long years of preparation that go into becoming a president.

Wilford Woodruff was succeeded by Lorenzo Snow. He was followed by Joseph F. Smith, who was first mentioned here when he was carried as an infant to see his father Hyrum and his uncle Joseph Smith while both were held in jail in Liberty, Missouri. As a boy of ten he had been a part of the great trek from Nauvoo to the Great Basin. He was succeeded by Heber J. Grant, a son of one of Brigham Young's councillors, and he in turn was followed by George Albert Smith, a grandson of Brigham Young's popular assistant. Even when Smith was succeeded in 1951 by David O. McKay there was no break, for McKay had been born three years before Brigham Young died and had served as a member of the Twelve for years before becoming President.

The New Century

It fell to Lorenzo Snow to be President at the turn of the century. Men's hopes were bright, and although the Mormons were far from recovered from the shock of the Edmunds-Tucker Act, they shared the general optimism of the period. The British Empire was at its flower; the United States, secure behind its oceans, maintained only token armed forces. The world was at peace. The Age of Invention had dawned, and with it the second industrial revolution. The world could not help but agree with President Lorenzo Snow when, with white-bearded, patriarchal mien, he stood before a filled Tabernacle on January 1, 1900 and prayed:

"The lessons of the past century should have prepared us for the duties and glories of the coming era. It ought to be the age of peace, of greater progress, of the universal adoption of the golden rule. The barbarism of the past should be buried. War with its horrors should be a memory. The aim of nations should be fraternity and mutual greatness. The welfare of humanity should be studied instead of the enrichment of a race or the extension of an empire. . . . May the twentieth century prove to be the happiest as it will be the grandest of all the ages of time, and may God be glorified in the victory that is coming over sin and sorrow and misery and death. . . ."[6]

From the present vantage point, looking back, one could only wish that it might have been as President Snow prayed. But the first half of the twentieth century furnished little peace to the world.

Chapter Twenty-two

TAKING CARE OF THEIR OWN

While we emphasized here the difference in Mormon economic development from the stream of concurrent history, the fact remains that it was a current within the larger river of contemporary events. The period of westward movement and colonization followed a parallel American movement. The great emigration of European Mormons to Utah paralleled a similar movement from the Old World to the New. And as the last years of the nineteenth century saw many European powers building and consolidating overseas empires, while America was content to consolidate its own empire between the oceans, just so the Mormons in the same period consolidated and strengthened their economy, building, investing, and developing.

Thus it was that while two world wars devastated empires and blasted the very idea of colonialism, both the American and Mormon "empires" were gathering strength. In the broad and imprecise strokes by which historical trends are measured, it might be said that the first half of the twentieth century was one of preparation while the second half is one of extending help and offering leadership, in their relative spheres.

The Mormons of today, no less fervently than their forebears, feel that time and destiny are on their side. It is against this background that the unfolding of the twentieth century in Mormon affairs should be viewed. To some extent the personality and the interests of the succeeding Presidents of the Church governed the trends, but these interests were naturally influenced by other factors.

President Snow had little choice but to be concerned with economic matters. He was fortunate in having among the Twelve able young Heber J. Grant, who had a mind for commerce and an awareness of his times. Since the Mormons were to be a part of the United

States and not a separate economic unit, he reasoned that outside capital should be brought in.

To this end he traveled to Wall Street, but found himself rebuffed. The times were not propitious; there was still doubt about the Mormons and their future; monetary affairs were depressed. The Mormons were advised to come back later. So President Snow called together some Mormons who had made personal fortunes. Their response was quite simple: outside lenders, they said, would not be interested in investment unless the Church proved it had the support of its own members and was willing to take leadership and responsibility in the risks involved.

These risks, however, were not to be taken simply on the basis of what would do the Mormon community the most good, but on the hardheaded basis of what would pay good profits. Actually, events were to show that these two approaches—good for the community and good for profits—were not always mutually exclusive. But to prove the point first required heavy financing from within.

This was accomplished when President Snow followed the advice of the leading Mormon businessmen by having the Church issue bonds to its members. One million dollars was thus raised, and it immediately put the Church in a positive fiscal position.

Sugar Success

Church leaders had never ceased to be interested in one of their industrial ventures of the 1850s—sugar. This commodity had to be imported at a cost of above $1,000,000 a year. While their earlier attempts had ended in failure, continued experiments were carried on elsewhere, and by the last decade of the nineteenth century successful, profitable beet-sugar mills were in operation in California and Colorado.

A Mormon horticulturist, Arthur Stayner, continued the work of growing sugar beets in Utah with ascending success. So a decision was made by the Church to back another effort at sugar production. There were several years of deficit operation, though good sugar was produced from the start from local beets.

A bond issue of $400,000, guaranteed by the Church, was sold to

Joseph Banigan of Providence, Rhode Island, a Roman Catholic, who said he believed the Mormons were a rugged mountain people who would not "be carried away by the ridiculous ideas that find circulation from time to time."[1] At the same time, Banigan got his $400,000 worth of bonds for $360,000, a favorable discount.

It was a good investment and it wasn't long before sugar mills were dotting Utah and Idaho. In 1907, largely at Church suggestion and Heber Grant's negotiations, these plants were all brought into a $13,000,000 consolidation now known as the Utah-Idaho Sugar Company. National tariff policies, based in some measure on a desire never to be entirely dependent upon sugar imports, have been good to the beet-sugar industry. The vision of the 1850s has been well justified, as thousands of Mormon farmers and workers obtain their livelihood from this. Today the company probably has a value in excess of $30,000,000 and the Church owns more than half of it.

Salt was a natural by-product of the Great Salt Lake and the Church always had some investment in one salt company or another. About 1890 the principal interest in Inland Salt Company was sold to a non-Mormon group in the Middle West and with the cash the Church participated in the long-held dream of developing a play area on the shores of the lake.

A sixteen-mile rail line with the rather grand name of Salt Lake & Los Angeles Railroad was built out to an oriental-style pavilion known as Saltair and comprised of bathhouses, a dance hall, and various amusement-park rides. The whole project cost about $600,000, and for several decades succeeding generations of Americans received postal cards mailed by friends from Saltair showing ladies and gentlemen reclining in the unsinkable water while reading the daily newspaper. Often attached to the card was a tiny cotton sack full of salt "from the Great Salt Lake."

New Plans

Saltair today has fallen victim to three things: a fire which partially destroyed the pavilion in 1925; changing patterns of amusement on the part of Mormons and others who prefer fresh-water bathing and water-skiing; and, no doubt most conclusive of all, the fact that diversion of water for irrigation combined with a cycle of drought and high rates of evaporation have served to leave Saltair high and dry about a mile from the lake shore. Dredging and pumping provide some waist-deep swimming pools near the old bathhouses, but it is a poor substitute for its former glory as a resort.

This is a source of regret to many who feel that the Lake could offer wholesome recreational attractions for residents as well as the thousands of tourists who visit "Mormon-land" every year. In 1963 the Utah State Legislature created the Great Salt Lake Authority and studies have been in progress since.

One of these studies advanced a proposal to build new bathing and recreational facilities suited to the present day on a part of Antelope Island, which lies a few miles north of Saltair and extends about fifteen miles into the lake. Other plans, or rather hopes, embrace development of the vast resources of calcium, iron, sodium chloride, boron, lithium, zinc, and rare minerals known to be present in the lake. Uses for many of these elements were not known in pioneer days, but their presence inspires many hopes today.

The Church led in the development of electricity in Utah. Power lines of higher voltage and greater length than any others then in use in the United States were built in Utah, partly with private capital and leadership, mostly with Church financing and inspiration. These investments were ultimately consolidated into the Utah Power and Light Company.

The Church was a major stockholder, but subsequently sold out to the E. H. Harriman interests, which by then also controlled the Union Pacific. Later the property came under Electric Bond and Share Company, but today a good deal of the investment is held by individual Mormons, not the Church.

The Church reacquired 25 percent interest in its original department store, Zion's Cooperative Mercantile Institute, ZCMI, with sales in the $35,000,000 class, and this has become one of the most progressive merchandising outlets in the country. It was one of the first to build a giant parking garage of the sort in which each car is placed in a virtual elevator cab of its own and stored in stacks, available at the press of a button. In the suburbs there is now a new $3,500,000 branch.

The Church's Hotel Utah has long been a western show place and never more than recently when millions have been spent on its re-furbishing. A seventeen-story annex is planned, and the hotel's motor lodge is one of the best.

Zion's Securities provided an eight-story home for the Church's Beneficial Life Insurance Company, having $535,000,000 in force. The Church's *Deseret News* is Salt Lake City's afternoon paper, with a circulation of nearly 100,000. And the Church has about a $20,000,000 investment in the Los Angeles *Times*, which is the largest paper there, but the holding results from a common interest in a paper mill, not an effort to control or influence media.

It owns the leading television stations in Salt Lake City, Seattle, Washington, and substantial interests in television stations and radio stations in Idaho Falls and Boise, Idaho, and elsewhere. The Church owns the well-known short-wave radio station WRUL (World Radio University) located near Boston and before and during World War II known as "Radio Boston." It has five transmitters, beamed around the world, but particularly to South America.

The Church also owns a trucking company, a clothing factory, several canneries, a pineapple plantation, but of much interest to some who inquire about the business side of the Church are the ranches. These have been acquired with different motivations. In Canada, for example, the Church had a good deal of cash which it was necessary, under tax laws and other regulations, to invest in Canada. It put its money into three large ranches and now has about 20,000 head of cattle grazing.

But much more dramatic are the Florida ranches. Incorporated as the Orlando Livestock Company, the original intention was to include it in the Church's welfare program, but as the low-lying scrub land, alternately the victim of torrential rains and long periods of drought, was studied, it became apparent that massive measures beyond the scope of local church groups would be required to bring it to optimum service.

Latest methods of drainage and of irrigation were applied, along with scientific methods of planting, a story of perseverance and wisdom almost equaling that of the Utah pioneers. Today, this story is held up in Florida as one of the all-time successes of the state. These ranches now exceed 700,000 acres, and feed more than 100,000 fine Aberdeen Angus and Herefords. The land, which was originally bought for about $3.00 an acre is now valued at above $100 an acre, representing a gain from $2,000,000 to $70,000,000 in land value alone.

Church interests certainly have a monetary value into very high figures. Income from investments is of course supplemented by tithings. Tithings are still the largest part of Church income. A complicating factor in estimating wealth is the near impossibility of putting a figure on the quickly rising values of Church-owned real estate around the world.

If all this seems a denial of the post-manifesto policy "to get the Church out of business," it must be recalled that times have changed; also that if the Church owns a newspaper, so does the non-Mormon community. If the Church owns one television station, other interests control two. The Hotel Utah has a rival down the street. The venerable ZCMI must compete with a host of lively locally owned and chain stores. Church-controlled banks compete against private banks. All this was not so in the pre-manifesto days of Brigham Young. One must judge the present against that past.

But that past is never too deep beneath the surface. Whenever the Saints need cooperative action to meet an economic need, the old pattern reappears. Perhaps the best example of that, one that is now almost a classic in American lore is the story of the bishop's storehouses.

The trend of the Church away from secular business continued in general through the presidency of Joseph F. Smith and into the term of Heber J. Grant. In the 1920s, under Grant's leadership, the Church regained a strong, even though no longer dominant, position in its fiscal affairs; but the world-wide depression of the early 1930s did not by-pass Utah. Indeed, it may have been harder, in some respects, in this region.

Many Mormon families were faced by the phenomenon that food was not worth harvesting while hundreds in the cities hungered. The wisdom of Brigham Young was recalled—that real wealth is food one can eat, clothes one can wear, shelter one can rest in. Gradually there was revived a system not unlike the early days in the Great Basin where under Church leadership crops were planted and harvested, canneries were rented and reopened, a clothing factory was set up. Unemployed Mormons worked full time at the projects. Others volunteered their spare time.

Government Aid Not Needed

It wasn't long before Mormon President Grant could call on Church members to avoid doles or unearned benefits. Federal relief for Mormons in Utah was not necessary. Mormons should take care of themselves. This example of what many considered to be a resurgence of American pioneer virtues thrilled the whole country and won the Mormons increased respect.

But it also gave the Mormons something new to think about. For it had been made tragically plain to them that like many millions of others they were vulnerable to economic forces quite outside their control, a prime cause for the *angst* and insecurity afflicting modern man. A refinement of the sort of problem that had confronted their forebears in England in Brigham Young's missionary time there had caught up with them in the United States.

Through rather simple means they achieved effective answers to a complicated problem. Church leaders began to advise their people that it would be a good idea if every family had in its basement or attic, or wherever it could have safe storage, a full year's supply of food, fuel, and clothing. With this sort of "real wealth" at its immediate disposal a family would feel greater security from the business winds. The Church encouraged members to seek reliable guidance on what to store, how to properly put it away.

This program that grew out of the welfare experience of the depression was carried forward through World War II and is today in greater scope than ever before. In fact the Church and its local congregations now own more than five hundred welfare projects, many of them local show places, and the total has a value in excess of $40,000,000.

In California, for example, they own fine ranches, and they recently sold their $125,000 Bountiful Farm in Virginia so they could purchase a much larger dairy and beef project in eastern Maryland. The New York Mormons have a New Jersey farm that has won state agricultural department awards for its efficiency. One citrus grove in California produces superior oranges for eating and trades its output for the smaller juice oranges of neighbors and thus boosts its juice output three or four times. A farm near Seattle grows beans for canning. Other farms produce cotton, wool, beef, pork, and all sorts of grains and fruits and vegetables. After all, five hundred enterprises spread over twenty-two states represent a massive effort. It provides about $10,000,000 worth of food and other goods yearly for charitable distribution by the Church.

How do they get the money to buy these farms? The initial down payment, or one quarter, must be raised by the local group. The usual practice of the congregation is to forego two meals a month and to donate the monetary value to a special or "fasting" fund. This is augmented in dozens of ways. Church suppers, musical shows, dances—all the usual ways in which American church groups raise money are employed.

When the farm is considered—and Church experts will supply advice on buying—the local group may, if it wishes, borrow the remaining three quarters from a Church revolving loan fund in Salt Lake City. Each farm is assigned a quota by Church authorities for supplying the Bishop's Storehouse, but anything above this quota may be sold for cash to pay off the Church-held loan. The object and desire is to retire the loan as quickly as possible.

Some of the farms have paid managers or hands, but they depend for the bulk of their labor on volunteers from the local congregations. On a summer weekend morning you may find bankers and bakers, clerks and teachers, and almost every other trade and profession represented as hoes and rakes are passed out for a cleanup job. Some of them, like Willard Marriott and Milan Smith, are millionaires; others like Senator Bennett and Ezra Taft Benson are noted political leaders. Indeed, the list of those laboring manfully under the direction of L. Blaine Liljenquist, the group's farming director, and in private life one of Washington's most prominent agricultural trade association leaders, would read like a *Who's Who* of capitol life.

But none is loathe to work with hands and backs in providing the means for others to help themselves. George Romney, presently governor of Michigan, was, as president of the Mormons in Detroit, a leader in getting started with the $200,000 model farm at Merrill, Michigan, and not too proud to spread fertilizer with the rest. This sort of work by the great as well as by all the members is, of course, in the tradition of their forebears who labored without pay on the Tabernacle and Temple.

In Salt Lake City one bishop's storehouse occupies a whole block on Welfare Square, and its contents and enterprise are reminiscent of the old tithing office. Products from the welfare farms are trucked into the storehouse. Cans of fruits come from the Pacific Northwest, canned vegetables from dozens of canneries—Welfare Square keeps 1,000,000 cans of food in stock most of the time—meat from all over the West, and a vast cellar holds potatoes and other root crops.

Dominating the square is a concrete grain storage elevator capable of holding 140 carloads of wheat. This elevator was built early in World War II in just eight days as 640 volunteer workers mixed and poured concrete night and day. It is kept nearly full, a defense measure of the Church, since wheat stores easily and retains its full food value.

The Mormons are a close-knit society; there is hardly ever a need among any of them that is not known to the bishop who watches over his ward with more exactitude and solicitude than any big city political ward leader. If a man is out of work, or if a widow is having trouble getting her children fed and in school, he knows about it and is there to do something about the problem. If it requires food or clothing or fuel, he has the authority to write out on the spot a bishop's order. This will do what cash could never do. It permits the bearer to take a pushcart, like those of any other supermarket, and to pick and choose her requirements at the bishop's storehouse. If she needs help in getting the food home, she is in better shape than many of her suburban sisters, for the people at Welfare Square will deliver it to her home in an unmarked truck.

But that is just a part of the story. Friends from the Women's Relief Society will have called to see what is needed in the way of clothes and household items, and these are supplied and a discussion is held to see what is needed to get the family back on its feet permanently and above the need for relief.

The stories are quite varied. In one instance a factory worker was incapacitated for anything but light outdoor work. All his life he had wanted to raise chickens, and his bishop was able to help him with the down payment on a small acreage and to find Mormon friends who would counsel him and guide him in getting off to a good start.

Another case involved a woman left a widow with small children. She had worked as a typist before her marriage. An elderly woman who needed a home was found to act as "grandmother" for the youngsters while the mother was helped through a refresher course at a business school and then located in a job where she could be self-sustaining.

In Salt Lake City such things may not be too difficult. The "grandmother" was probably a friend of the family for many years. The business school might well have been run by a first cousin, while a job in the Church offices or Church-controlled insurance company was probably not hard to locate. But Mormons far from Salt Lake City carry forward the same sort of projects, looking after their own.

And the spirit in which this is done is worthy of comment. For the Mormons do not call each other "brother" and "sister" without meaning. The widow who goes through Welfare Square picking out her food receives more deference and truly loving courtesy than is the common lot in the ordinary commercial market. The Mormons practice the art of being kind and gentle with each other, and all the more so if a need exists.

There are now two and a half million Mormons in the world and in a typical recent year some 80,000 were helped in one way or another. But the farms produced more than enough for that purpose; they helped fill Mormon bins for emergency relief for non-Mormons placed in need by fire or flood or other disaster.

To an outside observer, it would seem that the work has another aspect worth pondering, for the welfare farms offer a way for city people to get out, even for just a weekend, to the verities of wealth.

The businessman who hoes out the weeds along a row of tomatoes, and his wife who helps the other sisters prepare the midday meal, and the children who help in their own ways, have, it is true, a sense of service in knowing that the product of their labor may help feed someone in need, but they also know that they are contributing to the accumulation of a Church-controlled surplus that might help them if ever in need. And if they were in need, they would have the knowledge that in happier times they had helped provide for the dreary days.

Too, the welfare program conditions and helps them to follow their Church's advice and lay in a good stock of food and clothing for their own use. A year's reserve supply on hand should be a good tranquillizer in modern life for any family.

Chapter Twenty-three

THE OUTWARD THRUST

At the start of the twentieth century, The Church of Jesus Christ of Latter-day Saints had been organized seventy years, and as readers of the foregoing chapters are aware, it was a tumultous seventy years. Today, now that almost another seventy years has gone by, we can look back upon 1900 as a sort of halfway mark, and if one were to seek for some dominant characteristic of this latter span, it would probably rest on the international aspects.

During the initial period, using the first seventy years as a handy measuring stick, the principal trend was for the Church to pull inward to Zion. By contrast, this last seventy years has seen more of a pushing outward from Zion. Today it is not exclusively a "Utah church," nor even an "American church." It is true that Utah and the United States still supply it with a geographic base and the larger part of its membership, but yearly it is becoming more of a worldwide activity. And if a non-Mormon observer were required to forecast the trend into the future, it would be that this international thrust will continue. As we have seen, it fell to Lorenzo Snow, as President of the Church in 1901, to re-emphasize and rearticulate the world view. He called for a bigger vision, noting that Church leaders tended to become too involved in local Utah affairs. "It looks to me that our minds ought to extend somewhat," he said when dispatching Heber J. Grant to open the first mission in Japan in 1901. "The apostles—it is their business, by the appointment of the Almighty, to look after the interests of the world."

It was not given to President Snow, however, to do much more than point the direction. He was succeeded late in 1901 by Joseph

F. Smith, who in the first decade of the century stepped up a higher level of missionary work. To England, for example, the Church sent from a low of sixty-six missionaries in 1901 to a high of 190 in 1908 and 184 in 1909.

It was not easy going for these missionaries. In the first ten years of this century, for example, they baptized 7587 in Britain, compared with the 43,304 baptized in the 1850–59 decade. Elsewhere in Europe and in Scandinavia the results were in proportion. The reason seemed apparent: the Church was no longer presenting itself as a vehicle for removal to "heaven on earth." With little free land to offer in the New World, without a Perpetual Emigration Fund to assist with costs, the Church was forced to discourage emigration. In 1907 the *Millennial Star* said, "The Church is not using any influence to persuade its members or others to emigrate, but desires that many of them shall stay and build up the work abroad."

Thus was stated a policy, but for some years the policy worked against an increase in membership. People could be excited about the prospects of completely reordering their lives and moving to a "promised land" of fresh opportunities of all sorts, including that of living among brothers and sisters in a Zion apart, but it proved to be more difficult to excite people to remain at home and yet live apart in their religious beliefs and many social habits from relatives and friends. And there were other problems as the nationalism fired by Bismarck swept over Germany and other states, and brought fear of war to Europe.

President Smith went to Europe in 1907 and again in 1910, holding meetings with Church groups in England, Holland, Belgium, France, Switzerland, and Germany. He was seeking for some method of imparting a fresh inspiration. He was a sweet and patriarchal gentleman who won admiration and respect wherever he traveled, but the tide of human affairs was running against the gentleness of the Christian faith. In 1907, the year of his first visit to Germany, for example, the imperial government decided it could not brook anything but a state-dominated church and therefore announced that the Mormon teachings were "subversive of morality," with the result that President Smith had to order the withdrawal of one hundred missionaries from Germany to Switzerland.

New Attacks

In other European countries missionaries reported that once again they found themselves under the sort of attack that had greeted their fathers. Rocks were hurled at them; their meetings were disrupted by angry mobs, or police. In addition to the growing political tensions of Europe the Mormons abroad were in some measure being affected by troubles in the United States. In Utah the old issue of polygamy was being raised again, so much so that President Smith felt under necessity of issuing in 1904 a "second manifesto," reaffirming the original one. Fuel was added when several prominent Mormons withdrew, holding that they had interpreted the 1890 manifesto as applying only to the geographic limits of the United States. Specifically, they felt, it did not apply in Mexico, where some had gone to continue polygamy.

Mixed into this was a U. S. Senate investigation into the fitness of Reed Smoot to serve as a senator. Smoot, himself one of the Twelve, had been elected to the Senate in 1903. A group of non-Mormons in Salt Lake City protested that Smoot represented the interests of the Church but not those of the state of Utah. Others charged that he was a polygamist (which was disproved) but for two years the Senate Committee on Privileges and Elections heard testimony and counter-testimony about the power of the Church in Utah. Again, it was pictured as a virtual monarchy within the U.S.A., but when the Senate finally voted, Smoot was seated and in fact he remained in the Senate for thirty years, being replaced by a Democrat in the New Deal Franklin D. Roosevelt landslide of 1932.

But Smoot's victory did not silence the anti-Mormons in Salt Lake City. They continued to grumble and in 1910 and 1911 several large American magazines printed attacks on the Mormons. It was a time of "muck-raking" in American journalism, during which period almost everything was taken apart and very little put back together again. Timely help came to the Church, however, when on April 15, 1911, Theodore Roosevelt, beloved and respected late President of the United States, published a letter in which he strongly proclaimed the virtues and high standards of the Mormon people and at the same time refuted charges of improper political activities.[1]

As World War I came upon Europe, all the talk about Utah, or "Mormon-land," being a separate enclave suddenly vanished. The Mormons had supported with their prayers President Woodrow Wilson's efforts to maintain a neutrality, but when on April 6, 1917, Wilson asked Congress to declare that a state of war existed, the Mormons quickly responded to the call. They tried to excel all others in volunteering for service and in otherwise contributing to the effort. This was true elsewhere. A British newspaper commented that one branch of the Mormon Church had found every man of military age volunteering to serve in His Majesty's forces.

As with other churches, the problem of sending young men out to kill posed a difficult moral problem. President Smith's answer was to insist that in the face of conflict the spirit of the Gospel should be maintained. He declared that even in war the spirit of humanity and of peacemaking should prevail. He told young soldiers that they were ministers of life and not death and that they should go in the spirit of defending liberties of mankind rather than for the purpose of destroying the enemy.

President Smith lived to see the end of the war, passing away just eight days after the Armistice of November 11, 1918. When he had been sustained as President in 1901 the membership was 278,645. When he died it was 495,962, but perhaps of greatest significance was the fact that the rate of church-membership growth outside Utah was double that inside the state.

Heber J. Grant as President

When Heber J. Grant succeeded as President, the question many had was whether he would continue to emphasize overseas activities, for President Grant's mind was very much centered on Utah. He was born in Salt Lake City in 1856, the year that the first attempt to produce sugar was abandoned. His biographer concluded that he was a very practical man. "It is no disparagement to say that President Grant was not a poetic, highly imaginative man. He was neither a dreamer nor a doctrinaire."[2]

As a matter of fact, he was a banker and a substantial part of his time was taken up in forwarding the economic interests of the Church. It was he, for example, who had largely directed the second, and successful, effort to produce beet sugar, and was a principal architect of the Utah-Idaho Sugar Company, which to this day contributes significantly to the Church. But the forces that had acted before his term to inhibit the flow of emigration continued. Indeed, they gained in force. For the Mormons realized that Utah had its economic limitations and that, as the great agricultural revolution swept America, Brigham Young's ideas of real wealth had to be modified to meet the changing times.

It was a time when many Americans were leaving the farm for the city. Also, Mormon youth were found to be as adventuresome as their forebears. They, too, looked afield for opportunities. Many of them headed for California. By 1923 there was a sizable group in Los Angeles. And quite a few of the young people were attracted to the East. By 1934 there was a large permanent Church group in New York City.

In 1900, although membership was world-wide in scope, almost 90 percent of the Church membership resided in Utah and associated mountain area. By 1930 this was down to 75 percent. Today, the membership in and around Utah represents less than half the total Church membership, and the supposition is that this percentage will continue to decline as world membership increases.[3]

During the years after World War I the Church experienced some increase in its overseas activities. The mission to France was reactivated after some years of virtual suspension. Missionaries were once more welcomed into Germany and enjoyed some success, particularly in the northeastern, or Prussian, areas. Indeed, Germany was soon divided into areas of work, and a substantial mission in Austria was opened too. This was extended in 1929 to Czechoslovakia, which, as a part of the Hapsburg empire that had a state church, had always been denied to the Mormons.

A little earlier, in 1925, the first missionary work was undertaken in South America, and while the results were slow in manifesting themselves, the foundation was evidently good. Looking at the worldwide picture, there was a 28 percent increase in membership during the first decade of Heber Grant's presidency. This was certainly healthy, but it did indicate a deceleration from the 47 percent jump during the ten-year period, 1900 to 1910, and the 34 percent increase in the 1910–20 decade.

Then came the decade of the 1930s, miserable for everybody, when, as a wit of the period suggested, it might have been a good thing to take each year as it was completed and wash it and hang it out to dry.[4] The growth of the Mormon Church, reflecting this world problem, was at its slowest rate in all its previous century of existence. Yet the economic troubles of the times did force a return to some of the neighborly cooperation of Brigham Young's times and resulted in the reactivation of the welfare program described in Chapter Twenty-two.

The rise of Mussolini and Hitler and Stalin brought with it a heightening tension and foreboding of war which, as far as the Mormon missionary effort was concerned, meant that in August 1939 it was necessary to withdraw, first, the east and west German missionaries into Denmark, and then, as the war spread, to pull the missionaries from other countries as well. They numbered 697 at the time and the Church was hard pressed to find space on available ships to bring them all to the United States, but it was accomplished with minimum delay.

Many of the young men returning from missions hurried into uniforms as the United States increased its forces and prepared for the dangers that in fact fell when the naval base at Pearl Harbor was attacked in 1941. And, again, the Church was faced with having to tell its young men that mother earth had placed its faith in its own armaments, and turned from the Prince of Peace. Each had to make his accommodation to the facts, and terrors, that prevailed.

George Albert Smith

Like his predecessor, Heber Grant expired a few days after the end of hostilities in Europe and shortly before the end of the war in the Pacific. George Albert Smith became the eighth President. He was truly a child of the Church, his great grandfather having been an uncle of the Prophet and his grandfather the original "George A." He was seventy-five years old when he was sustained as President and he faced the gargantuan task of resuming the world-wide missionary work; but before that could begin, it was realized that first the wounds must be bound and the hungry fed.

Ezra Taft Benson was sent to Europe to see what needed to be done and what could be done. Everywhere he went he found destitution. While the Mormons in Europe had been faithful, they had suffered greatly. His reports to Salt Lake City aroused much sympathy, but although the Church welfare program had ample supplies of food, clothing, and bedding, there was little available shipping space. President Smith of the Mormons asked for an appointment to see the President of the United States, Harry S. Truman.

"He received me very graciously," President Smith reported, "and I said, 'I have come, Mr. President, to ascertain what your attitude will be if the Latter-day Saints are prepared to ship food and clothing to Europe."

"He smiled and looked at me, and said, 'Well, what do you want to ship it over there for? Their money isn't any good.'

"I said, 'We don't want their money.' He looked at me and asked, 'You don't mean that you are going to give it to them?'

"I said, 'Of course we would give it to them. They are our brothers and sisters and are in distress. God has blessed us with a surplus, and we will be glad to send it if we have the cooperation of the government.'

"He said, 'You are on the right track, and we will be glad to help you in any way that we can.'

"After we had sat there a moment or two, he said again, 'How long will it take you to get this ready?'

"I said, 'It is all ready.'"[5]

A year later it was reported that some of the European Mormon congregations looked exactly like meetings of Americans. "At least 80 percent in the audiences wore new American-made clothes, sent from church welfare!"

This practical demonstration of the value of Church affiliation no doubt had constructive effects on membership, and the return of missionaries to their fields also had an effect. By the end of 1946 3000 missionaries were already in the field and others were preparing to go. It was a time of much progress. It was found that in Japan, the Philippines, and other countries in the Far East Mormon servicemen had acted as part-time missionaries so there were new converts to greet the new postwar efforts. In a number of instances, released soldiers returned as missionaries and the work was given extra impetus. But it was still slow going. Missionaries averaged less than two converts a year apiece.

It was under the leadership of President George A. Smith that this postwar resurgence of missionary work occurred. Some feared that it might be set back when he died in the spring of 1951. But, as it turned out, there was no need to worry.

Chapter Twenty-four

DAVID O. MCKAY AND THE GREAT ACCELERATION

In 1850, the second year of the Perpetual Emigration Fund, and the first year on the job for the missionaries dispatched from Salt Lake City in the fall of 1849, a young man walked into Janetstown, a part of Thruso in the far northern Scotch county of Caithness. He had no particular family in mind, or any special house. He was just, as they said, "tracting," going up one lane and down another knocking on doors, visiting with anybody who would talk to him.

In time he came to a little stone cottage, a "but and ben" they called them, meaning living room and kitchen, that belonged to William McKay and his wife Ellen Oman. We have no record of what was said, but two days later, November 3, he baptized them, the first converts to the Mormon Church in that part of Scotland.[1]

From that moment on, they dreamed of going to Zion and join- ing the other Saints. Each month they awaited the arrival of the *Millennial Star* with its news of the fledgling settlement in the Great Basin. And, finally, six years later, 1856, the McKay family sold its possessions and joined a party of 764 other Mormons sailing from Liverpool. They ran out of money before they got to the Mormon settlement in Iowa, whence the wagon trains set out across the Great Plains. They had to pause and work to earn the price of a wagon and team.

When they finally did set out, Ellen McKay gave up her seat in the wagon to a young woman who was ill, and so walked with her husband and four children the full 1000 miles across the plains and mountains to the Great Basin. The McKay family arrived in mid-summer and Brigham Young advised them to settle in Ogden. It was just after the federal troops had marched through Salt Lake City and were still encamped at Camp Floyd in Cedar Valley. And it was a time when Young and his counselors were busy filling up the valleys of the mountains.

Soon after the McKays arrived in Ogden and put up a house at Twenty-eighth and Lincoln Streets, into Ogden trudged the family of Thomas and Margaret Powell Evans, including daughter Jennette, aged nine. They were from Merthyr Tydfil in South Wales, where they had known Dan Jones. They settled near the McKays, at Twenty-eighth Street and Adams.

Eight years later the youngest of the McKays, David, was married to the eldest of the Evanses, Jennette, and on September 8, 1873, on their new farm in Huntsville just above Ogden, was born their first son, David Oman McKay. Thus at the moment of birth he was a third generation Mormon. The Church was the dominant interest of his parents and grandparents and inevitably of him from his earliest recollections. The Church and its affairs and personalities was always the ascendant topic of conversation.

He went to local schools and possessed qualities of leadership from the first. Evidence of this was the fact that he was president of his class when he completed his studies at the University of Utah in 1897.

He was immediately sent to Scotland as a missionary, serving there two years in the northern area that included his grandfather's old home. Indeed, he found and visited the actual house and was directed to the "icy water where they were dipped."

Returning to Ogden he was offered a teaching job in Weber Academy, today a state college. He quickly rose to the presidency of this school, but within seven years, 1906, he was called to be an apostle. He was then thirty-two years old, indicating that he had won the confidence and support of his colleagues at an early age.

A Half Century of Experience

Soon after the end of World War I, he was sent on a trip around the world. This was to revisit and reappraise the overseas activities of the Church. It gave him an insight into local problems and opportunities of incalculable advantage later. In 1934 he became a counselor to the President of the Church. The practice is for the President to have two or more Counselors and these constitute the

First Presidency and are the highest authority within the Church. While the President has the final authority as "prophet, seer and revelator" of the Church, he counsels with his top advisers on virtually all matters of substance. So, it can be said that since 1906 David O. McKay had been continually in a position to be informed and active in the policy of the Church and since 1934 he had been continually involved in the highest administration.

When he was sustained as President in 1951 there were some among the non-Mormon observers who wondered whether the system of choosing leadership was as good as it might be, since a Church remarkable for the youthfulness of its founders had fallen into a pattern of being led by the elderly. President McKay, they pointed out, was seventy-eight. But of course this viewpoint failed to take into account the foregoing record of experience. As President he did not enter upon the unknown.

Moreover, it soon became apparent that years did not mean decrepitude to President McKay. When reporters sought him, they found that they had to get to his ancestral farm in Huntsville quite early, for even at 6 A.M. he might be out in the corral with a pan of oats trying to entice a favorite horse to take the bridle so there could be an early morning ride in the Utah hills.

Church officials soon found they had to persuade him to accept a chauffeur. And his travels were by no means limited to the mountains of the West. Within a year of becoming President he was visiting with President Juho Passokivi of Finland, dedicating a new chapel in West Berlin, attending a garden party given by Queen Elizabeth at Buckingham Palace, and personally looking over the site for the future temple near Berne. Never had the Church enjoyed a more traveled President. Soon it became evident that his leadership had two main thrusts:

1. Greatly expanded worldwide missionary effort.
2. A giant increase in church building.

The Missionary Effort

In 1952, a few months after President McKay had been sustained in his office, the full-time missionaries of the Church numbered

PLATE IX. The Mormon building program today extends into all parts of the world. Church members with skills needed in construction are called to go on missions to build meetinghouses and other needed buildings. Above, a father and his son from Seattle, Washington, are building a church in Japan.

The Los Angeles Temple (BELOW), dedicated in 1956, is located on a thirteen-acre hill-top tract overlooking the great Southern California metropolis. Before it was dedicated, more than 662,000 persons were permitted to view its interior rooms.

ET QUAND VOUS RECEVREZ CES CHOSES, JE VOUS EXH-ORTE A DEMANDER A DIEU, LE PÉRE ÉTERNEL, AU NOM DU CHRIST, SI CES CHOSES NE SONT PAS VRAIES, ET SI VOUS LE DEMANDEZ AVEC UN CŒUR SINCÉRE ET AVEC UNE INTENTION RÉELLE.

PLATE X. Young members of the world-wide Church are encouraged to participate in all functions. At left, a young French girl is shown speaking at Sunday school.

The Church of Jesus Christ of Latter-day Saints also has one of the largest programs in the world for Boy Scouts. The Boy Scout program is enjoyed by Latter-day Saints boys in all parts of the globe, even in Samoa.

PLATE XI. The Church education program enjoyed by these young South
Americans (ABOVE) shows the importance
of education reflected by the Mormon
Church.

At right, two young Dutch members of
the Latter-day Saints Church display one
of the scriptures they are learning in Sunday school.

Indien gij Mijne geboden
bewaart, zo zult gij in
Mijn liefde blijven ....
Johannes 15:10

PLATE XII. In Salzburg, Austria, three young girls run through the fields on their way home from attending the local Latter-day Saints Church meeting for young members.

Below, young Indians are given breakfast before continuing their journey to their new "white home" for the school year.

only 2,790, down some from the spurt of the immediate postwar years. The number of converts entering the Church from all over the world was counted at 11,839 that year.

Ten years later, 1962, the number of missionaries had almost quadrupled to 11,768 and the number of converts for the year was listed at 104,841.[2]

In the years since, these figures have stabilized at about 12,000 missionaries and upward of 180,000 converts a year. But the interesting figure to many non-Mormon church people is the figure of average converts per missionary. This has risen in the past decade and a half from under four per missionary to above nine!

This reveals that the acceleration is not due merely to an increase in missionary *numbers,* but even more significantly is due to an improvement in missionary *effectiveness.* It is a point of immense interest to other denominations, faced with the desire for more members.

During most of the Mormon Church's history, indeed until about the time of President McKay's accession, the bulk of missionary work was done by "tracting" or calling at one door after another, much as the missionary who converted the McKay family in Scotland. But in the years after World War II various leaders in the Church suggested that in the commercial world better methods were being found for an approach.

Every word of commercial solicitors is carefully worked out in advance to gain the interest and confidence of the person coming to the door; no fumbling with mumbled greetings. Right at the first crack in the door the missionary was instructed to introduce himself, show his credentials, and firmly state his purpose, which was to tell about his Church as an educational effort and to answer questions.

It was noted that in the commercial world a door-to-door salesman would frequently use his introduction merely as a means to seek an appointment for a regular interview. He would offer to come back with samples and, sometimes, a gift. Just so, the Mormon missionary was taught to seek the return interview so that he could come with pictures and exhibits. By 1952, these methods were being tested and refined by experience in the field. But a prime difficulty continued to be waste motion, which is to say too many calls before an interested person was happened upon. Again, in commercial terms, they needed some method by which the process might be speeded.

One opinion was to regard missionaries as rather specially trained experts and to use Church members to perform the screening work. Under this plan members would gather groups of friends and acquaintances in their homes for an evening and then invite a missionary team to present a film, or picture lecture. "Every Mormon a missionary," was the slogan with the goal of every Church member bringing in one additional member.

By 1960 one mission president was reporting that missionaries in his area were utilizing 90 percent of their time in actually teaching prospective members and only 10 percent in seeking contacts. Some working examples of the new missionary techniques are given in the chapter following.

The Breakthrough

This experimentation at the grass roots level, so to speak, was duplicated in the supervisory levels, and indeed changes are still going on. By 1960 it was clear that some breakthroughs were in process, and 1961 is regarded by many Mormons as a significant year in the history of the Church's missionary activity.

Starting on June 27 of that year, and continuing for a week, the first worldwide seminar for mission presidents was held. It reviewed what had been discovered about improved missionary work up to that point. As a result a so-called uniform system was adopted for world-wide use. It centered around teaching discussions designed to be used with persons sufficiently interested to investigate Mormonism. These discussions covered the basic beliefs of the Church, Church history, Church organization, and the part that individuals play in Church affairs.[3]

By the end of 1961 the word spread over Church headquarters in Salt Lake City that something important had happened: baptisms reached almost 80,000 that year, more than double the number of the previous year. Missionary work was at least twice as effective as theretofore.

Building Program

Tied in so tightly with the missionary program that it is almost impossible to separate it is the building activity. For as the new missionary procedures were successful, it developed that in addition to the theological teachings of the Mormons the new converts cherished the fellowship and activities of a Church-centered group. Zion could be found at home.

Just as in Utah many Church families found their entire social life revolving around Church activities, so many families outside Utah, and indeed in all parts of the world, discovered life was better for them if they had similar activities. And the missionaries found that a Church which offered a basketball court, a stage for dramatics, a room for dances and other activities for the young people quite naturally attracted young people.

President McKay was alert to this need, and even in the first year of his presidency was devoting almost one half the Church revenues to building projects. By 1956 almost five hundred new buildings were in process of construction around the world. The work by that time was in the hands of a General Church Building Committee with Wendell B. Mendenhall as chairman, reporting directly to President McKay and the First Presidency. Ten years later, 1965, the committee was reorganized with Mark B. Garff, a leading contractor, as chairman.

The committee is divided into three units. The first is a review group. It looks over applications and consults with Church officials on present and future prospects of the Church under consideration. If it is a fast growing suburban area, for example, considerations as to size may be different than if it is a group located in an older urban location considered to be in decline. If it is an area where missionary efforts are especially successful it makes a difference. In other words, practical outside judgments supplement those of the local group.

The second unit is concerned with plans. It has general ideas and plans developed by the Church architect. For example, it has been found that simplified buildings could be erected in most locations for half the cost of the conventional, or Colonial style, church edifice favored in earlier years. The Church architect works with local architects in designs and specifications.

The third unit actually supervises construction. It has experts in engineering, furnishings, landscaping, and—very important—acoustics.

So it is that a new church building in even remote parts of the world benefits from the international experience and continuous research of the Building Committee. There are two additional benefits: financial and the assistance of volunteer labor.

As a part of the outward thrust of the Church and because proper buildings are seen to be an integral part of the missionary program, the Church headquarters in Salt Lake City has a generous plan for financial assistance. In some instances the Church will put up as much as 90 percent of the total outlay. In the postwar years the Church has been on the lookout for good real estate investments, looking toward the future location of chapels and even temples. In some places, especially the crowded urban centers of Europe, these have proved to be fruitful investments and through consolidation and additional buying the Church has come into possession of many extremely valuable parcels for future development.

Church Builders

And not all of these are overseas. The New York City newspapers not long ago carried a front-page story to the effect that the Mormon Church owned a block of lots between Fifth and Sixth avenues and extending from Fifty-seventh to Fifty-eighth streets, one might say from the Plaza Hotel to Steinway Hall, definitely "the high rent area." Here it is planned to erect a skyscraper office building. It will house Church activities in the New York area, including a chapel, with space left over for commercial leasing.

But assistance with sites and with financing is only one aspect of help extended. The other part is supplied by the Church builders program. It will be recalled that in the early days in the Great Basin, a good deal of tithing was paid in the form of labor. A man would work for a period of time on the Tabernacle or Temple and be credited with the going wages on his tithing account. This practice became, as the years went by, less significant.

In 1950, however, the Church was putting up a school building in the Tongan Mission in the Pacific Islands, and five skilled supervisors from the United States and three from New Zealand had been dispatched to direct the project with instructions to hire local craftsmen. But no skilled workmen were available. The problem was solved by calling some of the local young Mormon men together and giving them the opportunity to serve the Church and in return to learn useful and needed skills from the Church experts.

It worked out well and a similar effort was made in Samoa. From there it spread around the world until today more than half the projects going forward in the world are assisted by the contributed work of local members.

At the beginning of a recent year it was reported to President McKay that there were at that moment—and it was typical for many in the past decade—868 building projects under way. Of these, 362 were in progress in the United States and Canada, 142 in western Europe, thirty-one in South America, fifty-two in the Pacific, including New Zealand and Australia, seven in the Far East, and four in South Africa. President McKay was hailed because more than 62 percent of the buildings in use around the world did not exist when he became President of the Church. By 1970 it is presumed that 90 percent of the buildings then to be in use did not exist in 1955.

Educational Activities

The emphasis in the above description of new buildings has been on chapels and other buildings relating directly to Church services and activities, but it would be improper not to underline, too, what is being done in the field of education.

It should be pointed out that some of the early American fundamentalist churches were not particularly keen about education. They felt that beyond the rudiments of arithmetic and a little reading and writing education was likely to corrupt the youthful mind and lead it away from the strict teachings of the Church.

The Mormons, at Joseph Smith's plea, never accepted this. Schools and the education of the young were always a lively concern. They never let fear that the highest education could corrode the beliefs of their young people limit their efforts and it is a notable fact that while many young Mormons undoubtedly go through the period, normal to all students, where they question and argue and sometimes express doubts, the actual number who fall away from the Church is remarkably small. Born and raised as Mormons they usually always remain Mormons, though naturally some are more active in the Church than others.

Thus, the Mormons have never had the slightest reason to fear education, but rather they welcome it. They have been proud of the fact that Utah has led the United States in its percentage of those having college degrees, and also proudly point to the fact that the Mormons have supplied presidents for several universities—in California, Minnesota, at Northwestern in Illinois, Arizona, Montclair, New Jersey to name some—in addition to colleges in Utah.

They list many men of science who, as is customary in that field, contribute to both the academic and business worlds. A list is always dangerous because space requires so many omissions, but a few that might be mentioned are Dr. Harvey Fletcher, formerly director of physical research at the Bell Telephone Laboratories; Dr. Henry Eyring, past president of the American Chemical Society and author of many important scientific papers; Philo Farnsworth, one of the inventors of electronic television and director of research for International Telephone and Telegraph Company; Nephi A. Christensen, director of the department of civil engineering, Cornell University; and the list could go on.

In business, the list of course is very long. It would include such names as Robert D. Bradford, executive vice president, American Smelting and Refining Co.; Lee S. Bickmore, president, National Biscuit Company; David Kennedy, president and chairman of the board, Continental Illinois National Bank; Robert C. Kirkwood, president, F. W. Woolworth Co.; G. Stanley McAllister, vice president, Associated Dry Goods Company and vice president of Lord & Taylor, New York; George H. Mortimer, attorney, Colgate-Palmolive Co.; C. Jay Parkinson, president of the Anaconda Company; William Snow, Jr., vice president, Bankers Trust Company; Robert Sears, vice president, Phillips Petroleum Co.; Isaac M. Stewart, vice president, Union Carbide Co.; Howard Stoddard, chairman, Michigan National Bank, and many many others.

In politics the Mormons have done very well. At this writing there are three United States senators who are members of the Church:

Wallace F. Bennett (R.-Utah), Frank E. Moss (D.-Utah), and Howard W. Cannon (D.-Nev.). There are usually at least a half dozen representatives who are Mormons, and Mormons are sometimes to be found in the President's Cabinet. Ezra Taft Benson has been mentioned before, and Stewart L. Udall served as Secretary of Interior under both Presidents Kennedy and Johnson. Governor George Romney of Michigan has been mentioned as a Republican Presidential nominee.

For all this representation in national life, the Mormons praise first their Church and secondly the relatively easy availability of higher education to their young people. This interest and belief in education is today at an all-time peak. The Mormon Church leadership is completely convinced that the best investment that can be made for the Church is in development of the Mormon young people.

Mormon education naturally starts with the primary grades. In pioneer Utah, most of the teaching was Church-centered in that it was a part of the extremely close Church-home relationship peculiar to the Mormons. But as public schools were established, the Mormons were drawn to them, although they still felt a need for secondary levels, or high schools, since in the last century education at that level was not always common.

The Church thus, in the last quarter of the nineteenth century, and the first decade of the twentieth, established twenty-one academies, most in Utah and the surrounding western states, although there were academies also in Canada and in Mexico.

But with the general expansion after World War I of the United States into the practice of providing a free high school education for all, the Mormons found their academies no longer answered the need, and some were closed and some were converted into junior colleges.

As the earlier primary schools and the academies were supplanted, the Mormons were faced with finding means to supply religious education. Several experiments were tried, such as building a seminary next to the public high school; to this Mormon students could be sent for special religious instruction.

But this plan is practical only in localities where the number of Mormon students is concentrated and large in number. In Southern

California, for example, where Mormon students may be spread over two hundred high schools, it was not feasible.

So, the plan of asking Mormon students to go to their Church for an hour's instruction before their regular school hours was begun. Parents rise at dawn, or before, in many instances, to drive their children to the classes, which in Southern California now include more than 6000 students in three hundred early morning seminaries. Worldwide, the figures are impressive—and more so to parents who have faced the task of getting teen-agers out of bed and off to school. There are now some 2000 such early morning seminaries in the United States and five foreign countries and they serve more than 90,000 students!

Brigham Young University at Provo, Utah, is the largest Church-owned school numbering around 20,000 students. The Church and its individual members have poured tens of millions of dollars into building a new and vastly enlarged campus. Additionally, the university in post World War II days has shown a leadership in adult and extension courses.

The Church has, in the postwar years, also established colleges in Hawaii and New Zealand. Church schools operate in Tonga and Papeete through the high school level, and (as described in Chapter Thirty) have begun interesting efforts in South America.

Applied Resources

Now that we have had a glimpse of the improvements in missionary techniques, a view of the gigantic new building program, and a summary of the expanding and changing education effort, it might be useful to see some of this activity in progress, to see how the resources are being applied. To do that, let us retrace some of the steps of the early Mormon missionaries and consider the changes since 1837.

Chapter Twenty-five

ZION WHERE THEY ARE

It is interesting to retrace the steps of the early missionaries in Britain today and observe the changes a century and a quarter have made. At the same time, one can discern how intelligently the Church has adjusted its appeal and its service to members. For almost a century —until wars and depressions and emigration restrictions and better times in their own countries—it was a driving urge on the part of newly baptized Mormons to "gather in Zion." This suited the economic no less than the spiritual needs of the times. But emigration is no longer easy or possible for many. Zion must be brought to them. Mormon activities and purposes no less than theology are being exported, and this is the key to present growth.[1]

Liverpool was in the midst of a building expansion even when the first missionaries leaped to the quay in 1840, therefore little remains today of that Liverpool. But succeeding generations of emigrants saw, as their last view of England, the old clock tower and the Liver building on the pierhead, and this view is pretty much as it was. Mr. John Alan Cubbon, a prominent baker and confectioner, was, at this writing, bishop of the Church in Liverpool and he has located some of the early centers of Church activity.

This was not done because of his own family's personal involvement with the early days—which is a factor with so many present-day Mormons—but because he has so many American visitors who ask about the buildings their forebears knew or served in. One of these, at 42 Islington Street, served the Church for many years as its principal European office and publishing center. While it still stands, the once handsome three-story red-brick mansion is now converted to commercial uses with a pizza restaurant on the ground floor.

Mr. Cubbon said he was himself an example of the workings of the present-day missionary efforts. Two young Mormons had rung his doorbell only a few days after he and his wife had returned from their honeymoon. The Cubbons had liked the two Americans and in time investigated the religious beliefs they presented, and which the Cubbons had scarcely previously heard about. Ultimately, they joined the Church.

When asked whether he had experienced the same sort of discrimination or loss of business that the early converts complained about, he replied, "Not exactly. Some members of my family were, of course, Church of England and they had a hard time understanding our course of action, but they were not unpleasant about it. My business associates found that I had to give a good deal of time to my Church work, especially after I was made a bishop, because this meant that I had to take care of those in need, visit the sick, be involved in marriages, funerals and the like. It's a busy job, and sometimes took me out of the office. But my associates were quite considerate about it. I certainly could never say there was a religious prejudice."

The Changes

After looking around Liverpool for a while for mementoes of the former days, Mr. Cubbon stopped by a brand new structure, with the usual extra boards and bits and pieces of masonry and other evidence of new construction lying around outside. This was the new chapel, quite similar in design and layout to many that can be seen in Southern California and Utah, a building divided between a fine modern chapel, which would seat perhaps six hundred, and a large recreation hall, not unlike the gymnasium that one might find in countless American schools. Even the basketball backstops were ready to be lowered for a game. There was a stage across one end, and nearby was a kitchen. This was to serve as a community center and it was clear the Mormons hoped to attract some of the young folks who otherwise spend their time downtown in dingy Liverpool cellars listening to the Beatles and their successors.

This new building illustrated the change in status of Liverpool. The city is no longer the staging area for emigrants. Those who do go to the New World these days rarely go through Liverpool. Other ports, and especially airports, have taken over that role. So Liverpool today is just another growing center of Church people who are building where they are.

This was the story in Preston, too, remembered in Mormon literature as the first center for Mormon activity in England. The old house in which Heber C. Kimball and one or two other of the first missionaries lived in Preston still stands, though almost derelict. The Cockpit, where once the early missionaries conducted their services, has long since been torn down. All that remains is a cement walk, perhaps twelve feet square, flanked by two park benches. On a nearby brick wall is a bronze sign that notes that "the building known as The Cockpit once stood here and that here it was that the total abstinence pledge was first taken."

Vauxhall Chapel is gone too. But the spot on the edge of the Ribble River, under the old bridge, where the first baptisms were performed, remains.

Ronald Hughes, president of the Church in Preston at the time of my visit pointed out the quiet eddy where tradition says the baptisms took place. Preston contributed its full share to the migration and for some years in the latter part of the nineteenth century and the early part of the twentieth, there was little Mormon activity in the town. But today, a city of approximately 150,000, it boasts a large chapel, built in 1951 and already outgrown. Mr. Hughes reported that membership grew from forty to 260 between 1960 and 1965, and he has strong hopes for a new building. When asked if old oppositions had disappeared, he said he thought so, although he pointed out a bronze marker on the chapel, intended for placement at the baptismal scene on the river, and he said that the city authorities had thus far refused permission for its erection.

Manchester

Activity in Britain in these times is so extensive that it has led to the division of the country into eight missions, each with its own president and missionary complement. One of the largest, and one that perhaps best typifies the way things are arranged, is the North British Mission, which includes the area where the first Mormon missionaries worked. It was headquartered for some time in a fine old mansion in an upper-class suburb of Manchester. The house is known at the post office as The Orchard, and the address is simply *The* Avenue. It has three acres of beautifully landscaped grounds and the building, of solid brick and timbered in the old English style, comfortably houses the twenty-one Mormons living there. During World War II it served as the seat of government-in-exile for one of the Baltic countries and one could only guess at the plots and intrigues its walls contained in those years. But today it has been completely renovated in the best of British-American style: British one might say in the pleasantly elegant Edwardian decor, American in the highly efficient oil furnace and comfortable baseboard radiators installed, along with the latest, and obviously costly, ceramic and chrome bathrooms.

The chief of this Mission—due shortly to be relieved when I visited him—was Rolland L. Jaussi. In private life he is a successful building contractor and construction man from Idaho. Like other Mission presidents around the globe, he was called from his business and asked to devote three years as a nonpaid chief in his assigned area.

Typical of the occupants of The Orchard at this time was Richard S. Rassmuson of Salt Lake City. He had been working in the Manchester area for nearly two years, and while looking forward to his return home and resumption of college, he would always have a second country in England and a second home in Manchester. He showed off the new Manchester Stake House—a "stake" serving the area—where Brother Beard, "first name Harry," was operating an electric floor waxer over the asphalt tiles. The building had been completed in the autumn of 1964, and followed the pattern of most new stake buildings, except that perhaps its chapel was larger than most, its recreation hall equal to that found in a new high school of moderate size in the United States, and its parking lot unusually big for Britain. This was obviously a prosperous congregation in a suburban area where many drove to church in their own cars. In design, size, and accommodations it was much after the modern American Church style in its soft colors and plain carpets, its laminated wood beams and arches, its acoustical ceilings and its central heating.

One feature Mr. Beard insisted on demonstrating was the baptismal font, a tiled pool, rather like an oversized sunken bathtub, with heated water. No more baptisms in the frigid rivers and lakes for the modern Saints!

When this was mentioned to President Jaussi he laughed and said that he wasn't in favor of chilling the fervor of converts under any circumstance. "When you look at the River Ribble in February and read how Heber Kimball, Wilford Woodruff and the others used to break the ice and go into the water several times a day with people who were eager, even standing in line in the cold for their turn to be baptized, you can only wonder at the saintly strength of those people. However, we do find people today of comparable faith."

He presented one such person, William Bates, president of a Manchester group. Mr. Bates has about the same rather heavily muscled stature, and some of the same homespun engaging personality that one associates with Brigham Young. Where Young was a carpenter, Bates is an engineer, with the strong, rough grip of a man who can use his hands.

Mr. Bates' Story

He related his story:

"In the Army during the war, I used to pray. You can bet there were plenty of times when we all did. But I did not identify my prayers with any particular church or set of beliefs. I just knew there was a God.

"After the war there was a tremendous rebuilding job to be done. Immense bomb damage, you know, and a vast housing shortage on top of it, due to increase of population and very little building for many years or during the depression, before the war, everybody doubled up, few new houses or flats. Out of my earnings I saved up $1000 and decided to start my own engineering or plumbing business, and such was the opportunity that I soon decided to go all the way, beg and borrow all I could and build a works to cost about $30,000.

"Of course I went out every day to see how it was progressing and I had to drive past a place where they were putting up a small chapel, or meeting house. LDS—Latter-day Saints—it said on a sign. What in the world is that, I thought.

"But it was evidently some sort of church and each day as I drove past I wondered whether they were meeting the same problems I was. Building in postwar England was not easy. Everything, including labor, was short. Since my plant and the chapel were proceeding at about the same pace, I decided that when both were complete I would stop in and say a prayer of thanksgiving."

He kept this promise and his visit to the chapel led to his meeting some of the local Mormon people and to his ultimately being baptized in 1951. During his period of investigation he had visited some of the other LDS groups and, generally, had found them very poorly housed. "Most were just in rented rooms, musty and uninspiring, to say the least."

A few years later, Mr. Bates took his family to New York, bought a new station wagon and made a 10,000 mile tour of the United States, mostly to look at Mormon church buildings. When he finally arrived in Salt Lake City, he saw Henry D. Moyle, then a member of the First Presidency. This led to his introduction to President David O. McKay.

"I found President McKay agreeing with my estimate. I said that there were two hundred buildings in Salt Lake City alone that were more beautiful and useful than anything we had in England. President McKay said that I must have been sent to him through divine means since he was at that very moment looking over proposed plans for a new chapel in London, the Hyde Park Chapel."

A Healing

Since that time the Church has set in motion its major building program. But so far as Mr. Bates is concerned, the Manchester Stake House will always have special relevance. He and his son, a lad of twelve, did volunteer work, and one day a heavy beam fell on the boy breaking his back in two places. He was taken to the hospital where the first question was whether he would live and the second whether he would ever walk again. The Manchester Stake observed a day of prayer and fasting. Elder Mark Petersen came down from London and laid his hands on the boy and blessed him. It is felt in Manchester that a miracle resulted. In any case, the young Bates certainly walks and runs today with the best of them.

When asked whether the fact that he had joined the Mormon Church had affected his business, Mr. Bates said:

"If it has affected it, it has been constructively. I believe that our Church teachings about honesty and full value carries itself to customers. In any case, the business that I started with $3000 and expanded into a $30,000 plant I recently sold for $800,000, and now I have a considerable brick business, so I can't say I have been discriminated against."

President Jaussi showed his office. One wall was lined with photographs of young men, part of the 1200 American missionaries in the field in Britain. Some of the names included Bertram S. Dalton, Richard Miller, Robert Glen Openshaw, Douglas R. Jensen, George Brooks, and William T. Evans.

One might suppose that because the missionaries are mostly young men of college age they reach mostly that age group in their missionary work.

"That used to be more true than it is now," President Jaussi said. "Indeed, just a few years before I came to this mission the effort was almost wholly focused on young people. The missionaries formed baseball teams (yes, they found baseball fairly popular in England), basketball and other activities for the teen and college age groups. But, quite naturally I suppose, we found many of these people had more interest in games than in church. They were getting the shadow and not the substance. So today we seek out more the young married families. This is not yet completely successful, but to give you an idea, last year we baptized 219 family groups, which is to say husband and wife and children above eight years. The actual number in this group was something short of nine hundred. Then, we baptized 376 couples, that is man and wife who have no children, or at least none over eight years in age. In addition, there were 848 adult men and 1239 adult women. There were only 181 of the sixteen to eighteen group. A few years ago I think you would have found that this sixteen to eighteen group was by far the largest. So you can see what we are trying to do."

"Do you still find a strong urge among your members to emigrate to the United States, to Utah specifically?"

"Yes, there is that desire. Of course we can no longer offer Church assistance, as we did through the Emigration Fund of Brigham Young's time, and we do all we can to encourage the strengthening of the Church community here. Nevertheless, some of our members, perhaps the most active and dedicated, find in themselves a desire to be part of a larger Mormon community. Possibly we lose a dozen families a year. I believe, however, that this is a diminishing thing and will diminish further as the new buildings are completed. These provide a center for expanding Church work and activity and brings together a larger number of people enjoying like interests. You will find as you go around that these new buildings play an intelligently conceived and central part in our new-style activities."

Chapter Twenty-six

THE LEGACY OF DAN JONES IN WALES

"Meet me at the Park Hotel at noon," came the soft Welsh voice over the telephone, "the airport car will know it well, in the very center of Cardiff."

Emlyn Davies, a delightful, rotund (or robust would be the better word) gentleman who had volunteered to retrace the steps of Captain Dan Jones in Wales said, "This is my first automobile, really the first my family has owned as times did not permit it before, so hold on, I'm a new driver!" And off we zipped up one of the famous Welsh valleys to his home at Merthyr Tydfil.

"The name of Dan Jones is familiar hereabouts?"

"One of the most beloved. But it was not he who brought first the Mormon teachings to Wales. That was done a few years earlier by some American missionaries from Liverpool or Manchester, I forget which, but Jones it was who really made the Church a living force in Wales, and more so I should say in Utah, though I have no personal knowledge having never been there, but I judge from what I am told by the many Americans who visit here. They speak of the Welsh in Utah."

Wales offered an especially promising land for the restored religion, since many of the Welsh had really never completely accepted any other Church teachings. In earliest times, of course, they had developed their own religious beliefs, symbolized by the many round church yards still to be found. The Romans had introduced Christianity but mostly it was absorbed into their own rites and worship. The Irish had brought Catholicism and it had its centers. The Church of England became official, but by the early nineteenth century, when Dan Jones came back here to his homeland from Nauvoo, there were more congregations of Baptists and Methodists, especially Methodists, than there were of the so-called Established Church.

"It's spelled D A V I E S, but in Welsh it's pronounced D A V I S."

On this side of the road are many houses which I am positive stood when Dan Jones was here. Merthyr was his home place and his headquarters.

"But you must understand that it was a long time ago. By the time Brigham Young had his first summer's wagon trains en route across the Plains, which is to say early spring 1846, Dan Jones was able to report to a Church conference in Manchester that the Welsh District consisted of twenty-eight branches and 687 members. Think of it!"[1]

New Era in Wales

"This house we are going to is on this little hilly street, and it has a plaque on it, which, as you can see, names it the birthplace of Jennette Evelyn Evans McKay. She was the mother of our beloved David O. McKay, President of the Latter-day Saints Church, and she left here for Utah as a little girl. The lady of the house, there, she knows President McKay. He has visited here when he was in Wales.

"Some of the Davies family emigrated, but my own forebears obviously did not. I have seen figures which indicated that the largest numbers went over in the ten years 1850 to 1860, but there seemed to be a steady flow of at least several hundred a year right up until World War I, when it all ceased. It never really regained momentum. I think the United States rather clamped down on people coming in. And times here grew just too poor for people to save the wherewithal to emigrate, and perhaps Salt Lake was not so encouraging. The records show we had only forty-six members in 1930. Then, we had World War II, which was quite bad for us.

"After the war we were visited from time to time by the Church people from overseas, but we had a very poorly group. We met in an old house that I can show you, not very proper, and while our faith was strong, we really had few works. The Church was a withering affair.

"Then, a few years after the war, maybe about 1950 to '52, we began to get a new sort of missionary. These were young Americans but grandsons, maybe great grandsons, of some of the old families that emigrated. Naturally, they had the keenest interest in old Wales. They began to visit up and down the valleys, no fancy cars or clothes, just trudging along, stopping by for a chat here and there.

"And one day we were told that we really needed a new chapel, true without denying, and that if we would all pitch in and work the way would open. Well, now, let me show you!"

We stopped in front of a bright and, compared with any other building in sight, a spanking new chapel, which Brother Davies showed off with evident pride. The chapel part of the building was finished in a light gray with natural oak, and a fine electric organ bore a plate noting that it had been contributed by a group of businessmen in Salt Lake City as a mark of esteem to the mother of President McKay.

Activity for All

The recreation hall was obviously much used. On stage was a setting which indicated that *Cinderella* was being played. A beautiful one-dimensional coach with tiny electric lights bulbs outlining it, leaned against a wall.

"Formerly the lights were on my Christmas tree," laughed Davies, "but take a look at the costumes. A room was filled with them. We can put on all sorts of plays and have the accouterments right at hand." Young people kept coming in and out, the young ladies obeying a hand-lettered sign pleading against the wearing of spike heels on the asphalt-tiled floor.

Some ladies were working in a small kitchen, while in another room the sounds of piano practice could be heard, keeping accompaniment to the whirr of a sewing machine. Clearly this was the center for busy community activity.

"We've never had anything like it before," confessed Davies, obviously tremendously pleased with the new upturn in LDS affairs in Merthyr. "We now have 294 members and I think a great many more will come in as a result of participating in our activities. Several hundred come to see one of our dramatic shows, and they become acquainted, and thus 'tis our group plays a useful and more important part in the community. It brings them into contact with our gospel teachings at least in a more friendly mood than Dan Jones found, and many are happy to find that they do not need to remove to Zion to be a Saint. They can be Saints in Merthyr, as they are glad to learn, though I suppose a good many would welcome the chance, still, to emigrate. Nowadays, you know, you must have a sponsor and a job and endless sorts of things."

Chapter Twenty-seven

A DAY IN LONDON

Inevitably London is today the center for much Mormon activity in Britain. The new temple, dedicated in 1958, is at Lingfield, just south of London, and the temple is of course the headquarters for the higher religious teaching. It is a trim structure, nicely adapted to the Anglican countryside, and was built under the direction of Sir Thomas Bennett, the noted architect who serves the Church as a consultant on building throughout Britain. The working offices, however, from which the missionary effort proceeds in the London area are on Exhibition Road, near Prince's Gate, Hyde Park.

There is located the London Chapel, dedicated in 1961. Built of Portland stone, with a tapering, needlelike spire reaching 131 feet high, the chapel is already a London landmark. When it was opened, the chapel attracted comment partly due to the fact that it incorporates an underground garage. Other features noted by the press include basketball backboards that disappear into the ceiling at the push of a button. On a mezzanine overlooking the chapel is a soundproofed room, twenty-five by thirteen feet, with a glass window looking out over the chapel. This is for restless infants who might otherwise disturb the services. On the first floor there are nine classrooms and a separate children's chapel. Nearby, on Exhibition Road, is one of the grand residences of Old London restored to house the head of the London Mission and serve as headquarters for his staff of missionaries. The work is carefully ordered. Where alternative methods for turning up prospects—or "investigators," as the missionaries call them—old-fashioned tracking is resorted to, but it is methodical. Maps are laid out and certain streets are assigned a two-member team. Such a team can ring about eighty doorbells in a three-hour morning session. That is a respectable number of rings.

One of the missionaries explains that he is from America, that he represents The Church of Jesus Christ of Latter-day Saints, known as the "Mormon Church," and that he would like an opportunity simply to tell something about his Church so that there will be a wider understanding and less tendency on the part of people to believe nonsense.

All that is sought is an opportunity to set forth the facts and answer any questions. If the person at the door evinces polite interest, and of course some do simply out of courtesy to two pleasant young strangers from over the seas, the missionary will say that he and his companion would like to call back at some convenient hour. They have some pictures to show, and they would be very glad to have other members of the family, and friends, invited in. About two of those granting the preliminary interview will let the young men return.[1]

Mr. "R."

It is impossible to label any one such return call typical, but an example was furnished recently by a call on a Mr. R., residing in a new block of flats near Marble Arch. While most such return calls are made in the evening, Mr. R. worked at night and preferred that the call be made in the early afternoon. When the missionaries arrived, it developed that Mr. R's wife worked during the day, so they alternated in caring for their twenty-month-old boy and it was clear that if there was a disciplinarian in the home, it wasn't the father; the little boy promptly got into the picture book the missionaries had brought and a certain amount of banana began to appear on the color plates.

Mr. R. began by stating very candidly that he was a Jew, but that he had noticed the activity around the chapel on Exhibition Road, especially observing that children seemed to be given much attention, and he had thought it might be something of value to his son, and that was the reason he had invited them to return. The missionaries quickly took the lead and brought out of a large brief-case and spiral-bound flip book. Its first picture was of President David O. McKay, and then followed illustrations of a typical church, a typical Mormon family, and a presentation of typical Mormon family activities. All this before any mention of the Prophet Joseph Smith, or Church history.

They knew Mr. R. was interested, not in the past but in the living present, particularly as it affected his family. Some of the activities of the Exhibition Road chapel were explained: the plays, the social hours, the meetings of mothers to exchange ideas on the proper raising of children, the sports for the younger people, "and," said one of the Missionaries, "we place a special emphasis on 'family night.'"

"And what is that?"

"One night a week it is suggested that each family plan on staying at home together. Let us say that it is Thursday night, though of course selection of the night is a family affair. Mother will plan an especially nice dinner. Then the family will play games, or maybe just talk. Father is encouraged to discuss his business with the family, so the family can share in his ups and downs and understand why the purchase of some things must be deferred, and why he is sometimes a little upset and grumpy. And if they pray together for a proper working out, they all have a sense of sharing when the good unfolds."

It was easy to see that the missionaries were hurrying to present the spiritual aspects of their religion. It is a fact that many of those with whom they talk express interest in such things as "family night," but to the missionaries such activities are but trifles when compared with the theological message they wish to convey. Possibly because the extraordinary "busy-ness" of Mormons with Church affairs is so familiar to them, and has been all their lives, they cannot see why those who haven't had this sort of experience are so interested in it. Of course, they may feel that nobody is likely to leave a lifetime church association simply to participate in amateur dramatics, or church suppers, and they are probably right, but there is no doubt that in Britain, and many other places, these temporal activities do arouse interest.

Present Revelations

After relating, with the help of their pictures, the story of Joseph Smith, one of the missionaries said something to the effect that "our Church has in the present time revelation from God, and it is the only Church that now has it."

Mr. R. broke in quickly. "On what authority do you say that your Church is the only one having divine authority?"

"Our Church is the only one, to the best of my knowledge, that even claims to be under continuing revelation *in the present time*. Many others claim to have had revelation in the past, but we assert that our Prophet, Seer, and Revelator, who is the same David O. McKay whose picture I showed you a moment ago, is receiving revelations from God as to Church affairs continuously, now, in the present time."

"But many people feel they are under God's guidance at the present time," protested Mr. R.

"Yes, but they believe that in one way or another God's will is made known to them, by revelation to the individual," responded one of the missionaries. "While we are speaking of revelation as affecting an entire Church, the revelation, we believe, comes only—at this time—to our Church, through its Prophet. We believe that Jesus established his Church on earth but that over a period of centuries his teachings were, shall we say, distorted, or at any rate the essential clarity was lost in what amounted to a great apostasy, or abandonment of Christ's true teachings. We believe that in our present time, through the means of Joseph Smith, that the true Church has been restored. Now, sir, may I ask, what is your view of Jesus Christ?"

Eighty Doorbells

Plainly taken aback by the directness of this question, Mr. R. pondered for a moment, and then replied, "Why, I've never thought much about it. I suppose that I believe that he was a very good man, and that he influenced the course of history immensely, though it is often said that few really and truly and fully follow his teachings. As to his birth, which so much is made of, I suppose it is possible that his parents were pure, as they say, but I am not prepared to go further. Let us say that in my view he was one of history's truly good men."

The conversation seesawed back and forth for a few more minutes with it left that Mr. R. would talk with his wife and find out whether they both couldn't come to the Exhibition Road chapel the following Sunday, bringing the baby with them, to meet some of the London Mormons and see something of the chapel building.

Thus, on a certain spring day, two young gentlemen, one from Utah, the other from California, rang eighty London doorbells, saw fifty Londoners, mostly housewives, some of them surly, talked with five briefly, and with one at greater length who might soon visit the chapel, and at least gave respectful and responsive attention to a thoughtful presentation. The missionaries counted it a good day's work.

Chapter Twenty-eight

SCANDINAVIA TODAY

Norway

Early in February 1965 a Mormon chapel was dedicated in Trondheim, Norway, some two hundred miles below the Arctic Circle and historically the farthest north of all the LDS churches. Except perhaps for an oversize furnace, the chapel design resembles the new ones we have seen in England, Wales, or even Utah.

It is a solid red-brick building of modern design with a contemporary steeple. It is ruggedly built for the rugged climate, but as usual with Mormon buildings, the distinguishing features are mostly inside.

There is the more or less conventional chapel area for services; there is the adjacent larger area for meetings, dances, games, dramatics; there is the kitchen equipped to serve up everything from smorgasbord to banquets. All this is a wonder to the good Mormons and others of Trondheim, but of even greater wonder to them is the fact that this benefaction came to them after more than a century of faithful, even though at times dispirited, meetings in a series of nondescript halls.

Although Norway was one of the first places to be visited by the missionaries who left Salt Lake City in 1849, progress of the Church was quite slow. There was the early period of hard opposition, described in Chapter Fourteen, followed by the exciting years of the "Great Emigration" when many Norwegians left for Utah. Nevertheless, the Church did not greatly prosper within Norway.

It was not that there was a lack of faith. At the Trondheim dedication it was remembered that a century before a Norwegian shoemaker placed Mormon tracts in every pair of shoes he repaired. One such pair was delivered to a widow, Anna Widtsoe, who subsequently joined the Church and with an infant son emigrated to Utah.[1] The son, John A. Widtsoe, later returned as a missionary, and in time, after a notable career as an educator which brought him to the presidency of two colleges, he became an apostle of the Church.

But even though such stories abound, the fact remains that it wasn't until the 1950s and 1960s when the new church building program came to Norway and offered new and purposeful centers for enlarged activities that interest in Mormonism was rekindled. Thus the effects of the surgent ideas of twentieth-century Mormonism began to reach as far as the Arctic Circle and the new chapel was projected for Trondheim.

A new building is under way in the Norwegian capitol, Oslo, the principal center for Norwegian Mormons; other cities are also on the list for future building. Throughout Norway there is a lifting sense of fresh activity.

Sweden

This lift among the Mormons is of interest, and is being commented on all over Scandinavia, for you are told that it runs against the common experience and, indeed, the common expectation. On almost all sides the inquiring visitor to Scandinavia, and particularly to Sweden, is told that very few people attend church these days. One estimate frequently heard is that 90 percent *do not* go to church.

And when it is asked whether this means that 10 percent *do* attend, the usual answer is that perhaps 10 percent of the people in the country do go to church but in a city such as Stockholm it is questioned whether as many as 4 percent attend regularly. It is pointed out, and casual observation supports the point, that many of the finest old churches are today hardly anything more than religious museums.

There is much public soul-searching about this in Scandinavia. Churchmen as well as laymen talk about it. They speculate on why it is that a country which has apparently found a way to balance out living at a high standard with a remarkable level of security for all, and with a record for preserving peace that is equalled in few other places, should have such a low degree of interest in religious experience. One remarks that simple gratitude would invoke other-wise.

The answers come in a multitude of ways. Some will point out that "religious experience" and "church-going" are not identical terms to Swedes. They will say that in some lands, and they include the United States, church-going is often not so much a religious experi-ence as it is a social activity.

Others are less defensive. They say that for a variety of reasons church-going has lost its meaning and appeal. "I will tell you why people do not attend church," said one Swede. "It is because the church is always answering questions that nobody is asking. They drone on in old words and outmoded texts. Now, when you step away from the question of mere sitting in a church and ask, 'Are the people really religious?' I have to answer, 'Yes, they are. They be-lieve in a power outside themselves, and they ponder the nature of that power, which they term God. They are not in the least above discussing their problems privately with pastors and if you counted up the work done by the pastors outside their pulpits, I believe you would find there is a great deal of religious activity, perhaps as much as ever. It is not just church-centered.'"

There is evidence to support this view—and some against it. Against it is a recent Gallup Poll in which some 53 percent of those questioned forecast a declining role for church. Only 23 percent felt the church would grow in importance; 24 percent had no opinion.[2]

On the pro side of the continued importance of churches, one has to consider that almost 90 percent of all Swedish babies are still baptized, that 91 percent of all marriages are performed in church. This point about marriages may be more important than at first appears, because in the modern Swedish drive for what they term "sexual liberation" emphasis on marriage in the old sense has a some-what different aspect.

Part of this is attributed by the Swedes to the desperate housing shortage that existed after World War II. Young couples twenty years after the war must get on lists for apartments or houses and in recent times the waiting period has sometimes extended five or six years.

The de-emphasis on formal marriage is illustrated in the larger Swedish newspapers, which refer to all women more than twenty years old as "Mrs." whether or not they are married. The term

"Mrs." simply signifies adulthood. The papers said they adopted this policy because they do not take similar note of whether a man is married or not. He is simply "Mr.," regardless. Although they do not say it, the newspapers may also have been affected by the problem of legitimacy of children. A point is made in modern Sweden of not condemning children born out of wedlock.

Yet despite all this indication, at least surface indication, of a new viewpoint, the fact remains that marriages are performed and most of them are performed in churches. Indeed, the vital records of most Swedish communities are kept by the churches. So no prejudice against the churches on that score can be said to exist.

And against the general tide running against a church-centered religious experience is the present Mormon saga. For the resurgence in Mormon activity in Scandinavia is distinctly, and distinctively, church-centered, just as we have observed it in Britain and elsewhere. Nearly a dozen chapels like the one in Trondheim exist, or are rising, in as many Scandinavian towns, and each draws and sustains its support not only by its religious teachings but also very markedly by the variety and commitment of its church-centered activities.

Denmark

As in the earliest missionary days, Denmark continues to be the most rewarding field for Mormon activity in Scandinavia and indeed the center for much of it. And this activity, while started in 1880, is lately of expanding dimensions.

In 1955, for example, at the time of the choir tour, when a concert for 25,000 people was given in the delightful Tivoli Gardens, there were but twelve missionaries in all of Denmark. As late as 1960 baptisms of new members were running between three hundred and four hundred a year.

Today, the number of missionaries ranges up to 185 and baptisms are approaching 4000 annually. Six new chapels are under construction. Frederick C. Sorenson, a mission president, drove to one now under construction in the Soborg section of Copenhagen.

On the way over, he related a story which, except in detail, could be heard from mission presidents in any part of the world. He had been engaged in selling agricultural machinery in Idaho and one evening arrived at a motel to spend the night. Awaiting him was a message asking him to phone Church headquarters in Salt Lake City. It was an invitation to come and talk with one of the top Church officials.

Mr. Sorenson's great-great-grandfather had been converted to Mormonism by Erastus Snow, the first mission president to Denmark. This fact had not been lost upon those who consider the appointment of mission presidents. Mr. Sorenson himself had served as a missionary in the Danish field.

The Church authorities knew that he was a dedicated member, as was his wife. They knew the children were grown and that a couple of years abroad would not destroy his business career. Indeed, he was employed by a firm owned by Church members. Within a month Mr. and Mrs. Sorenson were on their way; he to supervise the missionaries assigned to him, she to act as house mother and confidante to young people in the mission headquarters. As is the usual case in the missions, they found a lovely, large, beautifully furnished, and well-ordered mission home awaiting them. They could pick up from their predecessors and carry on without a pause.

When we arrived at the chapel it was just in the foundation stage of construction. A missionary from Nevada was checking the footings and remarked that building supervision was not difficult in Denmark, where conscientious workers take pride in what they do. The cost of this new building is estimated at $500,000. It will supplement a chapel built in the 1930s which lacked some of the facilities for teaching sports and for entertainment now found to be necessary.

Chapter Twenty-nine

A NEW "IMAGE" IN WESTERN EUROPE

Although the Nazis permitted church services, their ban on any such activities as youth meetings and church sociables were complete. So it was that, with the end of the war in 1945 and the start of the Occupation, freedom really began to come to the Mormons in that broad band extending from the Swiss border up to the occupied portions of the Lowlands and Scandinavia.

The interest of the authorities in Salt Lake City in sending relief supplies, and the interest of Mormon servicemen in the Occupation brought new hope and stability to members of a Church that had been regarded more or less as an enemy of the state for most of the previous century. And of course they are still viewed as enemies in East Germany and the Communist bloc.

Actually, it wasn't until 1955 that The Church of Jesus Christ of Latter-day Saints became legally recognized in Austria. At that time in Salzburg there were about fourteen local Mormons and perhaps as many more United States servicemen of the faith. The servicemen started a collection which soon mounted to $10,000. This was matched by the Church in Salt Lake City and a year later, 1956, the first LDS Church building in Austria was an accomplished fact, a three-story structure with meeting hall to accommodate 150 people, at a cost of $60,000.[1]

A certain prestige was given their cause and an elevation, no doubt, in the official mind, when Ezra Taft Benson was assigned to the West European Mission as mission president.

Very shortly the Mormons found they needed to have a building program. Each building project, of course, represents a church group large enough in fact or in potential to require a substantial center for the program of activities we have seen underway elsewhere in the world. From a handful at the close of World War II, Church membership among the German-speaking peoples has risen above 44,000. These are spread over 420 congregations, the largest single one of which is in Zurich, Switzerland.

American missionaries working in this west European field number 1100. Among the devices they use to interest prospective members is a film-strip machine. It is portable, easily set up in a living room with sound and pictures synchronized in a portable projector. The pictures and the sound track for this were worked out and produced in their own audio-visual laboratory and library. The latest in recorders, projectors, and editing devices are available.

Motion pictures and other materials are received from Salt Lake City and are kept here in shipping cases for immediate dispatch to missionaries requesting them in Switzerland, Austria—wherever German is spoken. This also serves as a distribution center for the missions in Holland, Denmark, Norway, Sweden, and Finland, with audio-visual materials in appropriate languages.

An Audio-visual Evening

On a typical evening two missionaries from Utah will take a film-strip machine around to the home of a German member of the Church. One of the two young men will speak pretty fair German. He has been in the country two years and has been living with a German family. The background of German which he had gained in two years at Brigham Young University speeded the process.

The second young missionary had just arrived in Frankfurt. His German is rough, but the guests invited to the affair were pleased and flattered by the effort the Americans had made to learn their language. They were eager to correct mistakes in grammar and punctuation. A few slips were great icebreakers.

The evening started off like most German parties in the home, with a sampling of a few cookies, a look at the new television set, and the older folks going off upstairs when it was announced that the young Americans had some picture slides to show their young friends. The screen was put up on its stand, the projector placed on a piano bench, and the lights were dimmed.

If the guests expected scenes of America and Utah, they were disappointed, for the opening picture was of the temple in Berne. The commentary with the picture said that the Mormon Church had a long history in Germany, going back to 1841 when Orson Hyde sailed up through the Rhineland and docked at Mainz. "He prepared literature to tell the people about the Mormons."

Ten years later, Elder John Taylor began publication of *Zion's Panier,* a publication in the German language. Then the pictures which had shown a drawing of Hyde and a facsimile of the *Panier* changed to show police arresting Mormon missionaries. Nevertheless, in 1852 John Taylor succeeded in having the German translation of the Book of Mormon published and the book gained wide circulation. A picture of the first edition of the Book of Mormon in German appears on the screen.

Next on the screen comes the picture of a young German professor. "Among the prominent converts to the Church during the early missionary days in Germany," says the voice, "was Dr. Karl G. Maeser, a well-known educator in Dresden. In 1855 Maeser heard about the Mormons and requested missionaries to come to his home and tell him more."

Another picture of Maeser appears and the voice continues, "At the time Maeser was a director of the Budich Institute in Neustadt, Dresden, and one of Saxony's most respected educators . . . a cultured and refined gentleman of the upper class."

The picture now changes to one of Maeser with two friends looking at a pamphlet. "Maeser and two other learned professors, Edward Schoenfeld and Edward Martin, invited the Mormon missionaries to Dresden, and fully expected to expose error and weakness in the doctrines they would present."

The picture now shows the three Germans with expressions of evident surprise. "But the simple message brought by an unschooled missionary, who could speak only a few words in German, made a deeper impression on the minds of the young professors than all the religious teachings and philosophies of their previous profound studies."

The picture shifts to a painting of the Germans and the missionaries with their hands on a table laden with books and literature. "After thoroughly investigating the Mormon teachings for several weeks, Maeser, his wife, two friends and others of their families declared they *knew* Mormonism to be true and requested baptism."

The next picture is a photo of a spot on the River Elbe. "The sacred ordinance was performed on October 14, 1855, in the Elbe River. So convinced was Maeser of the truth of the Church he had just joined that he pledged to support it all the days of his life, and, if necessary, even to give his life to its cause."

Maeser is then shown in a pioneer school, a log cabin with home-made furniture. "He could have remained in Germany and been assured of high position in his native society, but he chose to serve the Lord at the sacrifice of material rewards. In later life—as an educator in Utah—he said, 'Every one of us, sooner or later, must stand at the forks of the road and choose between personal interest and some principle of right.'"

The next pictures are of early schools in Utah, followed by modern views of Brigham Young University. "In Utah, Maeser pioneered an educational system among the Mormons that has endured to this day. As a result of his efforts Brigham Young Academy was founded in 1876. From this institution grew the Brigham Young University, now the largest church university in America. . . ."

Happy Mormons

The strip asks what it was in Mormonism that appealed to Maeser and then tells the Joseph Smith story, the persecutions, the martyr-dom, the trek across the plains and the mountains. Heavy emphasis is placed on the contribution that German-speaking people, like Maeser, have made to the establishment of the Church.

As a picture shows a throng of Mormons, obviously happy, the speaker says, "The forward-looking teachings and programs in the Church inspire German-speaking Mormons, like Latter-day Saints everywhere, to lead prayerful, purposeful, fruitful lives. Mormons are happy people, full of vitality, and sure of the faith which has brought them this happiness. In addition to Sunday worship services, they participate in a full round of character-building week-day Church-sponsored activities."

There is a picture of a dramatic production, followed quickly by a picture of group dancing, an orchestra, Boy Scouts, and children at play. The voice explains that the Church has activities for all ages, and that Mormons have a special interest in children "for they are the hope of the future."

The following picture is of a group of radiant-faced women. "These women are officers in a local Relief Society, which is one of the oldest women's organizations of its kind in the world. Among other duties, members of the Women's Relief Society help their bishop look after the everyday needs of church members in times of sickness, bereavement, or other misfortunes."

Then comes a photo of a new chapel and the explanation. "Mormons are builders . . . as their membership grows, scores of new church and cultural halls are being built in central Europe by the Latter-day Saints. Although most of the funds for the building construction come from Church headquarters in the United States, local members provide contributions of their own mostly in the form of time and by using their construction skills."

Then follows the story of church building around the world. Although the manner of the missionaries is quietly restrained, it is clear to those familiar with the commercial use of such machines that here we have an example of the "hard sell," the association of past and present greatness, the presentation of an exciting new way of life, a hint of help in case of need, and the promise of good companionship and fellowship in seeking after what are really the important things of life.

When interested people later learn of the larger Mormon beliefs concerning life both before and after death and the continuity of families, the appeal proves to be quite strong indeed. Denominations which sometimes think they should emulate the Mormons in their successful application of these missionary methods will have to face up to the fact that the Mormons do not go about it in any easy or offhand way; instead it comes close to being a model of professionalism in its application.

This thoughtful presentation of the Mormon story to younger people is duplicated in the careful way in which editors, officials, and others in authority are dealt with. In the mission president's home is kept a "very important person," or VIP, card file.

One such card not of a real person, of course, might read:

ALEXANDER, DR. JOHANN
Editor, Religious articles, Zeitung
Office: Universitasplatz 8 a. Second Floor
      Telephone: 35 87 94
Home: Wolfgartenweg 16
      Telephone 22 57 87

Dr. Alexander is regarded as a leading lay writer on religious subjects. Apostle Benson has called on him and he has visited the mission home for lunch. He has been given a copy of the Book of Mormon, and is friendly but requires frequent contacts to keep him informed of our work.

These cards are kept in alphabetical order and are cross-indexed. Missionaries are expected to keep the file refreshed with new names and data. Periodic review is made to see that contacts are kept alive and vital. While the Mormons are not large enough in number to represent a strong political force, they have succeeded in the past few years in making their presence known and felt, and respected. It is doubtful whether political or church leaders could as easily rule them off the course as they did half a century and more ago.

Prayerful Public Relations

As a part of their work, the missionaries are expected to read the newspapers of the localities in which they are stationed. References to the Mormons are clipped and sent to mission headquarters. Unlike some denominations that seek out errors and try to read defamations into even the most innocent of mentions, the Mormons take the trouble to analyze what has appeared in a given publication before, then they consult the file to see if they have any friends on the staff of the publication.

When they finally approach the paper, it is with solid homework behind them, and the request is seldom for a correction but for consideration of a constructive and, they believe, newsworthy story which they hope the editor will write about. This interest and care and good judgment have won many friends among the press of western Europe, a press that until very recent years was inclined to think and write about the Mormons chiefly in terms of amusement, or even derision. The Mormons who endured so much of this sort of thing are sometimes finding it hard to believe in the changing atmosphere, but to non-Mormon inquirers, editors agree that it has changed.

Several of the West German radio stations carry tapes of the Tabernacle Choir, supplied to them by the United States Information Agency, which finds the choir an eagerly sought cultural attraction. The choir's rendition of *"The Battle Hymn of the Republic"* is popular in Europe, as it is in America. The choir is also featured from time to time in films and tapes shown over European television stations.

While the public relations work is done by volunteers, a high standard is set by the mission president. Noting that good contacts are a help, he suggests that common sense, honesty, and efficiency in information work are far more important. The guide given the Mormon information coordinators:

This philosophy is applicable to the whole range of information activities in the missions. It is good to know important people, but far more important to do top-quality work. A single bit of poorly done work can undo all the good done by several well-prepared projects. We need, therefore, to avoid sending out press releases or calling press conferences when there is no news, making use of sloppy and unappealing displays, and giving carelessly prepared slide lectures—in short, anything that is less than excellent. Above all, we dare not attempt to "gild the lily" in information work, as everywhere else, we believe in being honest. The Church we represent to the public in the information service program is a divine institution. Everything we undertake to improve in the image of the Church in Europe must be worthy of its name and its sacred mission.

With direction and sentiments like that behind them, it is small wonder that the Mormon volunteer information workers do strive to turn in an excellent performance.

Chapter Thirty

THE LAMANITES AGAIN

When the famous American periodical *The Saturday Evening Post* sent a writer to Salt Lake City some months ago to consider what might be written about the Mormons, he quickly settled on a story that not even many Mormons knew about.[1] He went to Brigham Young University in Provo and there he saw almost four hundred Indian youngsters, ranging from eight to eighteen, and each with the stoical attitude so notable in the Red Man, or Lamanite, as the Mormons term them.

For to the Mormons the American Indian is not just a forlorn savage who cannot aspire to better things. To the Mormon, the Indians are descendants of the family of Lehi, who the Book of Mormon relates landed somewhere in America, probably South America, and spread north and south. Some of them sailed across the Pacific from Central America to the South Sea Islands and New Zealand. They were the Polynesians.

Joseph Smith sent some of his earliest missionaries to work among the Indian-Lamanites (see Chapter Four), and Brigham Young always abjured his people to treat the Indians kindly and fairly, and feed them when hungry. Today the Mormons are going much further. One of their main missionary thrusts is aimed at the Lamanites in South America and in the South Pacific. But before detailing that effort, it will be useful to look for a moment at what they are doing with and for the Lamanites, or Indians, in Utah and in the West, for this localized effort is basic to the effort elsewhere and hints of what may be expanded to a much wider effort.

Under the benevolent watchfulness of an apostle of the Church, Spencer W. Kimball, a grandson of Heber C. Kimball and a former Arizona banker and lifelong student of Indian affairs, and under the guidance of the highly effective Relief Society, the Church's women's auxiliary, Indian children are entering Mormon homes and living as members of the family. The four hundred children who arrived at Brigham Young University, as noted above, were there to undergo four days of health examinations by a staff of twenty-four doctors and dentists and a dozen registered nurses, all volunteering their skills and time, and to await a careful matching up by Relief Society social workers with prospective "parents."

After this orientation and testing, each child was introduced to a Mormon family with whom he or she would spend the school year. Most go into homes where there are children of similar age and they live as a fully cherished member of the family.

When the program was started soon after the close of World War II, considerable concern was felt about how children from the rigorous environment of the Navajo and Hopi reservations would get along with the privileged children of the Mormon settlements. But the answer is that they get along just fine.

Many Indian children have skills with the lariat that awe the Mormon boys and girls, Westerners though they are. Those scholars who believe they find basic differences in the competence of various races are bound to be impressed by this program of offering a change in environment. For as differences in school opportunities are equalized, progress tends to become equal.

The Mormon social workers strive to find families that will bring out the qualities of the individual Indian child. Thus a child who appears to have some musical ability is directed to a family where there is an interest in music and funds for lessons. This job of matching is yearly being made more easy because of the rising number of Mormon families eager to take Indian children into their homes.

Two-way Street

The problem of adjustment for the Indian children is eased by the fact that they come from reservations where The Church of Jesus Christ of Latter-day Saints is well known, and their Lamanite heritage, as seen by the white Mormons, furnishes a deep religious bond. But some do get homesick, and then it is up to the foster parents to use ingenuity in winning the visitors to decide to stay for the full school year.

One of the best ways, it has been found, is to give them some animals to take care of. Of course, this is not always possible in the city, but many Mormon communities still have enough of the country around them to permit an Indian child to have some chickens and possibly a lamb or at least a dog to care for. This usually does the trick.

This work with the Indian children has not been all a one-way street. Mormon interest in the Indians generally has been revived and with it a parallel acceptance in certain archaeological quarters that the Mormon view of the Lamanites may have more substance than some supposed.

The early observers of the western Plains Indians commented on the similarity of many of their beliefs and customs with those of the ancient tribes of Israel.[2] The Mormons have carried forward extensive archaeological and anthropological studies aimed at supporting their beliefs. And this has given, in recent years, a fresh impetus and direction to much of their missionary work. South America supplies one example.

Success in South America

Indeed, if you stand before a world map in Mormon headquarters in Salt Lake City and remark on the effort so easy to be seen in England, Europe, and Scandinavia today, there is agreement. But when asked where the greatest amount of missionary success is being experienced today, unhesitantly a pointer will move to the area starting with the Mexican border and extending southward through Central America to South America. There, it surprises most visitors to learn, is today's most promising field of Mormon activity.

While it is true that Parley P. Pratt visited some of the South American countries as early as 1851, about the time that the Scandinavian and west European missions were getting underway, he had to report to Brigham Young that he saw little opportunity at that time. Religious activity was regarded as political activity.

With their hands fully occupied elsewhere, the Mormons extended very little missionary activity in South America until 1926, when three church officials toured the area and made a fresh assessment. The leader of the party, Melvin J. Ballard, issued a statement which is today frequently quoted in the South American Mormon missions as having been notably prophetic:

The work will go slowly for a time just as an oak grows slowly from an acorn—not shoot up in a day as does the sunflower that grows quickly and thus dies. But thousands will join the Church here. It will be divided into more than one mission, and will be one of the strongest in the Church. The work here is the smallest that it will ever be. The day will come when the Lamanites here will get their chance. The South American Mission is to be a power in the Church.

Fresh Start

Thirty-five more years went by with only so-so missionary success until in 1961, under the more aggressive efforts that President David O. McKay and his counselors, especially Marion G. Romney, were pushing forward, a new mission president, Theodore Tuttle, was sent to South America. He was equipped with knowledge of the newest missionary methods being developed in Salt Lake City and was supported, within a short time, by 1200 zealous young missionaries. Their thrust was not aimed so much at the transplanted Europeans in South America as it was pointed at the native Indian peoples, the Lamanites.

In South America the Mormons found the Lamanites were often in virtual peonage, and when the Mormons brought word of their former glory many were eager to embrace the new teachings and practices. The number of baptisms began to rise as the enlarged corps of missionaries, furnished with the new methods, began to tell their old story.

At the end of 1960 the Church counted 1,701 new baptisms for the year in six of the South American countries in which they were active. By the end of 1961 this had risen to 3097 new members for the year; by 1962 to 6441; by 1963 to 8862, and above 10,000 new converts in 1965, where it appears to be leveling off.

Although these figures are exciting to Mormons, they are the first to point out that with a total South American population above 80 million, and only about 60,000 Mormons, there is a vast way

266   THE TWENTIETH CENTURY

to go. Moreover, in some of the South American countries, particularly those along the northern edge, they are still precluded from
missionary work by government regulation.

As the work with the natives has increased, it has at the same time
attracted a number of those of Italian, German, Spanish, and other
descent who comprise such a large part of the population. And,
of course, in South America, as elsewhere, there are few pure
strains of race.

The Mormon Church has looked upon its acceptance in South
America as a challenge for contributing to an improvement in the
way of life of their converts. For, as we have noted many times,
the Mormons have always believed that a religion which does not
prove its power to help people in a material way here on earth has
little to promise them in the life to come.

Church Schools

Visitors to South America cast up a variety of reasons for the
continent's problems. They range from the usual complaints about
political instability and the tendency of the rich to skim off the
money and export it to Swiss banks, to Church domination of a
superstitious people so immersed in poverty they can't even find it
in themselves to hope for a better day. But while the reasons for
South America's plight may differ, there is at least agreement on
one point: education of the young would help.

This is not a unique conclusion. It is, of course, a universally
held proposition. But in South America the problem of education
may offer larger aspects of challenge than in many other world
areas, if for no other reason than that it is in South America that
the world's present population explosion reaches its apogee. The
schools are inundated. The results are alarming. Mormons who
looked into the matter reported that in Chile it was common to
find that out of one hundred youngsters who entered the first grade
only two would remain to finish the twelfth grade and thus be
eligible for higher education. Indeed, out of a hundred who started
school, only sixty-five would finish the first grade. Thus at such
a young age they were cruelly judged to be lacking in ability to

progress further. Many stagnated in repeat grades for a few years and then dropped out.

Mormon parents showed Church officials rude one-room school-houses where in gloomy semidarkness students had no books, very little paper, and only stubs of pencils. Facilities, and motivation, were about nil.

By the autumn of 1962 those in charge of the Mormon missionary efforts in South America were under heavy pressure from Church members to do something to help the education of the children. While it was clearly beyond their scope to set up a complete educational plant in all parts of their mission work, they did feel that if they could set up one or two model operations it might spark imitation elsewhere.

Accordingly, they wrote to Salt Lake City headquarters requesting permission and a budget to open two schools. This was granted in early summer 1963 and plans were pushed ahead to open the David O. McKay School in Viña del Mar and the Hugh B. Brown School in Cisterna, adjacent to Santiago, both in Chile. An expert in education was borrowed from the Brigham Young University, teachers having Chilean certificates were recruited, arrangements were made to import, duty free, some of the teaching aids and materials that are taken as a matter of course in even the poorest American schools, and rooms were made ready in Mormon Church buildings in both locations.

In March 1964 the classes began. Church members, and others, were eager to enroll their children. One man appeared who said that he had four children but the family could afford the $1.00 a month fee charged by the school for only one child. Therefore, the family had held a meeting and decided that one daughter, Juanita, should attend and all the others in the family would work and pool their resources so that at least one in the family could attend the school.

This so touched the Mormons in charge that they arranged, with a little more pinching and saving, to get all four of the children into the classes. About seventy-five children could be accommodated in each of the schools, a total of 150.

When the time came around for grading the first year's efforts, it was found that every one in the school had passed, a 100 percent record! This was so astonishing that the Chilean state educational people looked into it. They personally examined the students and found that indeed all were qualified to pass!

The Chileans are quite proud of their wines and one of the examiners posed a question relating to the wine industry.

"Oh, but you shouldn't drink wine," an eight-year-old advised.

"And why not?" asked the kindly interrogator.

"The word of Wisdom says that it is not good to do."

The questioner remarked that the children were learning some useful moral lessons outside their textbooks and gave the school a high recommendation. Other South American educators are observing this relatively modest Mormon experiment and many are agreeing that it opens new prospects for them.

Equality of Sexes

Mormon officials are pleased with the fact that about an equal number of men and women are being converted in South America. In fact, the charts of baptisms indicate that membership is increasing most rapidly in the twenty- to twenty-five-year-old age bracket and for the most part represents young married couples, few of which yet have children in the over eight-year-old range. Children are not baptized until they are eight. Conversions in the over-thirty age group fall off rapidly. This is another fact of interest to non-Mormon church groups, for they normally find a much larger proportion of women joining than men, and, quite often, a greater interest among the older age groups.

As other denominations consider this success story, they might ponder whether they have available to send to South America 1200 dedicated young men of college age, which is to say pretty close to the age group being converted, who can carry a precisely oriented historical-religious appeal such as the Mormons carry to the South Americans, and with it provide the programs that will interest such age groups and cause them to become church-centered in a large share of their activities. This is not, obviously, a small order and illustrates why the Mormon Church is growing at so fast a rate.

The missionary effort is helped, as it is elsewhere in the world, by the building program. Twenty new chapels and recreational buildings have been completed since 1962 and in 1966 about fifty were still under construction. No end to the need for new buildings is in sight.

And, as elsewhere, voluntary labor represents a substantial part of the building program, though it has a local variation known as the Kilo Program. A kilo, of course, equals slightly more than two pounds in United States measure, and the plan is for each member family of the Church to donate a certain number of kilos— the number depending on its resources—of food to the building program. This food is given to those members who volunteer to work on the building program.

The plan includes building up reserve stocks of kilos, and Church groups which have no immediate building project can donate to others with assurance that they will be able to draw upon the central stock when needed in the future. Apart from the practical result of supplying food to those working, the program has clear psychological advantages in involving Church members with a group project in which they can participate as well as have pride.

Chapter Thirty-one

OCEANIA AND JAPAN

The success enjoyed by the Mormons in South America is duplicated in the islands of the South Seas. As the reader will recall from the previously told story of Addison Pratt, the Mormons have, since the days of Nauvoo in the 1840s, been active in the Pacific and Hawaii particularly contributing in substantial measure to the development of the islands. In James A. Michener's important book on Hawaii recognition is given to the early Mormon missionaries and the fact that they almost alone did not shun working with the lepers.

The Mormons account their success in this broad expanse from Hawaii south to New Zealand to precisely the same reason they attribute their success in South America—they consider the Polynesians to be descendants of the ancient Lamanites. The legend of the Polynesians is that they left a narrow strip of land that connected two immense islands, taken to mean North and South America, and sailed in canoes to the islands.[1]

It is a fact that they respond to the Mormon story of the Lamanites as bearing a relationship to their own chants of history, and have from the earliest days of the Church been enthusiastic converts. Some even attempted to make the move from their tropical homes to Utah, but usually found the change too great and returned to their own style of paradise.

It is said that people of original Polynesian stock are rare, as racial purity is rare indeed throughout the world, but in the Islands the range of color of skin seems especially wide, from light bronze to deepest black. Those who sometimes suggest that black people are not welcomed in the Mormon community should visit one of the churches in the Fijis. There they will find Mormons of darkest possible hue passing the sacramental bread and water.

New Zealand

While Mormonism went to Australia by way of English converts who carried it with them, the Mormon teachings reached New Zealand chiefly by way of the South Pacific Islands and until recently has been largely concentrated in the native or Maori population. The Maoris, by agreement of their own legends and the opinions of most anthropologists, are Polynesians.

Mormon missionaries were extending into New Zealand as early as 1851 and won endearing respect among the natives because they assisted in preserving their rights to farm lands against the demands of the *pakeha,* or European colonists. As the Mormons learned more in Utah of advanced agriculture, their missionaries carried this knowledge abroad.

By 1915 the Mormons had established an agricultural college in Hastings with a student body of eighty. In 1959 this college was moved two hundred miles north to Temple View, just outside Hamilton, nearer the population center, and of course much enlarged in number of students and scope of academic offering.

It has an enrollment of eight hundred now and represents a major opportunity for the native Maori Mormon to rise in scholastic, and hence in economic, well-being. Many of the teachers are from Utah and bring with them the educational concepts and teaching aids familiar to them at home. The college has boarding facilities for virtually all of its students and excellent sports equipment, including an Olympic-size swimming pool.

This work is attracting the attention of more and more of the European settlers, and many are joining the Mormon Church. In fact, about 35 percent of the New Zealand membership is now European. The largest single Mormon group is located in Wellington and numbers about 2500. The Mormon population in all of New Zealand is just under 30,000. They are served by forty church buildings, eleven built since 1960. It has not shown the spectacular rise evidenced in some other places, such as South America, but it has been steady, and the Mormons feel it provides a sound foundation for the unfoldment they see coming.

Australia

The New Zealand and Australian Mormon missions have always progressed along their separate ways. There was little opportunity in Australia to work with the natives, or Aborigines. And the early Australians were not particularly interested in the Mormons, although from the mid-nineteenth century there have been organized Mormon groups in Australia. They have felt that they were handicapped in not having the economic and social prestige enjoyed by the Mormons in the United States and that this hampered their missionary efforts. The Salt Lake City headquarters has been trying to help them in recent years by sending some of its better-known leaders to Australia to meet with local groups and state officials in an effort to more prominently identify the movement.

Whatever has been done, it has been successful. The Mormon Church is enrolling new members and officials are satisfied that the establishment is sound and thriving.

Hong Kong, Manila, Taipeh

Between Sydney and Hong Kong the principal Mormon activity is in the Philippines, where new converts average above 250 a year, but where the Church is really just getting a start. Hong Kong has seventy-two missionaries at work among the teeming 4,000,000 population and about 3000 members, spread over the four hundred square miles of the Crown Colony. To give an idea of the crowding of Hong Kong, civil authorities will tell you that if all the Mormons were bunched together in proportion to the jamming of the general population, the entire group would live on one acre of land! Of course, they would live, like most in Hong Kong, in high-rise apartment units.

Somehow, despite this lack of space, and a consequent premium on it, the Mormons have been able to gain possession of eight church buildings. One of these, Kum Tong Hall, is of special interest to Hong Kong visitors. It was built as the residence of one of the most noted of the old Chinese merchants, Sir Robert Tong. Its reinforced concrete frame is faced with red brick imported from England, and the exterior has a Georgian elegance. The interior has been remodeled by the Mormons to include a beautiful, though plain, chapel, the usual recreation hall, classrooms, a baptismal font, and offices and living quarters for missionaries.

Mormon activities in Red China are nonexistent. But in Nationalist China, which is to say Formosa, missionaries have been welcomed for the past ten years and about 1000 converts have joined the Church.

With the usual help from Salt Lake City, a beautiful new chapel building has been erected in the capital city, Taipeh, a building not too distinguishable from new ones in Trondheim or Santa Ana. A successful American contractor from Utah came to supervise construction and in time remarked, "These wonderful, simple, timid, underprivileged people have humbled me. My sense of values has changed. I know that happiness does not come through wealth. For the first time in my life I am completely happy and contented with myself, knowing that I am serving with all my mind and strength. All I ask is that the Lord will keep my rice bowl full, give my family and me health, and I will serve without question or complaint."

Japan

Before describing the recent Mormon activities in Japan, it will be useful to clear up one or two popular misconceptions. The first of these is that Japan has a strong religious tradition of its own.[2] The fact is that the indigenous religious beliefs were not very sophisticated parallels of those of the Greeks and Romans. In short, they were pagans who had a family of gods representing humanlike qualities and who were supposed to rule over such things as the sky, the sea, and the winds.

Buddhism came in from China and represented more of a philosophy than a religion, and while widely adopted as a way of life, the Buddhists in time began to build political and military power, centering in fortified monasteries. This inevitably led to power struggles which in the sixteenth century signaled the decline of Buddhism as a power.

About the time of the putting down of the political Buddhists there was landed in Japan by Portuguese sailors one of the founders of the Jesuit order, a man enlisted by Ignatius Loyola himself, the missionary who was to become known as St. Francis Xavier. Finding that his robes of poverty failed to impress the Japanese and in fact barred him from entry to the great court of the Shogun, St. Francis clothed himself in all the panoply of Rome that a papal nuncio could find in his baggage, and again presented himself.

The Jesuits soon found themselves accepted and making numerous converts. St. Francis remained in Japan almost three years and felt that this populous and highly civilized land was certain to become a Christian bulwark, and so reported to Rome. But after his departure it was evident that much of the Jesuit popularity was based not so much on the doctrine of peace and good will which they preached as on their knowledge of seventeenth-century European firearms and fortifications. And when the Spanish, some fifty years later, poured in Franciscan and Dominican monks, sharp cleavages became visible between them and the Portuguese-sponsored Jesuits.

The rulers of Japan at this period, which roughly corresponds to the time of Elizabethan England, had much of the same international spirit as the British. They longed for expanded trade and used the missionaries primarily as ways and means with which to open new avenues with Europe. They even elevated a wandering British sailor and shipwright, Will Adams, to what he compared to a lordship, complete with ninety servants and a palace, so that he would teach them the art of making sea-going vessels and sailing them.

At this period the Japanese traveled widely. Emissaries visited the Pope and the Court of Philip at Madrid. Reports came from all quarters and many of these stressed the fact that the Christians in Europe failed to practice the virtues they preached in Japan. Moreover, they were greatly impressed by the Protestant revolt.

The growing political power of the Jesuits was causing more concern in Japan, for it was noted that the Christian converts were required to put loyalty to Church above loyalty to their Japanese rulers. This was, of course, a central and unforgivable error, as viewed by the Japanese rulers.

As a result, Christians came under intense persecution. Priests were banished. Japanese Catholics were commanded to renounce their faith on pain of death. As just one illustration of the depth of feeling, early in the spring of 1638 some 30,000 Christians, many of them women and children, took refuge in a castle near Nagasaki.

End of Christian Tolerance

The Japanese authorities told them they must recant or be exterminated. The Japanese Christians chose martyrdom and for three months held out. The military, however, finally forced some Dutch ships then in the harbor to bombard the castle and virtually the entire 30,000 were killed.

This ended active and visible Christian influence in Japan and signaled the lowering of a curtain on the outside world, which in fact remained lowered for two centuries until Commodore Perry sailed into Japan in 1853, and it was not until twenty years later and resultant increase in intercourse that the ban on Christianity was lifted. During that long period of isolation there was only one tiny point of contact kept open. Because of their assistance in the massacre, and because they were obviously interested only in trade and not in proselytizing, the Dutch were permitted to operate one small port and to bring into it one ship a year from Holland. But the Japanese had no other reason than to regard Europeans as contemptible.

The foregoing is, of course, familiar to all students of Japanese history, and is touched upon here simply to underline that it was not fear of the unknown which condemned Christianity in the minds of the Japanese for so many years, but rather too much knowledge of what they understood to be the Christian way of doing things. When the curtain was again lifted toward the end of the nineteenth century, fresh attempts were made to bring Christian beliefs into Japan and they were in small measure successful. Even the Roman Catholics were able to convert a few of the most distinguished Japanese, especially in the commercial fields, while various Protestant sects, too, became active.

This was the situation when in 1901 the Mormons sent Heber J. Grant to open a mission. These efforts had a limited success up through World War I, even though the old Japanese international spirit re-emerged and they could scarcely wait to imitate Western ways, even religious beliefs.

But adoption by the United States of the post-World War I emigration policies, which excluded the Japanese from emigration, dealt a crippling blow to missionary efforts by Americans in Japan. This, coupled by the ascendancy of militant nationalism, ended all possibility of missionary success. In fact, the Mormon mission was closed in 1924. There were then only 160 Mormons in Japan.

During the occupation, following World War II, it happened that a number of the troops were Mormons. They made friends among the Japanese and, as is inevitable among Mormons, baptisms became frequent. Projects to care for Japanese orphans were undertaken, classes in English language were established; the call went to Salt Lake City for support and enlarged missionary work, and the call was answered. A new mission was opened in 1948.

While the growth of the Mormon Church has not been spectacular, it has been rewarding. There are some 160 American Mormon missionaries now working in Japan. Their instructions are that they must learn the language, eat with chopsticks, and sleep on the floor like Japanese. This requires, as anybody who has tried it will admit, dedication of a sort that could come only from religious zeal.

Mormons are converting an average of 1500 Japanese a year, and some 10,000 members today stretch over 1500 miles from Okinawa to the north Island of Japan and center in twenty-nine branches of the Church, each in some stage of a building program. In a land of a hundred million people this may not seem large, but against the background of history, and against the fact that early in this century the Church missionaries labored mightily for twenty-four years and gained only 160 members, it is regarded in Salt Lake City as significant news indeed.

Chapter Thirty-two

SALT LAKE CITY IN THE JET AGE

Visitors are always welcome in Salt Lake City. Indeed, the state legislature substantially increased its appropriations in recent years for advertising in behalf of tourism, and it doesn't need to be remarked that the Latter-day Saints and their works are a featured attraction. Many reminders of Brigham Young and his times remain. His Bee Hive House, so named because of the bee hive ornament atop the roof, is kept open several hours a day for a stream of visitors. His Lion House, standing beside the Bee Hive House, still has the carved lions in front.

Down the street is Temple Square, dominated by the gray granite structure that Brigham Young never saw completed but over the plans and foundations of which he labored lovingly and long. Near the Temple is the famed Tabernacle, which served as his principal forum during his later years. There is the sea-gull monument, and a log cabin, a typical rude structure in which the pioneers first found shelter.

But across the street rises the new seventeen-story building erected by the Church's Zion's Security Corporation for Zion's National Bank and the Kennecott Copper Company. On another corner the old red-sandstone Deseret News-Union Pacific Building has been refaced with gleaming marble and glass in the modern style that is adding a fresh, if not universally approved, appearance to America's postwar urban centers.

In fact, as one looks out over the city from the rooftop restaurant of the Hotel Utah, done over in the "modern rococo" decor of Dorothy Draper, one observes that nearly everywhere the new is thrusting up among the old. Naturally, this brings the question whether this is not symbolic of what is happening to the Mormons.

Such generalizations are too simple, but it is a fact that immense changes are in process. When Brigham Young visited England (Chapter Eight) he commented on the social and economic revolution then underway, as farmers left the land and entered the factories. Today he might observe something similar happening in Utah. A recent report to the state legislature[1] indicated that since 1960 more than half the counties in Utah had shown a decline in population while the state as a whole has gained 11 percent! The gain was in Salt Lake City and the area immediately surrounding, as even a casual automobile drive through the new suburbs will confirm. In fact, a wide band around Salt Lake City now accounts for most of the state's nearly 1,000,000 population.

What has happened in Utah is only a repetition of what has happened all over the United States, and indeed much of the world, as mechanized and even industrialized agriculture has offered less and less employment to the young people of the rural areas. They are driven, not too reluctantly it must be admitted, from the sun-baked fields to the air-conditioned offices, factories, hotels, and motels of the urban and suburban districts.

New Mormon Economics

Although this trend is directly opposite to the Jeffersonian views of Brigham Young, who felt that the people would thrive best on small farms and in small communities, it has not been opposed by the present Church leadership. As early as 1948, President McKay was welcoming the $3,000,000 plant of the Thermoid Company to Nephi, Utah, an area of declining farm income. Since that time defense plants and other factories have enjoyed the tacit if not active help of the Church in finding locations, capital, and a willing work force.

Some economists felt that the Mountain West of the United States suffered disproportionately from the depression of the 1930s because it was too dependent on marginal agriculture and marginal mining.[2] One reason they were marginal was simply because Utah was so distant from large consuming markets. But the postwar years have seen a measureable correction of this because of the growth of population in California and other parts of the nearby Southwest.

Thus, such companies as Thermoid, U. S. Steel, Litton, Remington-Rand, Hercules, Thiokol, and others find that markets are moving closer to them and that they can afford to take advantage of the natural resources, to say nothing of the honest and hard-working human resources. This brings industrial pay scales, not farm pay scales, to Utah, but it also tends to bring the Utah economy and ways of doing business more and more into parallel with the economies of other states.

The question naturally arises whether this trend has caused a concomitant lessening of Mormon influence. The new industrialization has inevitably brought managerial representatives of the larger corporations investing in Utah. Certain numbers of workers have also been attracted from the outside. While in early times Salt Lake City was populated by 80 to 90 percent Mormons, and the surrounding state by probably at least 90 percent Mormons, the figures most frequently heard today give Salt Lake City itself a 50 to 60 percent Mormon population and the state outside Salt Lake about 70 percent.

This is still a heavy political majority and one might suppose that it means a complete domination of the state's politics, but this is not the case. Since statehood, the Mormons have divided between Republicans and Democrats and the vote has tended to follow national patterns in a general way. Republicans have over the years been generally in the ascendancy, much as they have in other western farming areas, but in years of strong Democratic sweeps the state has, for the most part, gone along with the trend. The state was strong for Eisenhower, weak for Nixon, strong for Johnson. The Kennedy victory was not big enough to carry a state Democratic sweep, but the Johnson landslide was.

It is difficult, therefore, to see either party as enjoying dominant Church support. The high councils of the Church tend to be conservative, but this is not expressed in a dedicated loyalty to either party. On balance, it is probably true that a responsibly conservative Republican, which is to say not an extremist (contrary to some reports the ultraright has not done well in Utah politics) would enjoy larger Mormon support than a responsibly liberal Democrat who was not regarded as an extremist. All this does is simply to make Utah fit into the larger national picture. It suggests that the Church does not participate very much in politics.

As in other places, the battle between the liberals and the conservatives in both parties waxes warm at times. This is, however, completely in the Mormon tradition where each individual is expected to be informed, to have opinions and to express them forcefully regardless of the position, or supposed position, of the Church officials. And this carries over into Church affairs, where some members may exhort for more liberal or progressive policies while others declare for the old ways of doing. Discussion and expression of views are not discouraged and no doubt the debates are heard by the higher authorities and weighed in their conduct of Church affairs and in decisions in matters not dictated by recognized Church doctrine. In affairs involving doctrines political lines fade fast.

For example, though it is possible to introduce bills in the Utah legislature favoring amendments to the present strict liquor laws (liquor can be obtained now only in regulated state stores), or measures which would legalize pari-mutuel betting, they cannot be much more than introduced. Nonpartisan opposition from the Mormon majority regardless of party does not usually let them get to a seriously advanced stage.

Political observers both inside and outside Utah have been watching with much interest how the state would respond to the growing national clamor for civil rights. The Mormon theology has taught that the Negro race is not eligible for certain priesthood activities, although Negroes are welcomed as Church members, and, as previous pages have detailed, missionary work is certainly not limited to the so-called white races.

This view of racial background caused many to suppose that Utah would find it hard to comply with the bundle of new definitions of rights as emanating from the Congress and the courts. But the 1965 legislative session came out with state laws that are in some respects, though not all, in advance of the national legislation. For example, Utah's equal accommodation law does not exempt such service businesses as barber shops and beauty parlors, as does the national law, but on the other hand, a fair-housing bill was not passed.

Governor Calvin L. Rampton, a Mormon and a Democrat, was displeased by this and told the legislature that a bill should be adopted "because the government of this state owes a solemn, abiding moral obligation to effectively guarantee these rights to all its citizens." In this he was repeating the often-expressed sentiments of another Mormon governor, a Republican, George W. Romney of Michigan. No Church disagreement is discernible. Indeed, Church authorities have repeatedly said that they embrace no doctrine which would adversely affect any person's civil rights.[3]

At the October 1963 conference officials did the best they could to state their position clearly. On behalf of President McKay, President Hugh B. Brown declared:

"During recent months both in Salt Lake City and across the nation considerable interest has been expressed in the position of the Church . . . on the matter of civil rights. We would like it to be known that there is in this Church no doctrine, belief or practice that is intended to deny the enjoyment of full civil rights by any person regardless of race, color or creed.

"We say again, as we have said many times before, that we believe that all men are the children of the same God and that it is a moral evil for any person or group of persons to deny to any human being the right to gainful employment, to full educational opportunity, and to every privilege of citizenship, just as it is a moral evil to deny him the right to worship according to the dictates of his own conscience.

"We have consistently and persistently upheld the Constitution of the United States, and as far as we are concerned this means upholding the constitutional rights of every citizen of the United States.

"We call upon all men everywhere, both within and outside the Church, to commit themselves to the establishment of full civil equality to all God's children. Anything less than this defeats our high ideal of the brotherhood of man."

The next day, October 7, Albert B. Fritz, president of the Salt Lake chapter of the National Association for the Advancement of Colored People, was quoted in the Salt Lake *Tribune* as responding:

"We feel this will certainly put Utah in line with other liberal states in the West which have come out in favor of civil rights.

"We have urged all NAACP members, interested church groups, civic organizations, labor unions and individuals that have been working toward passage of civil rights legislation in Utah to work in harmony with all LDS Church officials, and members, where it is possible.

"We want to build a stronger Utah. If we work in harmony, we will have a better state."

Mormon Organization

With the Mormons clearly supplying a majority of the population, and energizing most of the civic, social, and political activities of the region, it is natural that those interested in the state today do not customarily call first at the state capitol building, which rises so high above most of Salt Lake City. Rather, they make their call at a smaller but equally elegant building set between the Hotel Utah and Brigham Young's Lion House.

This building houses the offices of The Church of Jesus Christ of Latter-day Saints. The headquarters dates from just before World War I. It is a solid granite edifice, four stories high, finely built, with liberal use of bronze and marble and hardwoods. Although it seems quiet and peaceful as one enters the front doors, the building is actually teeming with activity. Here the First Presidency sits in a large board room, interesting itself in the incredible number of the worldwide activities of the Church.

President McKay set no precedent, but he did alter the custom that had prevailed for some years when in late 1965 he increased the number of his counselors from two to four. Hugh B. Brown and N. Eldon Tanner were augmented by Joseph Fielding Smith, senior member of the Council of Twelve and by Thorpe B. Isaacson. Presidents Brown and Smith had enjoyed long service in important positions in the Church, while Presidents Tanner and Isaacson were successful businessmen. President Tanner was a Canadian oilman while President Isaacson was a leading insurance executive.

The First Presidency has much need for business talent, for into its office flows daily reports and requests for decisions on matters ranging from the multimillion-dollar welfare program to financing new buildings and stores on its real estate holdings, described more fully in Chapter Twenty-two.

These interests close to home, so to speak, are not the end of the story. The Church now has many holdings around the world. So many transactions have taken place in the field concerning land needed for the Church Building Program that it would be impossible to describe them, but many have added up to a multiplying of values. And these are the sorts of business considerations that flow into the

First Presidency for final action. These are the sorts of things that bring reporters from the *Wall Street Journal, Fortune, Business Week,* and similarly oriented publications to Salt Lake City. For a church that has business acumen and which invests and thrives in the best tradition of the free enterprise system (and let it be noted without special tax advantages because the Church insists on paying taxes on its business dealings) appears to be a novelty and, therefore, news.

But it must be quickly apparent to visitors that such things really do not dominate considerations of Church leaders. They will answer responsively questions about business affairs, but will try to make it clear that they feel such things are a small part of their lives. They can point out that if making money and running businesses were their principal aim, they could have done much better. They might add that while the Church played a useful and indeed some-times irreplaceable part in initiating and financing some of the im-portant economic assets of the area—the utilities, the railroads, the mines, and the like—the Church turned these over to private busi-ness interests as soon as practicable. Its business interests are related to the needs of the Church and its members, not to general economics and money making.

Their Real Interest

The real interest of the Church leadership unquestionably lies in how their Church is progressing as a church. They are all interested in and devoted to the world-wide missionary effort. This too, of course, is the responsibility of the First Presidency and missionary work is realigned and redirected by the President; but day-to-day direction falls under the guidance of the Council of the Twelve Apostles. The world is divided into twelve regions, each with an apostle in charge. Thus, starting with the West Coast of the United States, the Western American Mission, at this time of writing we find LeGrand Richards responsible. The intermountain area, which includes Utah and most of the western states and the principal Indian missions, is under Delbert L. Stapley.

The vital mid-American area, covering all the Middle West from Canada to the Gulf, is under Richard L. Evans, and the heavily populated east and southeast American region is the charge of Harold B. Lee.

Those areas of the southwest United States that are largely Spanish-speaking, and Mexico and Central America, report to Marion G. Romney, who has labored in this field for many years. South America, so rapidly growing in Mormon membership, is under Spencer W. Kimball. The South Pacific, including Australia, New Zealand, and the islands, is under Thomas S. Monson. Hawaii and the Orient are the responsibility of Gordon S. Hinckley.

The British Isles, rich in Mormon history, are under the direction of Mark E. Petersen. Western Europe, which includes the Scandinavian countries as well as Belgium, the Netherlands, and France, is under Howard W. Hunter, while the Germanic area that includes West Germany and Berlin, Austria, and Switzerland reports to Ezra Taft Benson.

Many of these names have been associated with other missions in past years. One of the valuable resources of the Church is the flexibility, and one might say the universality, of its top personnel. Elder Evans is as much at home in London as Chicago, and Elder Petersen has been at various times as acquainted with the problems in Hong Kong as he is with those of London. So it could be multiplied, literally, a dozen times.

These men headquarter in Salt Lake City, but the coming of the jet plane has immensely facilitated their activities. They seem to be in constant touch either in person or by phone, cable, or air mail with the areas of their chief responsibility for mission work. Each has an assistant directly supervising the area and reporting to him.

But though the missionary work ranks first in many of their considerations, it must be remembered that each of the apostles has many, many other interests and responsibilities. For example, one will be entrusted with primary responsibility for the welfare program; another with genealogy; another with the temples; still another with the Church's educational concerns, and so on.

Small wonder that the first impression a visitor to headquarters gets is that he is seeing some extremely busy men. There are, of course, elevators in the church offices building, but it is noticed that the marble steps on the stairs are well worn. The working day for some begins as early as six. President McKay himself has been known to schedule appointments for that hour, and not for breakfast!

Besides this sort of dedication and energetic effort, one notices that a great deal of the work follows after consultation and seems to be virtual committee action. Much secretarial time is spent setting up meetings so that several minds can be brought to bear on solving a problem. A not unusual conversation between secretaries might run, "Could Brother A meet with Brother B and Brother C at three-thirty next Tuesday? The Indian children, you know. No, well Brothers B and C could make it at two the following Monday. How would that be?"

Sometimes it is necessary to schedule these meetings two and three weeks in advance. No wonder that when the meetings do take place the participants are prompt, prepared, and ready to get right down to decisions without delay. Time is their most precious asset. In addition to this sort of formally arranged meeting, there are countless poppings in and out of each other's doors for a quick word. And every Thursday morning the Twelve solemnly meet with the First Presidency in the Temple for prayerful review of outstanding matters and for counsel and direction.

As one talks with these men and their many assistants one cannot help but feel that the dominant impression is that these are people who care. They are deeply involved in what they are doing. If you talk with a young man who is in charge of a certain aspect of the schools in Chile, you notice that tears come to his eyes as he describes the tragic magnitude of the job the Church faces. Another official concerned with missionary work among the Indians, or Lamanites as he will call them, tells you that like his father before him he has devoted most of his life to trying to improve the lot of the Red Men on the reservations. You know without being told that he would go anywhere any time to carry the story of the needs of the Indians to anybody who would listen.

Another official who is concerned with missionary work in the Far East exhibits no smug satisfaction over how well the work is going, but rather an urgent sense of wishing he could find better ways in which to expand the work. The Church's business and its political interests are in the minds of these men only a very small means to quite large ends.

They feel that their Church, and their own human experience, are devoted to humanity in the best sense. All else is passing dross. About some things affecting the Mormons and their cause some writers who visit the scene might disagree, or come away with different interpretations, but about the sincerity of the Church leaders there could be no question. Again, these are people who care.

Relief Society

If this is the dominant impression one carries from the headquarters building, it is certainly the ascendant one found around the corner in the little white-marble jewel box that houses the Relief Society. Founded in 1843 in Nauvoo, it has served to formalize the educational and charitable work of the Mormon women through the years. There are now 5000 units of the Relief Society spread over the world and all their activities stem from the direction of President Belle S. Spafford and her counselors, Marianne C. Sharp and Louise W. Madsen.

The members are the ones who carry the love and dedication the Church wants to express into the homes and lives of the Mormon families. It is one thing to say, in arithmetic, that in a typical year Relief Society members will devote almost a million hours to such compassionate services as visiting and caring for the sick. Or it could be noted that the society lists more than 115,000 teachers who in a year make about 4,500,000 home calls to work with Mormon women in religious and other instruction, which may range from sewing classes to social studies.

But such figures and words fail to communicate the direct and intimate transmission of the concern for members. This is the way the young bride is helped to prepare the big dinner for the night her husband brings the boss home. This is the channel through which the young mother is made to feel at ease in caring for her child. This is the source that the puzzled parents can turn to for outside views on why Johnny is not doing so well in school. To one from the outside looking in, it almost seems as though every young Mormon mother has a hundred grandmothers she can call upon.

In this sort of atmosphere, with more than a century's background, the visitor finds himself wondering how polygamy could ever have flourished here. It is not a question easy to ask, for it is quickly apparent that these Mormon women of today don't understand it either. They will be courteous, but one can tell they are a little embarrassed if one brings the question up. They read from time to time the sensational stories in the press alleging that polygamy still flourishes in Utah. They are puzzled. If there were such flagrant violation of the local, state, and national laws, they would suppose federal officers and the local police would be doing something. But when infrequent arrests are made, it usually turns out to be a woebegone backwoodsman from some remote area whose family is so lacking and so removed from late twentieth-century living that it might be more easily a tragedy located on Mars than anything relating to modern Salt Lake City. Only an itinerant unfamiliar with the continuous, purposeful, home-building visits of the Relief Society members to every Mormon family could suppose otherwise.

On the way to the Salt Lake City airport, the driver suggested a little detour. As we neared a large new building, designed after the Spanish mission style, we heard the music of guitars and Latin rhythms. It was Lucero Ward, composed of more than five hundred Spanish-speaking Mormons, mostly from Mexico, Central and South America, but a few from Puerto Rico, the Dominican Republic, and Cuba. The gay melodies rang out while Fernando Paredes and Elvia Romero, in full and colorful costumes, were exhibiting the Mexican hat dance.

It was a new aspect of old Salt Lake City, a fresh touch to the cosmopolitanism of the City of Saints, originally peopled by so many from the British and Scandinavian and other European cultures and now beginning to embrace those of southern Europe, as transmitted by the Spanish-speaking ones. This is an impression of Salt Lake City today that is worth holding in thought as the mountain seat of the Saints continues to provide the headquarters for the energy and the treasure of the Mormon Church.

At the airport there is a great map of the world outlined on the floor, and nearby, the usual row of clocks giving the time in various centers around the globe. In Salt Lake City it is early evening, seven o'clock, and you can picture the eager choir members gathering around Mary Jack for their copies of the music for the night's rehearsal.

In New York, of course, it is nine and probably a committee meeting is still in progress at the headquarters on upper Fifth Avenue, across from the Metropolitan Museum of Art. Subject: next summer's Palmyra pageant. But in Los Angeles it is only six and the lights are just going on to illuminate the exterior of the temple on Santa Monica Boulevard, to be seen by thousands passing on the nearby freeways.

In Honolulu it is four in the afternoon and the last bus is picking up its passengers at the Polynesian Village to return the tourists to Waikiki. It is ten the next morning in Manila and Hong Kong, and eleven in Tokyo, a busy day in the missions already well underway.

From there on westward across Russia and India and the Middle East not much is doing in the world of the Mormons. And even in Berlin and Vienna and the Scandinavian capitals it is only 3 A.M. and not even the cooks are stirring. The chapel on Exhibition Road is dark and the moon rests gently over Preston and Liverpool and the Atlantic, which bore so many to this valley. One cannot help but reflect that at least for this instant of time the eternal order of the world without has a comparable moment in the Mormon world within.

BIBLIOGRAPHY AND NOTES

It has become, to some extent, the unfortunate, as I think, practice to use these bibliographies as a place for informal and often unkind reviews of the books of others bearing on the same subject. This is a problem doubled in spades when it comes to listing books about the Mormons. For as Bernard DeVoto concluded, there are really no impartial books about the Mormons. They seem to have all been written either by friends or by enemies.

Generally, too, this writer has found that the books tend to fall into two classes. The first are written by Church members either as official or approved histories, or as diaries or memoirs of events in which they participated. The writers walked with history, and they knew it and were eager to say, "this is how it was." These are useful, and often interesting, but they inherently are one dimensional in that they focus on a limited scene for a relatively brief period. The second group of writing seems to come from disaffected and often excommunicated Mormons who have a story to tell, usually their own, and in anger.

And today we are finding a third type of book. This comes from the second or third generations of Mormon families. Some evidently find the prevailing views outside the Mormon community affect their belief; others are simply examples of the turning from the faith of the fathers, notable in all churches since biblical times. Judgments as to motivations can best be left to the psychologists, but it does bring a spate of more or less cynical "now it can be told" sorts of writing. These really should be viewed against the background of the person who is writing.

Among such, one might list the popular account of Joseph Smith entitled *No Man Knows My Story* (New York, 1945) by Fawn M. Brodie, an excommunicated Mormon. Mrs. Brodie comes from a Mormon family and her father was a Church official. Far less cutting is *Kingdom of the Saints* (New York, 1957) by Ray B. West, Jr., raised as a Mormon. This is excellent as far as it goes, but of its 363 pages, 332 are devoted to the period that ended with the death of Brigham Young in 1877. So the exciting and meaningful events of the last ninety years, two thirds of the Church's history in terms of time, necessarily receive rather hasty attention.

The list could be quite long, but it only tends to support Mr. DeVoto's judgment. And the sheer volume of material precludes anybody from pretending to be expert in the literature. Some 20,000 titles are given in the Church Historian's Office as bearing on the life and times of Joseph Smith alone!

But in any list of works that must have consideration as original sources one must, of course, include Joseph Smith's own account of events during his lifetime. This runs to six volumes and is known as the *Documentary History of The Church of Jesus Christ of Latter-day Saints, Period 1,* published by the Church in Salt Lake City.

Closely linked with it is the *History of the Church* by B. H. Roberts, also published by the Church, and considered to be the official history.

Most useful for a more concise yet inclusive review is *Essentials in Church History* by the present official historian, Joseph Fielding Smith, and covering the sweep of events from antiquity to the present. This has been revised and updated from time to time and is published under Church auspices in Salt Lake City.

From December 16, 1851, until August 19, 1877, a period of twenty-six years, almost every public utterance of Brigham Young was taken down verbatim by reporters who traveled with him. Many of these sermons and addresses were published at the time in *Journal of Discourses,* which was issued by the Church in England in twenty-four volumes, from 1854 to 1886. But it remained for John A. Widtsoe, a college president and later an apostle of the Church, to go through this huge volume of material and sort it out into categories and then reduce it to the magnitude of a single volume. This he has done in *Discourses of Brigham Young* (Salt Lake City, 1961).

This gives not only the essence of Young's teachings, but the flavor of a man who, among other things, is an outstanding American example of the self-taught.

Many books have been written about Brigham Young, and that of M. R. Werner (New York, 1925) is considered to be the most complete. But in this author's opinion the really definitive work remains to be written.

Most of the early Church leaders, and later ones as well, kept good accounts of their works. Heber C. Kimball's *Journal,* for example; also William Clayton's.

Among the "disloyal," or second group books, one must include the *History of the Saints* by John C. Bennett (Boston, 1842), one of the early assistants to Joseph Smith. Bennett apostatized and wrote a bitter book greatly damaging to the cause at the time, and often misleading to this day.

A somewhat later account by an apostate is *The Rocky Mountain Saints* by T. B. H. Stenhouse (Hartford, Conn., 1874).

There have certainly been books that tried, and succeeded, in treating the subject objectively and with insight. Two frequently cited are *A Journey to Great Salt Lake City*, by Jules Remy (London, 1861) and *The City of the Saints*, by Sir Richard Burton (New York, 1862).

Remy was a noted French botanist, who approached his subject with scientific detachment. While many in the United States, and elsewhere, were condemning polygamy because they supposed it was forced on unwilling women, Remy very sensibly sought out and interviewed a Mormon "plural wife" and found she favored it, for the reasons quoted in this volume. Burton was a British explorer who brought a worldly tolerance to his examination of Zion at a critical period.

There is an interest in the Mormons because they are presumed to be very wealthy. By far the best estimate of that wealth and its accumulation is given in *Great Basin Kingdom*, by Leonard J. Arrington (Cambridge, Mass., 1958). Professor Arrington covers the period up to 1900, and indeed a little beyond, in an economic history that quite well sets economies in its related constellation of social and political events. He uses economics to make many things clear about Mormon history.

Anyone viewing the Mormon development must be struck with the vital part that emigration, particularly from Britain and Scandinavia, played in Utah development. It is true that this same comment could be made about the United States as a whole. The German and Polish migration to Milwaukee, the Swedish swarming to Minneapolis and St. Paul are examples that come easily to thought.

But in Mormon affairs it was planned, organized, financed, and it worked. Without it, there could have been no such development in the Great Basin. Here is a story implicit in the whole history of the Mormons from the earliest days onward. As is noted in this volume, there were Mormon Churches in London, Liverpool, Manchester, and several other places before there was one in Salt Lake City.

Richard L. Evans, in his *A Century of Mormonism in Great Britain* (Salt Lake City, 1937) and Albert L. Zobell, Jr., in his *Under the Midnight Sun* (Salt Lake City, 1950) tell the respective stories with interesting documentation. Elsewhere the story of early missionary work seems to be less than vivid. The author hopes he has in some part corrected this in the present volume, and has tried to put the contribution of the emigrants in proper relationship to the total Mormon story.

In the notes that follow, sources are given and commented on as the need arises.

NOTES

Chapter One

1. After World War II much more ordered and purposeful training of missionaries was undertaken, much of it along lines proven to be successful by commercial firms. As a consequence, effectiveness of the individual missionaries
was generally trebled. A description of methods and illustrations of application are given in Chapters 24, 25, 26, and 27.

Chapter Two

1. Joseph Smith wrote his own account of these early experiences and it
appears in his *History of the Church* (Salt Lake City, 1902).
2. *Ibid.*
3. Although Cowdery, Harris, and Whitmer were not consistent in their
loyalty to the Prophet, each always insisted on the truth of his statement
that he had seen an angel visitant and had been shown the golden plates.
And each reaffirmed this on his deathbed.

Chapter Three

The author has had so much help in his research, and deliberations, for this
chapter that he can only distribute praise to others for any merits that it has
and accept any blame himself. Much of the material results from conversations
with authorities of the Church who have patiently responded to questions.
1. Words from Mormon Hymnal.
2. The "Word of Wisdom" was contained in revelations of February 1833,
and are found in Doctrine and Covenants, Section 89. Brigham Young often
alluded to moderation in all things and few of his sermons lacked exhortation to "let tea, coffee and alcohol alone."

Chapter Four

1. From Pratt's *Journal.*
2. The Kirtland Temple still stands and is under the aegis of the Reorganized
Church of Jesus Christ of Latter-day Saints. This group, largely composed
of Mormons who did not emigrate west and who did not accept polygamy,
was formed about eighteen years after the martyrdom of Joseph Smith.

Chapter Five

1. Heber C. Kimball wrote home: "Elders Hyde, Richards and myself, being without purse or scrip, wandered in the streets of Liverpool, where wealth and luxury abound side by side with penury and want. I met there the rich attired in the most costly dresses, and the next minute was saluted with the cries of the poor. Such a wide distinction I never saw before. . . ." (Quoted in Orson F. Whitney, *Life of Heber C. Kimball*, Salt Lake City, 1888.)
2. *Ibid.*
3. *Ibid.*
4. *Ibid.*
5. Kimball's letter to his son.

Chapter Six

1. A full account of the voting at Gallatin and the reason the people were stirred up against the Mormons is given in Joseph Fielding Smith's *Essentials of Church History* (Salt Lake City, 13th edition, 1953). He states that the Mormons believed that William P. Peniston, a candidate for the state legislature, was convinced the Mormons would not vote for him and therefore exerted himself to prevent their being polled.
2. An illustration of the depth of the bitterness of the times is given in the orders issued to General John B. Clark of the Missouri Militia by Governor Lilburn W. Boggs, October 25, 1838.

   Sir:—Since the order of the morning to you, directing you to cause 400 mounted men to be raised within your division, I have received by Amos Reese, Esq., and Wiley C. Williams, Esq., one of my aides, information of the most appalling character, which changes the whole face of things, and places the Mormons in open and avowed defiance of the laws, and of having made open war upon the people of this state. Your orders are, therefore, to hasten your operations and endeavor to reach Richmond, in Ray County, with all possible speed. The Mormons must be treated as enemies and *must be exterminated* or driven from the State, if necessary for the public good. Their outrages are beyond all description. If you can increase your force, you are authorized to do so, to any extent you may think necessary. I have just issued orders to Major-General Wallock of Marion County, to raise five hundred men, and to march them to the Northern part of Daviess and there to unite with General Doniphan, of Clay, who has been ordered with five hundred men to proceed to the same point for the purpose of intercepting the retreat of the Mormons to the North. They have been directed to communicate with you by express; and you can also communicate with them if you find it necessary. Instead, therefore, of proceeding to reinstate the citizens of Daviess in their homes, you will proceed immediately to Richmond, and there operate

against the Mormons. Brigadier-General Parks, of Ray, has been ordered to
have four hundred men in his brigade in readiness to join you at Richmond.
The whole force will be placed under your command.

L. W. Boggs. Governor and Commander in Chief
To General Clark

3. Brigadier General Doniphan's courage in refusing the direct order of his
superior, Major General Samuel D. Lucas, on this occasion is celebrated in
American lore, and was dramatized in a National Broadcasting Company
television series based on President John F. Kennedy's *Profiles in Courage.*

4. With their usual care for detailed history, and firm in their belief that they
were recording a new dispensation in the time of God, many Mormons
described events as they occurred. This is taken from a letter of Amanda
Smith in the Church Historian's office.

   Years later, in Salt Lake City, she recounted how a cartilage had grown
to replace the bone shot away in her son's hip and that he lived to make the
trek and to settle in the Great Basin.

5. Letter of Mercy Fielding Thompson. This letter is quoted in a memorial
brochure issued by the Mormons in Independence on the occasion of opening the restored Liberty Jail, September, 1963.

6. *Ibid.*

Chapter Seven

1. This is described in Cowley's *History of Wilford Woodruff* and is commented on in Richard L. Evans' *A Century of Mormonism in Great Britain*
as giving considerable impetus to the missionary efforts at that time.

2. Cowley's *History* quotes Woodruff's *Journal.*

3. From Richard L. Evans, who rediscovered Hill Farm in the 1920s.

4. Cowley, *op. cit.*

5. *Ibid.*

Chapter Eight

The most complete account of the Mormon activities in England is given in
Richard L. Evans' *A Century of Mormonism in Great Britain* (Salt Lake City,
1937). This was begun with his own researches as a young man about 1928
while serving as a missionary in Britain and was finished for the British Mission centennial in 1937. Much of the material in this and the other chapters
dealing with the Mormons in England, Scotland, and Wales derives from his
work. Acknowledgment is gratefully made.

1. On August 31, 1856, Brigham Young, while speaking in the Bowery in
Salt Lake City, felt in a reminiscent mood. While sixteen very busy and
exciting years had intervened since his British experience, it was still evi-

dently very vivid in his thoughts. The account as given here appears in his *Journal of Discourses.*

2. Young's *Journal of Discourses.* Young said he actually had a note from Mrs. Benbow making her contribution a gift, but he insisted on repaying to her order.

3. This remarkably trenchent letter was written as a personal message to Joseph Smith and is preserved in the Church Archives.

4. Woodruff's report of the London experiences is given in the official *Journal History of the Church,* Vol. IV, pp. 182ff. (Archives of the Church, Salt Lake City).

5. Letter of October 12, 1940, from Heber C. Kimball, George A. Smith, and Wilford Woodruff to Brigham Young in Manchester in *Journal History of the Church,* Vol. IV, pp. 222–23.

6. Young, *Journal of Discourses.*

7. *Ibid.*

Chapter Nine

1. The revelation dated July 12, 1843, covers celestial, or eternal, marriage as well as the doctrine of plural wives. It is given in the *Documentary History of the Church* (Vol. V, p. 423) but was not announced publicly until 1852 in Salt Lake City.

2. Thomas A. Ford's *History of Illinois* (Chicago, 1854).

3. An account of the early Mormon missionary activities in the South Pacific was compiled by Doyle L. Green, managing editor of the Church's magazine, *The Improvement Era,* and run in installments in that publication during the winter and spring of 1950. This and subsequent references to Addison Pratt are drawn from Green's sources.

Chapter Ten

1. Governor Thomas Ford of Illinois had ample reason to be defensive about his part in the martyrdom of Joseph Smith, and spelled out his version of the affair in his *History of Illinois* (Chicago, 1854). This account is valuable not only because it gives his viewpoint but because it indicates how dominant the Mormon "question" was in that period. The governor could think of little else.

2. On the morning of June 26, 1844, Governor Ford granted the request of Joseph Smith for an interview and the conversation here is as reported by the Mormons who were present.

3. The conversation between Joseph Smith and Dan Jones, and the subsequent conversations with a member of the Carthage Greys and with Governor Ford

were reported by Jones, and are given here as recorded in *Essentials of Church History*, by Joseph Fielding Smith (Salt Lake City, 1953).

4. Governor Ford in his *History* appears to have foreseen that the martyrdom of Smith would be the chief reason for his own name being remembered.

5. Joseph Fielding Smith, *Essentials of Church History*.

6. Dan Jones in a letter dated July 8, 1847, to *Millennial Star*, Vol. IX, pp. 299–300.

7. Letter from Dan Jones to Orson Pratt, January 6, 1849.

Chapter Eleven

1. Eliza R. Snow, poetess who wrote the words to the hymn "O! My Father," quoted in Chapter Three, was described as the plural wife of Joseph Smith and later Brigham Young. She kept a remarkable journal, and much of the feeling and color of the early Mormon experiences that have been preserved must be credited to her sensitive reporting.

2. An interesting account is given in William Clayton's *Journal* (Salt Lake City, 1921).

3. Thomas L. Kane, *The Mormons* (Philadelphia, 1850).

4. *Ibid.*

Chapter Twelve

1. Brigham Young discusses his uncertainty as to the exact place the Saints should go, but his complete assurance that it should be in the West, and his own confidence that it was somewhere in the Great Basin. *Discourses of Brigham Young*, 1:279.

2. John C. Frémont and Jim Bridger were regarded as the two best sources of information about the Great Basin, and Bridger, already a legendary figure, was sought by Young and the Mormons for the guidance they so greatly needed. Young gives an account of his meeting with the famous Mountain Man. *Discourses*, 13:173.

3. This letter was the principal guide for the Mormons in Salt Lake City during the long winter of Young's absence. The text given here is taken from the original in the historical files of the Church.

Chapter Thirteen

1. The gull monument is a noted art work in the West. It was unveiled in Temple Square, September 13, 1913, the work of Mahonri Young, a grandson of Brigham Young.

2. Brigham Young had much advice for missionaries. These examples will be found in his *Discourses*, 6:276.

3. The Church kept very full records of those joining and especially noted the skills of newcomers from abroad. These people could thus be called upon at any time for their special services.

4. The Perpetual Emigration Fund has been the subject of much historical comment. These figures are taken from the *Mississippi Valley Historical Review*, 1931.

Chapter Fourteen

For a number of years the then assistant church historian, Andrew Jensen, a native of Denmark, compiled information about the early days of the Scandinavian Mission. This material was available to him in the official records and correspondence of the Church and in the personal memoirs of many of the Scandinavian emigrants. He published a *History of the Scandinavian Mission* in 1927.

This material as well as the results of subsequent research was reviewed and amplified by Albert L. Zobell, Jr., of the Church's publication, *Improvement Era*, as the centennial of the first mission to Scandinavia approached in 1950.

This research provides the basis for the material in this chapter.

1. Letter from Taylor to *Millennial Star* (September 15, 1850).

2. Prayer of President Snow, from his reports to the Church.

3. The "dipper" incident was also reported by President Snow.

Chapter Fifteen

1. Tithing was most fully explained and justified in *Epistle of the Twelve Apostles to the Saints of the Last Days*, issued December 13, 1841. Vol. IV of the Church history.

2. Alvin Allen's biography of his grandfather, *Ira Allen, Founder of Hyrum* (Logan, Utah, 1941) gives this account.

3. Bill Nye was a famous nineteenth-century Wyoming and Colorado newspaperman and humorist who was very familiar with the Mormons and frequently talked about them in his lectures. This excerpt was widely circulated in the West and this version comes from a Mormon source, Alexander Toponce, who said he jotted it down as he heard it.

4. This description of the General Tithing Office is from F. H. Ludlow's *The Heart of the Continent* (London, 1870).

5. From Brigham Young's sermon, April 9, 1852. Taken from his *Discourses*.

6. From "Ten Months Among the Paper Rags," *Deseret News* (August 20, 1862).

7. From message to the iron miners from The First Presidency of the Church as recorded in the *Journals* of Wilford Woodruff (Salt Lake City, 1909).

8. From Joseph Holbrook's *Diary*, Vol. VI, cited by Arrington.

9. Heber C. Kimball to William Kimball, *Millennial Star* (XVIII, 1856).

Chapter Sixteen

1. From letter of Brigham Young to Franklin D. Richards, in London, published in *Millennial Star* (July 30, 1855).

2. From letter of Brigham Young to Franklin D. Richards, *Millennial Star* (September 30, 1855).

3. From Chislett's *Journal,* quoted by Ray B. West, Jr., in *Kingdom of the Saints* (New York, 1957).

Chapter Seventeen

1. From President Buchanan's message to the Congress, December 8, 1857.

2. The Mormons believed that persecution was not only inevitable but useful and even helpful. Brigham Young spoke along these lines many times and a complete chapter (Chapter 30) of Widtsoe's compilation of Young's discourses is given over to this subject. One excerpt serves to portray his attitude:

   > I have heard a great many tell about what they have suffered for Christ's sake. I am happy to say I never had occasion to. I have enjoyed a great deal, but so far as suffering goes I have compared it a great many times, in my feelings and before congregations, to a man wearing an old, worn-out, tattered and dirty coat, and somebody comes along and gives him one that is new, whole and beautiful. This is the comparison I draw when I think of what I have suffered for the Gospel's sake—I have thrown away an old coat and have put on a new one.
   >
   > No man or woman ever heard me tell about suffering. "Did you not leave a handsome property in Ohio, Missouri, and Illinois?" Yes. "And have you not suffered through that?" No, I have been growing better and better all the time, and so have this people. *Discourses*, 13:147.

3. These instructions from General Daniel H. Wells to Major Joseph Taylor, dated October 4, 1857, were found on Taylor when he was later captured by federal troops and were published in a congressional report of the "war" (House Executive Document 71, 35th Congress). One who was much exhilarated by this Mormon attitude was Samuel Colt, inventor of the famous revolver. He sent Brigham Young two handsomely mounted guns. And soon the Mormons were manufacturing similar weapons in their own workshops. This gave rise to the speculation that because of Colt's great admiration for Young, he had given permission to use the patents. This is discussed in Jack Rohan's biography of Colt, *Yankee Arms Maker* (New York, 1935).

4. Several descriptions of the deserted appearance of Salt Lake City were made by the soldiers. This comment is from the *Journal* of Captain Albert Tracy, entry for June 26, 1858. Published in the *Utah Historical Quarterly* (XIII, 1945).

5. "The Mormons denounce the Mountain Meadow Massacre, and every act connected therewith, as earnestly and honestly as any in the outside world. This is abundantly proved and may be accepted as a historical fact." H. H. Bancroft, *History of Utah* (San Francisco, 1891).

Chapter Eighteen

1. Brigham Young had much to say about the benefits of social enjoyment. This excerpt is from *Discourses*, 1:30.

2. This description of the theater and Brigham Young's comments is from *The Heart of The Continent* by Fitzhugh Ludlow (New York, 1886).

3. From an address by Horace G. Whitney, Dramatic Editor, the *Deseret News*, before the Cleofan Society, Salt Lake City, January 27, 1915.

4. Related by Horace G. Whitney, dramatic editor of the *Deseret News* and published in *Improvement Era* (1915).

5. Ridges' story was told in his *Journal* and is quoted here from *A Century of Singing* by J. Spencer Cornwall, (Salt Lake City, 1958), an excellent account of the Tabernacle and its choir by a long time choir conductor.

Chapter Nineteen

1. *The Rocky Mountain Saints*, T. B. H. Stenhouse (New York, 1873).

2. In a footnote to his comments on the Mormon emigration procedures, Dickens quotes this passage from the report of the House of Commons' Select Committee's report of 1854.

3. From *A Journey to Great Salt Lake City* by Jules Remy (London, 1861). One of the best accounts of Mormon life of the times.

4. Conversation between W. S. Godbe and Governor J. Wilson Shaffer, reported by Stenhouse, *The Rocky Mountain Saints*.

5. *The City of the Saints*, by Sir Richard Burton (New York, 1862). One of the best books of the period written by a serious observer who was neither friend nor foe.

Chapter Twenty

1. Judge McKean is quoted thus in *Life of Brigham Young*, Edward W. Tullidge (New York, 1876). Tullidge was an official historian of the Church. Judge McKean made many similar statements, reported in the

Deseret News, for example, March 22, 1871, and October 18, 1871. His principal rulings were overturned by the U. S. Supreme Court.

2. These quotes from Brigham Young's sermons are selected from the *Discourses of Brigham Young,* compiled by John A. Widtsoe (Salt Lake City, 1961) and chosen from that wealth of material by this author as briefly exemplifying the sort of message that "Brother Brigham" gave his Saints in the latter years of his presidency. This selection simply reflects the author's own judgment.

3. From Brigham Young's will.

Chapter Twenty-one

1. President Woodruff's *Journal,* September 25, 1890, in Church Archives, cited by Joseph Fielding Smith in *Essentials in Church History.*

2. This is the essential paragraph in a longer explanation and justification taken from Smith, *Essentials in Church History.*

3. This interesting development is set forth in *Doctrines and Covenants,* Sec. 128:13, but is explained more fully in a letter from Joseph Smith to the apostles in England, dated October 19, 1840, and quoted in Smith's *Essentials in Church History:*

> I presume the doctrine of "baptism for the dead" has ere this reached your ears, and may have raised some inquiries in your minds respecting the same. I cannot in this letter give you all the information you may desire on the subject; but aside from knowledge independent of the Bible, I would say that it was certainly practiced by the ancient churches; and St. Paul endeavors to prove the doctrine from the same, and says, "Else what shall they do which are baptized for the dead, if the dead rise not at all? Why are they then baptized for the dead?"

> I first mentioned the doctrine in public when preaching the funeral sermon of Brother Seymour Brunson; and have since given general instructions in the Church on the subject. The Saints have the privilege of being baptized for their relatives who are dead, whom they believe would have embraced the Gospel, if they had been privileged with hearing it, and who have received the Gospel in the spirit, through the instrumentality of those who have been commissioned to preach to them while in prison.

4. *Church News,* January 18, 1964, describes machines then available. New apparatus is being continually examined and often is installed as the work expands.

5. President McKay's remarks were reported in *Improvement Era* (November 1955).

6. *Journal History of the Church.*

Chapter Twenty-two

1. Banigan's name is often spelled Bannigan in Utah accounts. The incident here is described in Wilford Woodruff's *Diary*, March 20 and 21 and August 23, 1893. But by far the best account of the Mormon's economic history in this and earlier periods will be found in Leonard J. Arrington's *Great Basin Kingdom* (Cambridge, Mass., 1958).

Chapter Twenty-three

1. Letter from Theodore Roosevelt, *Colliers Magazine* (April 15, 1911).
2. Heber J. Grant, *Highlights in the Life of a Great Leader*, Bryant S. Hinckley (Salt Lake City, 1951).
3. James B. Allen and Richard O. Cowan, extension publications of Brigham Young University, 1964.
4. Heywood Broun.
5. This account of President Smith's interview with President Truman was given in the Church Conference Report (October 1947).

Chapter Twenty-four

1. From *Home Memories*, Llewelyn R. McKay (Salt Lake City, 1956).
2. Figures as to membership are from Church records.
3. From articles in *Church News*, a supplement of the *Deseret News* (May, June, and July 1961).

Chapter Twenty-five

1. Material for this chapter was obtained in personal interviews by the author, and interpretations are solely his own.

Chapter Twenty-six

This chapter resulted from visits and interviews in Wales.
1. Dan Jones' report will be found in Chapter Ten.

Chapter Twenty-seven

1. This material results from actual field visits made in London, observing the methods and results of the missionary work. Names are of course fictitious.

Chapter Twenty-eight

1. John A. Widtsoe was born on the island of Froyen, January 31, 1872.
2. Gallup Poll as published June 1965.

Chapter Twenty-nine

1. The postwar development of the Mormons in the ancient realm of the Hapsburgs was reported by United Press International in a despatch from Vienna (January 8, 1966).

Chapter Thirty

1. Andrew Hamilton in *The Saturday Evening Post* (September 17, 1960).
2. *Wild Life on the Plains*, by W. L. Holloway (St. Louis, 1891). In an exceptionally interesting chapter, Mr. Holloway sums up the then prevalent views of those who had studied the North American Indians. He remarked:
    Passing down the Mississippi to Mexico and from Mexico to Peru, there once existed an unbroken chain of tribes, which either in peaceful or warlike manner, contained a connection and kept up an intercourse with each other. . . . After the discovery of America, Europeans were surprised to find in villages in Guatemala inhabitants wearing the Arabian masculine costume and the Jewish feminine costume. Travellers in South America have found Israelites among the Indians. This discovery strengthens the theory given by Garcia, a Spanish writer, that the Indians are the descendants of the tribes of Israel that were led captive into Assyria.

Chapter Thirty-one

1. The last few decades have seen an ample testing of Mormon beliefs regarding the movement across the Pacific. Most familiar, no doubt, is the *Kon Tiki* saga, that of sailing a raft along the currents from Peru to the islands.

2. Malcolm Kennedy, in his *A History of Japan,* published in London by Weidenfeld and Nicolson, and in New York by Mentor, 1964, contains an interesting review of the evidence that some Polynesians reached as far as Japan, joining with the main thrusts of emigration from Asia.

Chapter Thirty-two

1. Reported in the Washington *Post* (April 9, 1965).
2. Leonard J. Arrington, paper for Research Council of Utah State University (1965).
3. Governor Rampton's message to the legislature, 1965.

INDEX

The world-wid[e ...]nts.
Dots on the m[ap ...]ng projects.

Taber
Canada

Seattle
Washington

Tokyo
Japan

Los Angelos
California

Salt Lake City
Utah

Laie
Hawaii

Brisbane
Australia

Suva
Fiji

Sutherland
Australia

Temple View
New Zealand